EVERY BREATH YOU TAKE

"Affecting, tense, and smart true-crime. . . . A case study of the classic American con man crossed with the more exotic strains of the sociopath."

—Washington Post Book World

"Ann Rule has outdone herself. . . ."

—The Orlando Sentinel (FL)

"Absolutely riveting. . . . Rule excels at painting psychologically perceptive portraits." *—Booklist*

. . . AND NEVER LET HER GO

"Truly creepy. . . . This portrait of an evil prince needs no embellishment." *—People*

"[Rule] might have created her masterpiece."

—The Plain Dealer (Cleveland)

"Even crime buffs who followed the case closely [will] gain new insights." *—The Orlando Sentinel* (FL)

"[Rule] tell[s] the sad story with authority, flair, and pace."

—The Washington Post

BITTER HARVEST

"A must-read story of the '90s American dream turned, tragically, to self-absorbed ashes." *—People*

"Impossible to put down. . . . A tour de force."

—Kirkus Reviews

Books by Ann Rule

Green River, Running Red
Heart Full of Lies
Every Breath You Take
. . . And Never Let Her Go
Bitter Harvest
Dead by Sunset
Everything She Ever Wanted
If You Really Loved Me
The Stranger Beside Me
Possession
Small Sacrifices

Ann Rule's Crime Files:

Without Pity: Ann Rule's Most Dangerous Killers

The I-5 Killer
The Want-Ad Killer
Lust Killer

ANN RULE

WORTH MORE DEAD

AND OTHER TRUE CASES
ANN RULE'S CRIME FILES: Vol. 10

POCKET BOOKS
NEW YORK   LONDON   TORONTO   SYDNEY

An *Original* Publication of POCKET BOOKS

 POCKET BOOKS, a division of Simon & Schuster, Inc.
1230 Avenue of the Americas, New York, NY 10020

ISBN-13: 978-0-7434-4874-1
ISBN-10:   0-7434-4874-X

This Pocket Books paperback edition December 2005

10   9   8   7   6   5   4   3   2   1

POCKET and colophon are registered trademarks of
Simon & Schuster, Inc.

Cover design by James Wang
Cover photo © Rhydian Lewis / Getty Images

Manufactured in the United States of America

For information regarding special discounts for bulk purchases,
please contact Simon & Schuster Special Sales at 1-800-456-6798
or business@simonandschuster.com.

To my friends in the "Sporadic but Loyal Union Meeting Lunch and Gossip Club": Gerry Hay, Shirley Jackson, Rosalie Foster, Donna Anders, and the late Ione Kniskern who is truly missed. These great women have survived and triumphed over many vicissitudes of life, all the while doing more manuscript reading and book buying than any friends I have!

ACKNOWLEDGMENTS

There were dozens of people who led me through their personal memories of the circumstances and details involved in the five cases in this book. I was both impressed and grateful for their crystalline recall. There are some individuals who wish to remain anonymous because they are both private and modest people. Many thanks to you all, and thank you to the Internet, a miraculous tool for authors who must follow slender threads back into the past histories of victims, suspects, and investigators. I could never have imagined such a resource might one day exist.

"Worth More Dead": Hank Gruber, Joe Sanford, J.K., Ron L. Edwards, Greg Meakin, Doug Hudson, Myrle Carner, P.K., Doug Wright, Jim Harris, Lieutenant Lewis Olan, Chris Casad, Steve Sherman, Ginger Arnold and the Staff of the Kitsap County District Attorney's Office, Rudy Sutlovich, Sue Paulson, Mike S.

"It's Really Weird Looking at My Own Grave": Kathy Casey, Stacy C., Chuck Wright, Bob LaMoria, Frank Chase, and Cheryl.

"Old Man's Darling": Captain Joseph Padilla, Detective Betty Smith, Kirk Mitchell, Sean Kelly, Howard Pankratz, George Merritt *(Denver Post)* Lisa Ryckman, Brian Crecente, Sarah Huntley *(Rocky Mountain News)*.

"All for Nothing": Cindy Versdahl, Lee Yates, Lucas Fiorante, KOMO-TV's *Northwest Afternoon,* Robert Shangle, Verne Shangle, David Martin, and Paul R. and Ellen Martin.

"A Desperate Housewife": Denise and Gary Jannusche, Linda and John Gunderson, Patricia Eakes, John Henry Browne, and Antoinette Olsen.

Acknowledgments

With special thanks to Patty and Gary Guite of AAA Liquidating, Kevin Wagner, Matt Parker, and Jeremiah Hanna-Cruz.

There is no way I could turn out even one book without the team that stands behind me: Louise Burke, my editor Mitchell Ivers, Josh Martino, Felice Javit, Donna O'Neill, Victor Cataldo, and Steve Llano.

To my agents of so many years now that none of us wants to admit just how many: Joan and Joe Foley of The Foley Agency, and my theatrical agent, Ron Bernstein of International Creative Management.

CONTENTS

PREFACE

Human life is very precious to most of us; nothing is as valuable as drawing in breath and feeling the reassuring beat of our hearts. Most of us feel the same about the lives of other creatures, from fellow humans to animals, and this often includes even bugs' small lives. Some people eat meat but would never think of hunting wild creatures. Some are vegetarians or vegans. The majority of us feel sad and even cry when we hear of disasters halfway around the world in which hundreds of people we never knew have perished. This ability to empathize—to identify with the pain of others—is the part of us that makes us human.

Yet there are other people who feel no sorrow or empathy when someone else suffers or dies. When they want something, the end justifies the means. Their motivation is usually financial gain or sexual conquest, but sometimes they act out of a need for revenge. If they look back at all on the death of someone who got in their way, it is without regret or guilt. With those who have no conscience and no empathy, there *are* no lingering doubts.

Despite my having written about a thousand or more killers, the ability to understand those without conscience is, for me, the most elusive. I can deal with it intellectually—but not emotionally.

The title of this book came to me full-blown, almost in a nightmare: *Worth More Dead*. As disturbing as it is to accept that these murderers believed their victims were, indeed, more valuable to them dead than alive, I know that it is true.

The first case history is about a man I encountered in a courtroom many years ago and never expected to hear about again. That he kept bouncing back into the headlines amazed me. He may have been smarter than many cold-blooded killers, or he may only have been more devious than most. He was always circumspect about choosing someone else to blame. Had he held the death weapons himself? That was always the question, but I think I may have finally answered it.

"It's Really Weird Looking at My Own Grave" is the story of a serial killer and rapist who believed that if his victims were dead, they could not come back to identify him. Fortunately, some of them were smarter than he was.

"Old Man's Darling" is a Colorado case, curious to ponder. The woman involved looked like an action-movie heroine, but her obsessions didn't lend themselves to a romantic last chapter. How dare her aging lover cast her aside? Furious and desperate, she took action, and a terrible finale ensued.

"All for Nothing" is one of the most shocking cases I've ever written about, and my longtime readers know that that's saying a great deal. Was it the result of a love triangle ripped apart? Or was it simply the inevitable ending to the erotic games one brilliant woman played with the men she delighted in enticing? She didn't realize that one man was playing for keeps.

All of these murderers had what they considered a good reason to want their victims dead—be it financial or emotional—and the last case in this book, "A Desperate Housewife," seems to have been fueled by both emotions. It is one of the saddest I've ever written about, although certainly none of the cases I cover are cheerful. What happened was so unnecessary, so selfish, and it will probably haunt you as it has me.

Worth More Dead

This case or, rather, series of cases, defies categorizing. The true culprit behind a number of fatal, near-fatal, cruel, and serious felonies wasn't easy to spot. He—or she—was either really smart or really dumb. But then I've run across a number of killers who scored near genius in IQ tests but had no sense of how they appeared to others. And no common sense at all. Was this killer crazy? Probably not. Were his intricate plots brilliant and well designed? Sometimes. But sometimes not.

With every public document about this case that I have read over the last twenty-five years, I've become more incredulous. If the events weren't so tragic, many of them would be funny, anecdotes suitable for "The World's Dumbest Criminals."

Still, there isn't anything humorous about violent death, betrayal, and dark, emotional games designed to break hearts.

I don't even know where to start explaining this killer,

so I think I'll jump in the middle and try to bring all the edges together. That way, my readers won't ask, "What *did* you say?" as did a number of mystified judges when attorneys tried to detail the myriad felonies.

When even judges shake their heads in disbelief, you know you're dealing with a tangled tale.

1

For servicemen, there is good duty and bad duty. They are at the mercy of superiors who dispatch them around the globe, but few navy men would deny the many benefits of being stationed at the Whidbey Island Naval Air Station in Oak Harbor, Washington. There is also a U.S. Marine detachment stationed on the island. With Deception Pass to the west and Skagit Bay to the east, the setting is idyllic, a virtual vacation spot. Sailors—civilian and navy alike—anchor pleasure craft in Oak Harbor, and it has a small-town atmosphere: friendly, welcoming. Like most small communities, there are few secrets. Neighbors know neighbors' business, and gossip flourishes. Love triangles are rarely as clandestine as the participants believe they are. Most sexual straying there is uneventful, but the scandal and shock waves that reverberated throughout Oak Harbor in mid-July 1980 were of a magnitude seldom seen. When the dust settled, those involved and onlookers

3

hoped devoutly that nothing like it would happen ever again.

Because of what happened shortly after ten PM on that sultry Sunday night of July 13, 1980, four lives that had come together from widely scattered parts of the world were irrevocably changed. One man died instantly in a barrage of bullets from a .357 Magnum. The other three principals would tell divergent stories during a lengthy trial in Judge H. Joseph Coleman's courtroom in Seattle as the 1980 Christmas season approached. There was no question of holding the trial in Island County; there had been too much pretrial publicity, and there probably wasn't a citizen in the whole county who hadn't heard of the murder of Lieutenant Commander Dennis Archer.

I attended that trial. Much of the convoluted narrative that follows is either directly from court records or from my conversations with close associates of the principals and from detectives' precise recall. Some of it is from my own observation.

The testimony that was elicited in Judge Coleman's courtroom was so explosive that spectators lined up for hours to get in, content to sit packed into the rows of hard benches in the overheated room, eager to listen to the almost unbelievable sequence of events that led up to the brutal slaying of the high-ranking naval officer.

One of the defendants on charges of first-degree murder and conspiracy was Dennis Archer's widow, Maria Elena, 32, an exquisitely beautiful woman of petite stature. She could not have been more than five feet tall, and she wore her long dark hair pulled back from her face and loosely braided in shining waves. Once released from its braids, her hair would make a shimmering cascade reaching below her waist. She didn't look like a cold-blooded murderess. Her voice was soft and her clothing was feminine and demure.

But then, most murderers don't look the part.

The second defendant was a man Maria claimed she had never met. He was, she said, a complete stranger to her. His name was Steven Guidry. He was 26, a short man with a slight build, rather attractive with his sideburns and handlebar mustache. Guidry had come to Oak Harbor from his home outside New Orleans on the fatal weekend Dennis Archer was killed. But he had stayed a very brief time, unusual after traveling such a distance.

The third figure in an alleged plot to kill Maria's husband was not on trial. He would be a witness, but he had already confessed to conspiracy to commit murder. He was Roland Pitre, 27, and was also originally from Cajun country near New Orleans. Pitre was a Marine Corps staff sergeant and Maria's admitted ex-lover. To save himself, he had agreed to turn state's evidence and promised to take the witness stand to bolster the prosecution's case.

Roland Augustin Pitre Jr. was a good-looking man. He looked every inch the Marine, although he no longer wore the uniform. He wasn't much over five feet ten inches tall, but he was extremely muscular. He carried himself as a longtime military man is expected to. His part in this puzzling murder was clouded. Was it possible that he was admitting guilt to protect someone else? No one doubted that he and Maria Archer had enjoyed a consuming and passionate affair so intense, both of their marriages had been teetering on the edge of divorce. Murder made divorce unnecessary.

Just what part Roland Pitre might have played in

Archer's murder no one but the investigators and the attorneys yet knew.

What happened to make this man turn on both the woman he swore he loved and the man who had been his best friend since their boyhood? The first overt betrayal on Pitre's part proved to be only the onset of a quarter of a century's worth of crimes to come, tumbling down one after the other until justice began to seem not only blind but deaf, too.

Of course, none of us sitting in that courtroom could know that then. All we knew was that the engrossing trial was certainly not a slam-dunk case for either side. Nevertheless, observers expected it all to be over before the holidays so that the lawyers, jurors, reporters, and the judge's staff could enjoy Christmas and then move into the New Year and the next newsworthy case.

The female defendant, Maria Elena Archer, was born in Oruro, Bolivia. She had three older sisters and a younger brother, and her wealthy family could well afford to send her to private schools in Bolivia. When she left Bolivia in 1966, Maria had already completed the equivalent of two years of college; she was as brilliant as she was beautiful. And beautiful she surely was.

Maria went first to Ohio State University in Columbus, but the campus and the city were just too big and overwhelming for the 18-year-old, and she moved to Corvallis, Oregon, where she attended Oregon State University. Although even at trial some fourteen years later Maria still spoke with a lilting Hispanic accent, her grasp of languages was excellent. Indeed, she majored in languages, business administration, and psychology at Oregon State. She attended college there for almost three years, excelling in her studies and attracting the eye of more than a few male students.

It was Dennis Archer who won her love after they met in class and began dating. Dennis was a handsome, solid young man about to graduate with a degree in electrical engineering, which would make him a sought-after candidate for a career in the navy. The husky American and the flowerlike girl from Bolivia made a storybook kind of couple when they married in Corvallis on December 27, 1969.

Dennis's first duty station took them to Pensacola, Florida, for four months. Home of the Blue Angels, the navy's incredibly synchronized jet flying squad, Pensacola had charming old houses and white-sugar-sand beaches. They were lucky, too, when Dennis was assigned to a naval base in Corpus Christi, Texas. Again, they stayed just four months before another transfer.

The first permanent home the Archers ever had was in Oak Harbor, Washington, where Dennis was a Navy Air Arm navigator.

Oak Harbor and the Whidbey Island Naval Air Station became a true home base for the Archers. Their first child, a girl, Denise, was born there ten months later. Maria was saved the arduous chore of packing up, moving, settling in again every year or so, and the Archers remained in Oak Harbor for ten years, although Dennis was often away on deployment. Maria estimated later that Dennis's duties kept him away from home for at least four of their ten and a half years of marriage. Service wives have to accept that. When they cannot, their marriages usually end in divorce.

Dennis Archer rose rapidly through the ranks, and he was a lieutenant commander by the late spring of 1980. He and Maria purchased a home on North Fairwood Place in Oak Harbor, and she was involved in activities both as an officer's wife and as a member of the community. On the witness stand, Maria recalled that her marriage was one where she literally worshipped her husband. She said she had always placed Dennis "on a pedestal." That attitude may have been the last vestige of her Bolivian upbringing.

She was totally devoted to her two children (a son was born a few years after Denise). Besides keeping an immaculate house, Maria loved to cook, to paint, and to study. She particularly enjoyed reading in the field of psychology, as she was fascinated by human behavior.

Surprisingly for a woman who appeared so delicate, Maria Elena had always been interested in exercise and physical activity; she took Middle Eastern dancing lessons (belly dancing is the more familiar term) and followed those up with jazz, tap, hula, and folk dancing. She became so adept that she taught dance classes at the Katherine Johnson Dance Studios in Oak Harbor and at Skagit Valley Community College in Mount Vernon, Washington. She directed and planned a Spanish night at the officers club and sewed costumes for and performed in local pageants and drama groups.

Like all service wives, she had to make a life for herself and her children, one that was not dependent on her husband. When Dennis was home, they were a regular family. But for much of the time she was basically a single mother.

"I was alone so much," she remembered. "I spent a

lot of time doing things with my children; I like to help other people and to get involved in the community."

As idyllic as it sounded, things were not rosy in the Archer marriage. Their story is far from unique. Maria took much of the blame for the trouble, wondering if their relationship had faltered because she worshipped Dennis too much. "We weren't on the same level. There was a lack of communication," Maria said softly. "Dennis wasn't willing to work out the marriage problems. His job was very important to him, and there was family pressure. We had counseling about four or five years ago, but I just couldn't get close to him."

As Dennis Archer trained to leave on another deployment in November 1979, Maria prepared to be alone again. She and the children would be alone for Thanksgiving and for Christmas. She testified that she was never unfaithful to her husband, even during the long months while he was away. To forestall temptation in a life without sex she deliberately kept herself very busy.

Maria explained that one of the activities that took up her time after the midsummer of 1979 were the judo classes that she—and the children—attended several times a week. The classes were very popular with service dependents in Oak Harbor. Marine Corps Staff Sergeant Roland Pitre's instruction in self-defense and martial arts drew packed houses. His reputation was such that there were waiting lists for his classes.

Maria recalled that she initially went to the judo classes because of her interest in sports. She said she also went because she was sometimes frightened at night when she was all alone in the house with the youngsters.

Roland Pitre was the instructor, and Maria was only one of many judo students. Then something changed—gradually, subtly, at first. Maria said she wouldn't deny that there was a strong physical attraction between herself and the Marine who taught the judo classes with such grace and strength.

Roland Pitre didn't talk much about his Cajun roots in Louisiana, but he still had a trace of the accent that was partly French and partly the melody of the bayous. He was not classically handsome; his chin was a little weak, and he had a small brush of a mustache, the same reddish color as his wavy hair. But he had a tautly muscled body and moved like a tiger. Although he wasn't particularly well educated, Pitre was innately intelligent and had a quick mind. There was also a sense of danger about him, nothing overt, more like electricity in the air before a storm, the kind that makes the hair on your neck and arms stand on end.

Maria Archer's and Roland Pitre's magnetic attraction to one another was stronger than her loyalty to Dennis or the fact that Roland too was married. He and his wife, Cheryl, were married in May 1976. By May 1980 they were headed for divorce. She had moved back to Pennsylvania with their 18-month-old daughter, Bébé, to stay with relatives while they tried to sort their marriage out. Whether Cheryl knew all the details of Roland's womanizing is unknown. Probably she didn't. He had been like catnip to females since he was in his teens. Usually, he managed to keep his various conquests apart so that they had no way to compare notes.

Detectives one day winked as they said that besides his having well-toned abs and biceps, rumor said that Roland Pitre was exceptionally well-endowed and that that was one of his secrets in seducing the opposite sex.

Maria never mentioned that, of course. Later, she recalled that she was attracted to him because he seemed "a good person" and he adored children, as she did. She had felt a little sorry for him. He told her he'd spent six or seven years in an orphanage as a youngster, that he'd come from a home torn by dissension. "His first judo instructor changed his life," she once told an Island County detective. "That was the first person who showed him he could be good at something. And he wanted to help other kids."

What happened next was perhaps inevitable. Maria Archer never denied that after Dennis Archer went to sea, she and Roland Pitre began a physical affair sometime in the latter part of 1979. According to Maria, the affair continued until late March or early April 1980. They made no effort to hide it, and the liaison was an open secret in the small town of Oak Harbor. The couple were often seen out together, and they even entertained together. Maria admitted to having serious doubts that she could continue in her marriage.

Roland Pitre's marriage blew sky-high, and his wife remained in Pennsylvania. Cheryl threatened to file for divorce, and he didn't try very hard to dissuade her, although he did seem to be heartsick that he was separated from his daughter.

Maria insisted that her relationship with Pitre had nothing to do with the breakup of his marriage. She said that it was already over by the time she and Roland began to sleep together.

As for her own marriage, Maria had been torn. She wrote to Dennis and said, "If I can't make you happy, I'm sorry, darling—but maybe we should try some other way."

Maria recalled that she was surprised by her husband's answer: he wrote that their problems were largely his fault, that he expected her to do everything. She wrote back and said part of it was her fault. "He opened up for the first time.

"He said he loved me very much, but he'd never contest a divorce. In late March or the first part of April 1980, I was planning to try my marriage again."

According to Maria, Roland Pitre took her resolution to attempt to mend her marriage with grace. "He said, 'I'm just a good friend. I'll always be your friend. I just want you to be happy.'"

Dennis Archer was not due to return to Oak Harbor until June 1980. Still, Roland's attitude toward her changed well before that. He seemed to accept her decision to end their affair but remained a constant in her life. They were no longer lovers, but he told her he considered her his closest friend. He would come to her house to babysit her children, and he was a great friend of the neighborhood children. She was busy sewing costumes for a town pageant and Roland even helped with that.

The Marine from New Orleans, who was four years younger than Maria, had lost his wife, his child, and now his mistress, but according to Maria, he accepted all of it with equanimity. He had asked her to divorce her husband and marry him, he had told her he loved her, but that was all in the past. Now, she was only his good friend: "the best friend he'd ever had."

Roland still needed Maria's advice. He wanted to gain custody of his daughter, Bébé. Maria pointed out that a little girl should be with her mother. He didn't agree with her. Maria didn't know Cheryl Pitre, but Roland was adamant that he would make a more reliable parent for his toddler daughter.

In June, Dennis Archer returned home. "We were going to be a family again," Maria testified sadly. "My husband always said, 'You don't have to tell me everything,' but I thought I would—but I didn't want to hurt him." Dennis seemed to accept her confessions, and she said their last weeks together were good. "My husband had changed. We would talk until four AM. We were going to leave and go camping. I told Roland I could finally express my feelings to my husband."

Everything appeared to have come together flawlessly like the seamless ending of a romance novel. Maria's husband appreciated and communicated with her now. She said he had forgiven her for her few months of infidelity. And her lover wasn't the least bit upset that she had gone back to her husband. According to her astounding revelations, Pitre had moved smoothly into the position of her best friend. No one was jealous. No one had an axe to grind, or revenge to seek. All the ends were tied up neatly, too neatly for a skeptic to believe.

His divorce papers filed, Roland Pitre traveled to the East Coast and returned with his 20-month-old daughter and his sister around the first of July. He moved them into a new apartment in Oak Harbor. He called Maria to see how things were going with her. She remembered that she wasn't really that happy to hear from him. She told him a little sharply, "It's none of your business. My life is my life."

Apparently, she no longer needed him as a best friend at that point, and after that, she said she didn't care to see him at all. Maria was totally reconciled with Dennis. Or so it seemed.

2

It was 11:34 on Sunday night, July 13, 1980, when Maria Archer's frantic phone call came into the Island County Sheriff's Office in Coupeville, Washington, ten miles south of the Archer home. The dispatcher had to calm the female on the phone before he could understand what she was saying.

"Someone has broken in and shot my husband!" she cried.

The dispatcher was finally able to get the address, and he radioed the call to Deputy A. J. "Bud" Graves, who arrived at the residence in minutes. Graves found Maria and a neighbor waiting at the house on North Fairwood. She appeared very agitated, which was to be expected. She and the neighbor led Graves to an upstairs bedroom, where a man she identified as her husband, Dennis Archer, lay motionless.

There was no question that Archer was dead; the front of his polo shirt was one giant splotch of crimson, and still-liquid blood stained the carpet beneath him. Still, Graves knelt next to the body, and felt in vain for a pulse. Whatever had happened had happened very recently. There was no rigor mortis, no lividity; the body was still faintly warm to his touch. Nevertheless, Archer was dead.

Graves radioed for backup from Captain Robert E. Sharp, the head of Sheriff Richard Medina's Criminal Investigation Unit. Detective Sergeant Ron Edwards was next up on the list to respond. Edwards was a ten-year veteran of the sheriff's office, and he was about to become the investigator who would be principally responsible for probing into the baffling case.

He quickly ordered deputies to cordon off the house and yard to prevent curious bystanders from contaminating any evidence that might be there.

On the surface, the motive for Archer's murder appeared to have been burglary: a stereo and other belongings of the family were stacked near the front door in the living room. Yet that was strange. The Archers, while comfortable, hardly seemed prime targets for a burglary. Nor did it seem prudent for a burglar to enter a home whose occupant, a husky, six-foot-tall 33-year-old naval officer was still awake. Far better to enter in the wee hours of the morning when the lights were out and the residents were sleeping.

Trembling, Maria Archer told the investigators that she had been out during the evening. She had driven a friend of one of her children home after baking pizza for her family and the other youngster. She left her children with Dennis so that she could visit a woman friend, Lola Sanchez,* who was also a Latin-American navy wife. Maria said she had intended to stop for a few breakfast

---

*Some names have been changed. The first time they appear, they are marked with an asterisk (*).

items at a convenience store on her way home shortly after eleven but had decided it was too late and she had driven straight home from Lola's house.

When she entered the house, the front door was unlocked, Maria said, but that wasn't unusual. She called out, "Hi! I'm here," expecting to hear her husband answer. Instead, she heard first silence, then her children screaming from somewhere in the basement.

"They were screaming, 'Mommy! Mommy! Daddy locked us in the closet!' I wondered if my husband had gone out of his mind," she told Edwards. "Nothing made sense. There was a board across the door to our darkroom, and I wrenched it off to get my children out. The kids said a man came in the house. I looked around, but I was afraid. I was trembling inside, but I'm strong, a mother. I thought maybe someone was in the house, and I had to protect my children. The receiver was off the hook, and I called my neighbor and said, 'Please come right now.' The kids were blubbering. I left them with my neighbor, and I went upstairs."

Maria Archer told the detective that she found her husband lying in the bedroom with his hand blocking the door. "His eyes were open. His mouth was open, and he was white. I knew he was dead. I kissed him and said, 'Darling, we'll always be together now. I'll never leave you now.' I moved his hand and shut the door."

Maria said she was most concerned about her children and that she'd put them to bed, trying to calm them as they cried, "Daddy, where's my daddy? Where did they take him?"

Then she went downstairs and told her neighbor that Dennis was dead and that she must call the sheriff.

It was a most puzzling case for the Island County investigators. If robbery was the motive, why wasn't anything missing? Why did the supposed thief leave his loot still stacked in the living room? Had he been frightened off as Maria arrived home? A canvass of nearby homes by deputies elicited little information that might help. One neighbor thought she might have heard a shot approximately twenty minutes before Maria arrived home to find her husband's body. Other nearby residents had neither heard nor seen anything.

Dennis Archer had been a well-liked and respected neighbor; no one could fathom why he would have been a likely target for murder.

The children, almost hysterical, could offer no help. Nor could Maria.

3

It was a long, long night for Captain Sharp, Sergeant Edwards, and the investigative team as they diagrammed the crime scene, gathered the lethal .357 bullets, vacuumed for fiber samples, and cut sections of carpet from beneath the body. Dusting for latent prints proved to be fruitless. They didn't find any useful possibles. There *were* tire tracks in the front yard of the Archers' home, but they were faint because the weather was hot and dry; there wasn't any mud to hold a good impression. Still, they painstakingly took samples of dirt and grass from the yard, hoping they would later use them to match debris caught in the undercarriage of a suspect vehicle.

There was one odd note that long night: Roland Pitre, who identified himself as a close family friend, made three visits to the Archer home, each time demanding to see Maria, insisting that she needed his emotional support. But Maria declined to see him until, at last angered by his continual prowlings by the house, she asked to confront him to tell him to go away. The detectives asked her not to do that. In fact, the Island County investigators were beginning to find Pitre's presence highly suspect.

His stubborn refusal to leave was so questionable that they arrested him. He was soon charged on suspicion of first-degree murder. Detective Edwards drew up an affidavit and obtained a search warrant for Roland Pitre's apartment, a residence approximately seven miles from the Archer home. The search warrant also listed Pitre's van.

Their sweep of Pitre's apartment unearthed one bizarre item: a spiky black wig. His van contained a duffel bag stenciled with the name "D. E. Woods." Inside, they found only jeans and miscellaneous clothing. The duffel bag and its contents proved to have been reported as stolen by a D. E. Woods in a complaint filed three days before Dennis Archer was shot to death.

Subsequent lab tests found no fiber, dirt, or grass matches between the crime scene itself and Pitre's home and vehicles.

For Detective Edwards, the father of small children whose wife was expecting another in November, the months ahead meant hours and hours of overtime, many trips across the country, and the wildest assortment of witnesses' stories that any investigator had ever uncovered.

Virtually none of the principals had told the absolute truth going in. It didn't take Edwards long to find out about the seven-month affair between the widow Archer and Roland Pitre. Maria Archer willingly gave Edwards an hours-long taped interview a few days after the murder, an interview in which she freely admitted that she and Pitre had been emotionally and physically involved from November 1979 until April 1980. She told Edwards of her resolution to rebuild her marriage at that point and of Pitre's seeming acceptance of her decision.

More telling, she also admitted to Edwards that she had not in fact been with her friend Lola Sanchez on the Sunday evening her husband was killed. She had been at Roland Pitre's apartment. "It didn't have anything to do with anything—where I was—so I didn't think it mattered."

By late June, when he returned from the East Coast with his little girl and his sister, Maria said Roland Pitre had changed dramatically in his attitude toward her. Where he had seemingly released her from all obligations to him, he suddenly began to cling to her like a drowning man. He didn't seem to be able to handle anything by himself: raising his daughter, helping his sister, planning his life. Maria told Edwards that she was appalled to realize how weak Roland really was.

He bombarded her with phone calls, begging her to come see him "just one more time . . . one more time."

He had become the very opposite of what attracted her in the first place. Scornful that a man could be so powerless, Maria told Edwards that she nevertheless felt she had to help Pitre with all his problems.

She said she saw him in her regular judo classes between July 1 and July 13 and then he dropped in at her friend Lola's one day when she was there. She agreed to have ice cream with Pitre and his sister one evening at his apartment. And she even invited his sister to her home for lunch one day. She wasn't very surprised when Roland showed up too, and she had no choice but to let him join them. He then wangled an invitation to ride to Seattle with her to pick up costumes for the Spanish pageant on the pretext that his sister wanted to see the sights there. It was on that occasion, Maria believed, that he purchased a black wig, but she didn't know what it was for.

"What happened on that Sunday night, the thirteenth?" Edwards asked Maria.

Maria deeply inhaled her cigarette's smoke and recalled the last night of her husband's life. She said Pitre called her that afternoon and pleaded with her to drop over in the evening to discuss his problems. She hadn't really intended to go. She and Dennis had had a busy day: taking her children and their friends swimming, baking pizza for her family. She asked her son's friend to spend the night, but his mother called to say that he had a doctor's appointment early the next morning and that he'd better come home. So Maria had to deliver him there about eight. Then she visited with his mother, talking about the boys' teacher and their school. Maria said she left and decided to drop in to see Roland, hoping that maybe she could finally get him straightened out so he wouldn't be so fixated on her.

"I am very independent," she said proudly. "I never knew anyone could be so dependent."

When she arrived at Pitre's apartment, she intended to stay only about twenty minutes. But she found him very anxious, and he said his sister was with friends for the evening. Maria said she meant to leave in plenty of time to get to the store to buy milk and bananas, but ended up talking with Pitre from about nine until eleven. She tried to explain to him that "responsibility is all around us—not just ourselves."

Edwards's mind was calculating the time sequence

of the murder with Maria's story. While she said she was in Pitre's apartment, *talking* for two hours, someone stealthily entered her house, locked her children in the basement darkroom, and shot her husband.

Sergeant Edwards asked Maria the most cogent question: "Do you think Roland Pitre had anything to do with it [Archer's murder]?"

She shook her head slowly. "Putting the pieces together, I asked myself, 'Why did he come back? How could anybody do that?'"

Edwards wasn't sure what she meant. "Why did *who* come back?" he asked himself. Did she mean, "Why did Pitre come back from the East Coast? Or why did he come back to her?" But she was talking freely, so he didn't interrupt her.

Maria stated vehemently that she wanted only the truth. "I just want one thing. I pray to God. I don't want to think he had anything to do with it. I've studied psychology. I thought he was all right."

Maria seemed absolutely baffled that this man who showed such love for her, for her children, for all children, who seemed such a good person, could possibly be responsible for the death of her husband. And yet— and yet, he still loved her so much. She realized that he never really stopped adoring her, never accepted that she had totally gone back to her husband.

It was clear that she was painting herself as a woman who loved her husband, who had no reason to want him dead, and at the same time describing Roland Pitre as a besotted man who might well have done *anything* to win her back.

• • •

Ron Edwards interviewed a number of people who verified that Roland Pitre and Maria had been—at least for several months—a flaming duo. Jo and Mick Brock,* who categorized themselves as good friends of Pitre's and more casual friends of Maria's, had some electrifying information. Jo Brock said that before Dennis Archer returned from deployment, Maria had discussed her affair with Pitre.

"She said she loved Roland and she was afraid Dennis would keep her children if she divorced him. I told her to keep her family together and not consider Roland's feelings."

Jo Brock recalled that Roland begged her to call Maria and arrange a meeting between him and his lost love in the Brock home on the first or second of July and that this was after Dennis Archer returned from sea. "I did that, and they talked awhile in the living room and then went upstairs to our bedroom to talk for a couple of hours. When they came down, Maria rushed out and we could tell that Roland had been crying."

Jo Brock said her husband had helped Roland move on or about July 1 and that Mick had been terribly upset afterward. "I finally got him to tell me what was wrong. He said Roland told him that he and a friend of his from back home [New Orleans] were going to kill Dennis Archer and make it look like an accident. We went to our chaplain and told him about what Roland had said. That was on July 5. My husband tried to talk Roland out of it. He didn't know if he'd succeeded or not, but Roland thanked him for his concern."

Jo Brock recalled that she had seen Roland Pitre three times on Sunday, July 13, the day Dennis was murdered.

Roland lived only a half-block from the Brocks. He was "quite hyper" that day. "He came over around three to three-thirty, and he sat in the kitchen juggling brightly colored balls. He had dressed up like a clown the day before and juggled for the kids, and he promised to teach them how and to have a party for them. Then he came back at six to six-thirty and asked if his sister could spend the evening with us—because Maria was coming to see him and he wanted to talk to her alone. We liked his sister, so we said, 'Sure,' and she came over that evening about eight and stayed until eleven-thirty."

"You said you saw Roland Pitre three times that Sunday?" Edwards prodded.

"Yes. Roland came over again at twelve-thirty, and he was so hyper that his hair was literally standing on end. He said he thought something had happened at Maria's because he saw police cars there. He wanted me or Mick to drive over there with him. I was afraid of him. I thought he might hurt me or Mick—or maybe that other person he'd talked about would—but Mick went with him."

Of course, something *had* happened at the Archer home.

Roland Pitre seemed to have had a motive for murder as old as the history of man: jealousy. Despite his later insistence that he and Maria had become only platonic friends, he had told others that he planned to kill Dennis Archer.

Edwards discovered that a .357 Magnum gun belonging to a friend of Pitre's had turned up missing after he'd had a visit from the judo expert. Pitre borrowed a truck from another serviceman on the day of the murder, a truck that turned up—inexplicably—at the Seattle-

Tacoma International Airport (Sea-Tac) the morning after the murder. The parking ticket for that vehicle, from the machine at the airport gate, read "12:16 AM, July 14." That was just after midnight on Monday morning.

There were so many parts to this puzzle, and they were such extraneous fragments that they could not be forced to mesh into a working mold. Dennis Archer had been gunned down on July 13 between nine and eleven PM. During that exact time period, Maria Archer swore she was with Roland Pitre and that neither of them had left his apartment.

If the two lovers had arranged Dennis's murder and were telling the truth about being together, there had to be a third individual who had done the shooting. Was it the "friend from home" that Pitre told the Brocks about? Jo Brock had seen a dark-haired, mustached man wearing a blue plaid shirt walk away from a truck near Pitre's apartment on Sunday afternoon. Even though he was a stranger, she felt she could identify him if she ever saw him again.

Edwards looked for this mysterious man as the case became curiouser and curiouser. Roland Pitre's mental condition deteriorated rapidly in jail. He mumbled about a killer named Targan who was responsible for Archer's death, he constantly carried around a blanket that he said was his small daughter, and he urinated on himself. He appeared to be in a catatonic state. He was either crazy or was doing a very good job of pretending to be. When he grew even more disoriented, he was taken first to a local hospital, then transferred to the Western Washington State Hospital for observation.

While Pitre babbled incoherently and pretended not

to understand what psychiatrists were saying to him, the Island County sheriff's investigators learned that a close friend had indeed visited him in Oak Harbor on the weekend of July 12 and 13. This was Steven Guidry, 26, another man of Cajun descent, who normally lived in Hanrahan, Louisiana, a suburb of New Orleans. Airline records confirmed that Roland Pitre had prepaid a round-trip plane ticket through a travel agency for one "Billy Evans" to travel coach from New Orleans to Seattle. Edwards found that this ticket was canceled and that Pitre wired money to Steven Guidry instead.

A "Billy Evans" *had* been on a flight that arrived at Sea-Tac airport around noon on July 12 (Saturday) and had departed Sea-Tac for New Orleans on a seven AM flight on Monday, July 14.

Having been declared sane at the Western Washington State Hospital, Pitre was returned to the Island County Jail. On July 21, he visited in jail with relatives, and then asked to speak to Captain Sharp. His statements at that time gave the Island County Prosecutor's Office probable cause to arrest Steven Guidry on suspicion of first-degree murder in the death of Dennis Archer. Sergeant Edwards flew to New Orleans and assisted in the arrest, bringing an apparently bewildered Guidry to jail on Whidbey Island.

The second arrest hit the community by surprise. Then the thirty-four-page statement that Roland Pitre gave to Edwards on September 2 led to yet a third arrest, one that sent shock waves through the tight community. Maria Elena Archer was booked into jail on September 6 on murder charges.

The sheriff's office tried to maintain a tight lid on information about the murder, but rumors spread furiously. Still, the curious would have to wait for the trial before any of the actual statements made by witnesses and the principals were revealed. A change of venue from Island County to King County was granted and the Seattle courtroom was jam-packed as the trial for Maria Archer and Steven Guidry began in early December. Many of the "Islanders" had taken the ferry from Whidbey Island to the mainland to listen to testimony.

It seemed ironic that Roland Pitre was not on trial. With his statements about the guilt of Maria, his lost love, and Steven Guidry, he had cleverly manipulated his plea bargain. He had been allowed to plead guilty to a lesser charge of second-degree murder in exchange for his testimony.

If Pitre ever had been crazy, he had quickly recovered his wits and made sure he would do himself the most good. During the trial, Guidry was still in jail, but after spending several weeks in custody Maria was released on bail. She was free to come and go from the courtroom, to have lunch in downtown restaurants, and to mingle with trial observers in the marble hallways of the King County Courthouse.

The twelve jurors and two alternates in Judge H. Joseph Coleman's courtroom did not have an easy task before them. They would hear the three different and completely contradictory statements regarding the murder of Dennis Archer. Just about the only thing that the prosecutors, the defense lawyers, and the defendants agreed on was that Dennis Archer was dead, that he had been sent to his grave by three bullets in his chest.

It was strange to see the two defendants in the courtroom. They were both small people who looked as if homicide would be completely alien to them. Steven Guidry sat at the far end of the L-shaped cluster formed by the two defense tables, next to his lawyer, Richard Hansen. Maria Archer sat three chairs away, beside her lawyer, Gil Mullen, a former Seattle police officer. During the three-week trial, Maria and Guidry never even glanced at each other.

It was quite possible that they *didn't* know each other, although the State contended they almost certainly knew *about* each other because of the plotting between Maria and Roland.

David Thiele, the Island County prosecutor, presented the State's case, and Sergeant Ron Edwards of the sheriff's office assisted the prosecution, sitting close by Thiele to help with information on the details of his investigation.

The first row of the gallery was reserved for the media. We were packed so tightly that we could barely scribble on our yellow legal pads. The second row was made up principally of friends and family of the victim and of Maria Archer. The rest of the long oak benches were up for grabs by a long line of spectators.

The Archer-Guidry trial in 1980 was one of the very first in Washington where both television and still cameras were allowed into the courtroom, and cameramen from all major stations and newspapers in Washington took turns filming the proceedings. Maria, completely beautiful from any angle, was their chief subject. Sometimes it appeared that she was unaware of the cameras focused on her. Sometimes she seemed to pose for them.

Roland Pitre, the former Marine Corps staff sergeant, the judo instructor, the admitted ex-lover of the female defendant, transfixed the crowd and had the jury's full attention for four days as he laid out a story of passion and conspiracy to commit murder.

Pitre maintained that he had been totally in love with Maria and that it was she—not he—who had convinced him that the only way they could ever hope to marry was to have her husband killed.

He testified that Maria was terrified that she would lose custody of her children if Dennis divorced her and that she couldn't bear that. According to him, she begged and nagged him to help her until he finally agreed. "I was doing something that I didn't want to do. I knew it was wrong," Pitre earnestly told the jury.

He described how the pressure from Maria to kill her husband built during the last days before Archer's murder. "I felt I was losing my grip on things." Pitre said he thought about seeing a psychiatrist and that he spent some time reading *I Never Promised You a Rose Garden* (a book then popular about a young woman institutionalized for schizophrenia). Try as he might, he testified, he was unable to stop the inexorable progress toward murder. He sighed as he said that he himself could not bear the thought of murder, but then he couldn't stand to lose Maria, either.

Pitre recalled that Maria had first brought up the matter of killing her husband a few weeks before the murder. They were making love on the floor of his apartment when she initially broached the idea after he asked her, "How can I really make you mine?" He told the jurors that she had answered quickly: "The only way I can really belong to you is if you kill Dennis."

He was shocked, he said sadly, to hear her say that.

The witness said he tried at first to suggest the demise of Dennis Archer in a nonviolent way. Pitre admitted that he purchased three bottles of Sominex—an over-the-counter sleep aid—and gave them to Maria, hoping that she would believe they might poison her husband and therefore trust that he, Pitre, was sincere in helping her. That didn't work. She told him he'd better find a more effective way to kill Dennis.

Killing Dennis had to be a sure thing, not just something that would give him a stomachache or put him to sleep for a day. It needed to be death by gunshot or knifing or bludgeoning.

Because the community knew of his affair with Maria, the couple realized that neither of them could actually carry out the act of murder. They had to find someone totally unconnected to Dennis Archer, someone no one would recognize or remember who could do the killing. Stranger to stranger, the most difficult kind of homicide for detectives to solve.

The jurors, transfixed, watched Roland Pitre as he glibly told them a story that sounded as though it had come out of a film noir.

The plan had been refined, Pitre testified, to the point where he and Maria decided that he would contact his old friend, Steven Guidry, in Louisiana and fly him up to Washington, furnish him with plans of the Archers' house layout, give him a gun, and send him off to do the job. Guidry would have firm instructions to make Archer's murder look like the by-product of a burglary that he had interrupted. If this *had* been a forties movie, the plan would surely have called for Guidry to die, too, after he had accomplished his deadly assignment.

Pitre said he *had* contacted Guidry and offered him $5,000 to do the killing. Guidry countered by saying he would do it for nothing. This was very hard for the jury and the gallery to swallow.

Pitre testified that he picked up his old friend around noon on Saturday at the airport south of Seattle. He immediately drove him to the Whidbey Island ferry and then to his apartment. There he gave Guidry a key to the Archer residence and the gun, explaining that he and Maria would be miles away from the murder location. After Guidry had determined that Dennis Archer was indeed dead, he was to call Pitre and give him the code words "Bernie Garcia."

The witness said he explained to Guidry that the gun was to be dropped off the Deception Pass bridge as they drove to Sea-Tac airport after the murder. The water below was so deep that no one would ever find it.

The plot to murder Maria's husband sounded so cold-blooded as Roland Pitre spun it out. Cold-blooded it was and planned to the minute. On Sunday night, July 13, Pitre testified, he took his sister over to the Brocks' home to visit as he planned. He had been very careful that no one in Oak Harbor saw Steve Guidry and kept him hidden in his van until the moment came for him to leave for the Archers' house. Maria would not be there, of course, because they had planned for her to leave her home well before Guidry got there. The children were not to be hurt; they were to be shut up in the basement so they would not witness their father's murder.

After Pitre dispatched Guidry to commit murder, he said, he spent his time waiting for Maria, "frying fish, and watching *Mork and Mindy.*"

The judo expert then described to the jury a Maria Archer who was completely different from the loving mother and penitent unfaithful wife that she portrayed herself to be in her statements and testimony.

"She got there, and we sat on a sofa for a while," Roland Pitre told the jurors. They gazed at Maria Archer as she sat at the defense table, her head slightly bowed, her hands clasped in her lap.

"I was laying down with my head in her lap, and she asked me to make love to her," Pitre continued. "That was about twenty minutes after she got there. We went upstairs. During the time we were upstairs, she asked several times what time it was and whether I thought it had happened yet. I told her I didn't know. It was supposed to happen when it was dark. But the time wasn't specific."

Pitre recalled that Maria rose from the bed, began to get dressed, and was brushing her long, dark hair about 10:30. She had then made a couple of phone calls, including one to her friend, Lola Sanchez.

"Maria told me that Lola had told her she shouldn't be seeing me and that Dennis was going to find out about us and she was going to lose everything," Pitre testified. "Then she said, 'You know, she's right.' Maria said it would be better for me and my daughter and for her and her kids if we not see each other anymore."

"I said, 'You know, Maria, Dennis is probably dead now.'"

"She said, 'I know,' and then she left."

Roland Pitre said he had realized suddenly at that point that he had been "tricked" and "manipulated" into arranging his lover's husband's murder and that Maria had never intended to marry him at all. He had been duped. The thought of what he had done for a love that didn't really exist ate at his mind like acid. Not surprisingly, he said his mental problems had grown worse after his arrest, that he had stopped eating and drinking and that he even lost his memory for long periods of time. He actually began to believe that it was an evil being named Targan who made him do the bad things he did to keep Maria's love.

Still, he recalled that Maria came to visit him once in jail and that she mouthed the words "I love you" during that visit.

But she never came back.

Roland Pitre was supremely convincing as the betrayed lover, who was now facing years in prison because he had been seduced by a wanton woman and used to carry out her murderous desires. On the witness stand, he managed to hide the muscles of a trained judo expert and looked like the pathetic loser he claimed to be.

Now it was time for the defense. Maria Archer's lawyer, Gil Mullen, one of Seattle's most effective criminal defense lawyers, tore into Roland Pitre during cross-examination. Mullen aimed at Pitre's credibility as a witness, which he showed was highly suspect by quoting lies in several statements Pitre gave to the Island County lawmen since his arrest. Pitre's statement that Steven Guidry arrived from Louisiana wearing only rubber thongs as footwear seemed one of the more minor oddities in a case already so strange. But then what are the rules of dress for someone contemplating murder? Suit and tie? Trench coat? Hip boots? Whether Guidry wore thongs or sneakers didn't seem to have much to do with his guilt.

Now Gil Mullen smiled sardonically as he pointed out that Pitre's insistence that Guidry was such a loyal friend that he offered to be the triggerman for nothing, refusing $5,000, money he needed badly, defied credulity.

And what are the limitless bounds of friendship? The jury was considering these peculiarities when counselor Mullen hit on an area that shocked most of the gallery.

Mullen elicited an admission from Roland Pitre that he had considered murdering his 20-month-old daughter earlier in the summer of 1980. For profit. Pitre admitted that he had insured Bébé's life for as much as he could, an amount the State estimated at $45,000. He said the thought of killing little Bébé, who had been entrusted to him in temporary custody, had seized his mind—but for only a day or so. Then he said he dismissed the idea.

"But the thought did occur while I was putting Bébé to sleep for her nap," Pitre testified. "I said 'Nothing better happen to you, or I'll be a rich man.'"

"What method did you consider when you thought of killing your daughter?" Mullen probed.

Pitre said he had considered killing the child with a drug overdose by giving her access to his medicine cabinet or maybe stuffing her into a plastic garbage bag so that she would suffocate or throwing her from his moving van. He hastened to add that Maria had known nothing of these dark thoughts.

Pitre was asked about various statements he had

made about Dennis Archer's killing, with Mullen often pointing out discrepancies. Pitre answered that everything he said in each statement was "true at the time."

Targan, the evil being, was blamed for the murder in a statement Pitre gave on August 28.

"Is Targan still with us today?" Mullen asked.

"No, he's not."

"Targan had nothing to do with it?" Mullen probed.

"No, but at that time, I thought he did."

"You once claimed to be a hit man for organized crime in New Orleans. Was that true?"

"I was making a joke," Pitre said with a smirk, as if it were laughable.

Pitre maintained in court that he felt overwhelming guilt about Dennis Archer's murder. He said that there were times when he found it was difficult even to look at himself in the mirror to shave. But he was resolute about his testimony that Maria Archer had been the one who pushed and prodded him into arranging her husband's killing.

"I was used," he said flatly.

As the trial moved into its second week, Maria Archer herself took the witness stand, seemingly undisturbed by the television and still cameras that recorded her every movement. She appeared to have no stage fright in a courtroom filled to overflowing with the curious. It was easy to believe Maria. She perched on the edge of the witness chair, looking almost childlike, so tiny that her feet hardly touched the floor. She wore a plaid pleated skirt, a dark blazer, and a ruffle of white at her neck, and she smiled often, although it was a subdued smile, one suitable for a young widow.

Her voice was so soft that even with the amplification

of a microphone, it didn't reach to the rear of the courtroom. The jurors leaned forward in their chairs, straining to understand her words.

By testifying in her own defense, Maria opened herself up to cross-examination, but she seemed prepared for that. Her own attorney asked her many of the "tough" questions, aware that they would be forthcoming from the prosecutor, David Thiele, on cross. Mullen used this effective technique to defuse any of her answers that might make the jury think badly of her. If he asked them first, they wouldn't have as much impact when the prosecutor asked them.

Maria repeated the story that Detective Edwards taped two days after her husband was killed. The jurors had already heard that tape, and it was one of the most compelling pieces of evidence that the State had against her.

Now, on the witness stand, she once again admitted her affair with Roland Pitre. "Was it a physical affair?"

"That's what I always understood an affair was," she said a little condescendingly, toward even her own lawyer.

Maria said she believed that Roland understood her wish to return to Dennis, but then she said she was horrified at the way he began to cling to her. Once he came back to Whidbey Island with temporary custody of his daughter, he didn't seem to know what to do. Yes, she admitted that she saw Roland Pitre almost every day for two weeks prior to the murder, but that had not been her choice. It was because he dogged her trail, confronting her everywhere she went. She could not avoid him, and she felt sorry for his sister. She recounted the meeting around July 1, 1980, in their mutual friends' bedroom.

"I did not want to see him. But I went there. Mr. Pitre

started talking to me. He was extremely apprehensive. He started crying. I thought he would not want to be embarrassed so we went to the bedroom to talk."

Roland Pitre (whom she occasionally referred to as "Sensei," a Japanese word for "teacher" used frequently in martial-arts training). "He was different from the nice friend who'd left. His hair was different, blond instead of dark. He sat on the bed. He was trembling. He asked if he was going to see me any more beyond judo class, and I shook my head no. 'That's what I was afraid of,' he said. He cried, and he caressed the air around me. He was afraid to touch me. I yelled at him and preached at him a lot.

"I told him: 'You are a blind man touching a big, gigantic elephant, touching just the tail and you think the tail is the whole elephant. You can't pray for anything you want! You are not a good Catholic.'"

She said that she had called him a fool.

As far as Maria was concerned, she testified, the affair was over, dead, cold.

"Did you ever at any occasion suggest anything that could have sounded like killing your husband?" Mullen asked.

"No. Never."

"Did you talk to him about drugging or poisoning your husband? Did you say anything about giving him some Sominex?"

"Never. Never."

"Had Mr. Pitre ever discussed his plan to kill your husband with you?"

"Never. He wouldn't discuss my husband with me. Never."

Maria's scathing answers were spat out as Mullen

asked her if she'd agreed to a plan to leave her children at home while a third party—Steven Guidry—went to her home to kill her husband. "Did you agree to expose the children to that danger?"

"I am not demented!"

The questions became more difficult after Prosecutor Thiele rose to cross-examine Maria Archer. Thiele asked, "You lied about being with Roland Pitre on the night your husband was shot. You asked Lola Sanchez to tell your husband you were with her?"

A. . . . it was not the truth . . .

Q. You lied to the police on that first night?

A. But it had nothing to do with it.

Q. Why did you tell them you were at Mrs. Sanchez's?

A. Wherever I was, it was none of their business.

Q. In the statement you gave to Sergeant Edwards, you said you'd told Lola Sanchez to "just tell him [Archer] I was at your house?"

A. I was under Valium. I don't remember the statement.

Thiele suggested that Dennis Archer had planned to move into a mobile home the Archers owned when he returned from deployment in June 1980, but he couldn't do that because Maria had sold it while he was gone. He asked her if it was true that there would be no "quarters allowance" from the navy if Archer didn't move back with her because of the problems they were having over Roland Pitre. He pointed out that she had financial motivation to reconcile with her husband.

Maria appeared not to understand what he was getting at. When Thiele asked her if she had—or would—derive any financial benefit from her husband's death, Maria Archer said she couldn't hear him. He repeated the question in a slightly louder voice. There was no way she could claim to be that deaf.

Thiele asked specifically about the three insurance policies: $25,000 from Old Line of the South, $20,000 from Servicemen's Life Insurance, $3,000 (a navy policy), and mortgage insurance on the Archer home, which had recently been sold for $72,000.

Maria Archer barely acknowledged this information. Thiele then pointed out that all the money that might be coming to her was frozen because of litigation brought by Dennis Archer's family. They were suing Maria in civil court through the Slayer's Act (which denies insurance benefits or inheritance from wills or profits from writing about their crimes to someone who has caused the death of the benefactor).

Thiele led Maria through the many meetings, phone calls, judo classes, and the countless hours that Maria had spent with Roland Pitre since her husband's return. Still, she was adamant that she had merely been trying to help a man who was as dependent upon her as a baby.

With her chin tilted up haughtily, Maria denied absolutely that she had wanted her husband dead.

Now, two versions of the strange case had been told. It was almost Christmas, and outside the courtroom the first-floor lobby of the King County Courthouse held a towering, decorated fir tree, but there was no holiday spirit at all inside.

Steven Guidry had said nothing during the trial. He

had barely glanced up from the yellow legal sheet that he filled with scrawls during the long court sessions. Now it was his turn to tell of the events leading to the strange and fatal weekend in Oak Harbor, Washington, in July 1980.

Guidry was neither timid nor cocky as he took the witness stand to be questioned by his lawyer, Richard Hansen. The second defendant recalled that he and Roland Pitre were best friends from their early teens until Pitre joined the Marines. And it was Steve Guidry, not Pitre, who first became interested in judo. The defendant said he joined the Jefferson Parish Junior Deputies (an organization the sheriff's office sponsored to stop crime among juveniles) when he was 12 or 13. Steve took to the judo instruction with enthusiasm, and he persuaded Roland, who lived a few blocks away, to join, too. They both became adept in the martial art.

After Pitre left for the Marines, Steve said he saw him four or five times over the years and that Pitre sent him postcards and letters from Japan. He didn't know Pitre's wife well, although he and his wife double-dated with the Pitres on one occasion. He didn't feel that Pitre's wife was well suited to him but didn't explain why.

Steve Guidry said that life wasn't going so well for him in the late spring of 1980. He was working on a pipeline repairing gas detectors and mud-monitoring equipment, and he wasn't contented with the work. The apartment he shared with his wife and son had a broken-down air conditioner, which in New Orleans in the summer made the rooms like ovens. His wife took their child and moved to her parents' home. Since Guidry didn't get along well with them, he moved in with his mother and sisters.

"I wanted to buy a house," Guidry told the jury. "But I couldn't see how I'd ever be able to pay for one, so I joined the Marines, thinking I'd learn a specialty and eventually be able to afford a house for us."

Guidry spent every day in late June and early July 1980 with Marine recruiters, taking tests, talking about the opportunities in the Marines. "My test results were so high that I qualified for every school they offered. I wanted electronics, but the only thing available in that field at the time was refrigeration school, and I didn't really want that."

For the first time in a long time, Guidry had called his old friend, Roland Pitre, "to discuss the Marines and what schools I might want to get into."

Guidry said Pitre urged him to wait until the avionics school was available. Steve followed his advice, delaying his departure for basic training until sometime in September. It left him with several weeks of free time on his hands; he'd quit his job and had virtually no money. He testified that he was really pleased when Pitre called him a few days later and invited him to come up to Washington State for a visit. It would give him the opportunity to look over the Marine installation in Oak Harbor.

It turned out that Roland's life wasn't running smoothly, either. He told Steve Guidry that he was in terrible trouble, something he couldn't discuss over his phone, which he said was tapped. "He told me I was the only person he could trust. He offered to pay for my ticket both ways and all expenses if I'd fly up."

Guidry testified that he agreed to fly to Washington. He was supposed to leave during the week of July 14 to July 19, but he had received an eviction notice from his landlord and had to wangle an extension from a Hanrahan constable. He called Pitre and said he couldn't make it. "He told me I had to come—it was so important—so I told him I'd come for a couple of days anyway."

Guidry said he thought it was kind of strange that Pitre didn't want him to fly under his own name, but he finally agreed to fly under the name "Billy Evans." He flew into Sea-Tac airport on Saturday morning. He brought one change of clothes, and, yes, he had worn his usual rubber thongs for footwear.

"Roland met me about noon on July 12. I axed [*sic*] him what the trouble was, but he told me to wait till we were in his van. First, he bought my return ticket, and then we headed for Oak Harbor. I axed him again what the big problem was, and he started talking about his affair with his girlfriend and how much he loved her and how he wished he'd met her before he met his wife and how no woman ever treated him like that before. It seems like she was married and her husband was back from deployment. The guy being back presented a big problem. Roland said that the guy knew about him and the wife and was going to have Roland sent to a military prison because you can't go out with an officer's wife while he's gone on duty."

Then Roland said, Guidry testified, that he really brought Guidry up to Washington State to kill his girlfriend's husband.

"He says he wants me to kill the husband because of the prison threat and that the guy found out because he'd tapped the phone and heard his wife and Roland talking. He said the guy had beat the girlfriend and her kids up, too."

Guidry said he'd been shocked and told Pitre it was ridiculous to plan to kill the man. "But Roland ignored me. He showed me a pistol, ammo, and some maps in a duffel bag. It was a .357 pistol."

Guidry said he'd called Pitre "crazy," and Pitre assured him that nothing could go wrong, the killing had been planned for weeks. The maps and diagrams were of the house where the man was to be killed. Pitre explained several plans that had already been considered and discarded. In one plan, Pitre was going to have someone fly to California or Oregon under Dennis Archer's name. Then Pitre was going to kill Dennis and dispose of the body, and it would look as if Archer had simply disappeared from the flight. In another, Pitre was going to talk Archer into climbing a ladder, from which he would fall and break his neck. Guidry testified that he was dumbfounded. None of his old friend's wild imaginings sounded like the Pitre he knew.

The current plan was for Guidry to be the hit man while Pitre spent the time—set for Monday evening, July 14—with friends at the Globe and Anchor Bar so he'd have an alibi.

Guidry told the jurors next about a less than delightful "vacation" weekend in Washington State. He said that Pitre had insisted that he spend most of his time waiting in Pitre's van, because Pitre didn't want his sister to see him. Oddly, Pitre has taken Guidry to the Globe and Anchor (where Pitre worked) on Saturday night and introduced him around, but then he stashed him right back in the van parked outside Pitre's apartment.

By Sunday, Guidry said, he was getting pretty annoyed. Pitre had taken him for a ride and bought him a couple of Big Macs, for a picnic on the beach. Then he started in again on how it was up to Guidry to shoot Dennis Archer.

The jurors glanced from Steve Guidry to Maria Archer and back again. Everyone involved in this case was talking and talking a lot. Whom were they going to believe?

Guidry testified that he never saw the Archer home and never saw Maria, but that he probably was the man walking near the truck that Jo Brock saw on Saturday afternoon. "Roland took me with him to borrow it because he said he needed it to move."

Guidry said that he had finally had enough of Roland Pitre's constant pressure to shoot Dennis Archer. "I told Roland that I was leaving Monday morning. He said he couldn't take me to the airport Sunday night, because he was having company, or Monday morning, because he had to work. We started to bicker. We got back to his apartment about 5:30 on Sunday afternoon and Pitre told me again to 'wait in the van' until his sister left. I told him I was going to leave that night, and I needed transportation to the airport or I'd hitchhike. I got my suitcase and said I wanted to leave before the sun went down. Finally, he tossed me the keys to the truck, and I left."

It was Guidry's testimony that he drove out of Oak Harbor around seven. He took a wrong turn on his way to the airport, some 118 miles away, and ended up north of Oak Harbor in Anacortes instead of south heading for Seattle. Retracing his path, he finally headed in the right direction. He said he stopped once to go to the bathroom and ask directions and once to get something to eat.

Guidry swore on the stand he had nothing to do with Dennis Archer's murder and that he'd told Pitre the whole plan was ridiculous.

The Archers' children would probably have been the only witnesses anyone could believe for sure. Although they were nearly hysterical when the deputies responded to their mother's phone call on the night of the murder, they had conveyed that their father had been shot and killed in his home by a "strange man."

According to the medical examiner and neighbors' statements, the shooting had probably occurred around ten PM.

At ten PM, Maria Archer, by her testimony, was with Roland Pitre. At ten PM, Roland Pitre, by his testimony, was in bed with Maria Archer in his apartment. At ten PM, Steven Guidry, by his testimony, was driving toward the Seattle-Tacoma Airport. The driving time between Oak Harbor and the airport, which is fifteen miles south of Seattle, is just over two hours if one adheres to the speed limit.

Maria Archer left Roland Pitre's apartment to return home at eleven PM. After her husband's body was removed to await autopsy, Maria remained home for the rest of the night. She made one phone call at around 2:30 AM. That call was to her friend Lola Sanchez, who reported that Maria said, "Someone broke into our house and shot my husband. It must have happened just when I was talking to you on the phone from Roland's apartment."

Roland Pitre spent most of the night driving by the death house, occasionally stopping and attempting to talk to Maria. Steven Guidry spent the night at the Sea-

Tac airport awaiting the flight to New Orleans, which he boarded at seven on July 14.

In short, if one believed all of the testimony given in the three-week-long trial, none of the principals could have shot Dennis Archer. Each pointed a finger at someone else. It was the sort of stuff that can boggle juries' minds.

Prosecutor David Thiele bluntly told the jury in his final arguments: "It is an either-or situation. There are only two possible murderers of Dennis Archer: Pitre or Guidry. Evidence has proved that the actual killing was done by Guidry."

Thiele reminded the jury of Pitre's testimony that he and the victim's wife were in his apartment making love at the time of the murder. "Roland Pitre would not have had time to go out and do the killing himself. Roland Pitre was not the triggerman. Steven Guidry was the triggerman, and Maria Archer was a participant in the plot."

Thiele pointed out a "fourfold" reason for Maria's wanting her husband dead: "She wanted to rid herself of a husband she no longer loved or [even] liked." Added to that, Archer's death would clear the way, Thiele said, for Maria to marry Roland Pitre, give her financial gain in the amount of $120,000, and protect her from losing her children in a custody suit stemming from a divorce action.

Gil Mullen, Maria's attorney, struck hard at Roland Pitre's credibility as a witness. "The state's case has got to rise or fall on the testimony of Roland Pitre. And Roland Pitre is a thief, a faker, a cold-blooded, violent, confessed murderer and an unmitigated liar!"

Mullen did not attempt to paint Maria as a saint. "Maria Archer admits she had an affair with Roland

Pitre, and she was ashamed and not very proud of it; but she is not here on trial for having an affair. She is not here on trial for committing sexual indiscretions. She is here on trial for murder—premeditated murder."

Richard Hansen, Steven Guidry's attorney, enlarged on the defense's belief that Pitre was a liar. "If you convict these two innocent people, that is going to help Roland Pitre. He has a strong incentive to help convict these innocent people to help himself. It would cut off half or probably more of his sentence."

By testifying against his former mistress and his former best friend, Roland Pitre was now allowed to plead guilty to second-degree murder, and he would indeed have a much shorter sentence than life in prison.

4

And so, on New Year's Eve 1980, the tangle of evidence and testimony went at last to the jury. The press bench vacillated. As one reporter remarked, "One day, I think 'guilty' and then the next I think 'not guilty.' I wouldn't want to be on the jury."

After eleven hours, the jury came back.

The verdicts . . . Steven Guidry: first-degree murder, not guilty; conspiracy to commit murder, not guilty. Maria Archer: first-degree murder, not guilty; conspiracy to commit murder, not guilty.

Steven Guidry broke into tears. Maria Archer's face was void of any expression. Then she smiled. Afterward, she told the press, "Anybody who had any sense could see what was right and what was true. It was ridiculous—having to go through all this."

She spoke of her former lover, Roland Pitre, "I'd like to feel sorry for him. Sometimes I do. But that does not change the fact that he's a liar and the most unscrupulous person I ever met."

Maria said she didn't care about the financial benefits derived from her husband's death. Looking toward her former in-laws, she said, "I don't care about the money. I'm not fighting them. They can keep it."

If ever a murder case was over but yet not over at all, it was the bizarre killing of Dennis Archer. It was possible, some observers felt, that the man about to be sentenced for his murder, Roland Pitre, might not have committed the actual crime. The only eyewitnesses, the Archer children, were blocked from testifying in court by motions by the defense that stated that the children, at 7 and 10, were too young to be accurate witnesses. (That isn't necessarily true. It depends on the child; in retrospect, it was probably far more beneficial to the children to keep them from testifying against their own mother.)

If they had seen a "strange man," it might well have been Roland Pitre in his spiky new black wig.

Only one thing is certain. Dennis Archer most assuredly did not shoot himself in the chest three times. The gun never turned up, and it is probably still buried in the silt at the bottom of the limitless depths of the water at Deception Pass.

Detective Sergeant Ron Edwards of Island County would not forget this case. In the years ahead as an investigator, he often wondered if perhaps someday, sometime, the corrosive nigglings of conscience would force someone to speak out. A careless word to the wrong person.

That never happened. But the story of Roland Pitre was far from over.

5

Because he turned state's evidence against his ex-mistress and boyhood friend, Roland Pitre drew only a thirty-five-year maximum prison sentence. His former wife, Cheryl, remained in Pennsylvania with their little girl, Bébé. Maria Archer went on with her life, never to make headlines again. Steven Guidry was far away in New Orleans, undoubtedly much relieved that he had been acquitted of murder.

Those of us who witnessed their trial in 1980 assumed that Roland Pitre would stay safely behind bars in the federal penitentiary on McNeil Island. It is located, as Alcatraz was, in an isolated spot surrounded by deep water. With good behavior, he might conceivably be released on parole in ten to fifteen years. But he had demonstrated that he wasn't always who he appeared to be, so as charismatic and appealing as he often was, Pitre seemed an unlikely candidate for early parole.

Still, true sociopaths often make model prisoners,

giving corrections officers little trouble. They learn that
the way out is not to fight the system but to respond to
those who are temporarily in control with charm and an
earnest mask. No one could be more cooperative than
Roland Pitre.

During his time on McNeil Island, he obtained his
Associate of Arts degree from Centralia Community College and his B.A. degree from Evergreen State College
through correspondence and prison courses.

Back east, Cheryl Pitre had never really stopped loving
her ex-husband, and she wanted very much to believe
his letters protesting his innocence in Dennis Archer's
murder. Perhaps even more compelling, Roland wrote
of his tremendous regret that he had been unfaithful to
her. His reasoning made more and more sense to her because he was telling her what she needed to hear. He
had always been extremely persuasive, and he was very
attractive to women. When he first proposed to her in
the seventies, Cheryl was both grateful and baffled. She
was not a beautiful woman, and she knew he had dated
many gorgeous women in the past. She had thick chestnut hair and lovely blue eyes but was a little plump and
somewhat plain. Where Maria Archer was tiny and slender, Cheryl was large-breasted and big-boned. Her confidence had been severely shaken when she learned that
Roland was cheating on her with Maria.

But now he was back in her life, telling her all the
things she thought she would never hear. Cheryl took
into account that he was in prison, where there were no
women for him to cheat with. Still, he truly seemed to
have come to appreciate her letters and her renewed

loyalty to him. He wrote that he wanted to start over, to be a father to Bébé, who lived with Cheryl. If only, he wrote, he wasn't stuck in prison for years.

It worked. They remarried in December 1981 while Roland was still in prison.

Cheryl made up her mind that she would do everything possible to help him achieve an early parole. She longed to be with him again. He explained that his only chance to get out before he was an old man was to have someone to come home to, someone with a solid reputation who had a house where he could move in. Someone who would arrange to have a job waiting for him, too.

Cheryl promised Roland that she would be that person for him. As she had before, she accepted him on faith. Just how much Cheryl knew about Roland's life each time she married him may never be known. He was—and always had been—a man with an astounding gift of gab, and he was also a man with many secrets. He was a chameleon, changing his demeanor and attitude to suit whatever situation he was in. He always had many male friends and—this much Cheryl knew—any number of women who had loved him.

Roland usually told women that he suffered through an abusive childhood, but that may very well be only one of the lies he told to draw people to him and gain their sympathy. He was born in Donaldsville, Louisiana, on October 30, 1952, and was named after his father; he was Roland Augustin Pitre Jr. He was built exactly like his father, thin but tough as steel cable, with ropelike muscles.

Aside from his longtime friendship with Steve Guidry, Pitre's early childhood in the New Orleans area is murky. He was born the third of six children, the second of five to survive. His parents, Roland Pitre Sr. and Emily Gros Pitre, apparently had a successful marriage that lasted until death parted them. There were five boys—Roland Jr., Danny, Michael, Rodney, and Wade—and one girl, Sherry. Tragically, Wade died at the age of 2. Roland's father, 28 when Roland was born, was a truck driver with the Teamsters Local 207 in New Orleans and a Marine Corps veteran of World War II. His mother worked as a waitress. Both Roland's parents were Cajun French, part of a large population that lived the rich culture handed down by their ancestors in Louisiana, enjoying zydeco music, spicy gumbo and crawfish cuisine, and folklore and ghost stories. They often spoke Cajun French in their home.

Roland would always have a trace of a French accent, although his bonds to Louisiana and his family were not particularly close. He attended St. Rita's parochial school through the eighth grade, then went on to East Jefferson High School in Metairie, Louisiana. He dropped out of school in the eleventh grade.

Like his father before him, Roland enlisted in the Marine Corps when he was in his late teens. He flourished there and obtained his GED high school degree in the service. His fellow recruits called Roland "Pete" and admired his judo proficiency. One of his Marine buddies recalls a visit to Louisiana with Pitre in 1972.

"We went to New Orleans on a four-day weekend," he says. "Five of us drove down from Cherry Point, North Carolina. We went to see Pete's fiancée, who was named Debby."

Roland had a large Marine Corps tattoo on his upper left arm and had DEB tattooed on his right arm.

"He always called her Deb," his fellow Marine remembered. "He once told me that if he ever got into trouble and was asked about it, he would say his tattoo stood for *his* initials, and that his name was Donald Edward Buschere. It was a long time ago, and I'm not sure of the spelling."

Pitre didn't explain why he expected trouble or an arrest or why he might need an alias. The Marine, remembering Roland Pitre almost thirty-five years later, says he was impressed with Deb's family. "We stayed at Deb's parents' house, a nice, upper-middle-class neighborhood. And they treated us like kings. Deb's father was a fairly successful businessman, and her mother was a great cook. They seemed to think the world of Pete."

Deb, who hoped to marry the dashing Marine that Roland Pitre was in 1972, was very petite and "gorgeous." She rounded up two of her girlfriends to be blind dates for the two Marines who accompanied Pitre to New Orleans.

"We all went to the French Quarter one evening for drinks and dancing," one of them remembers. "We visited Roland's father—but only briefly—in this town outside New Orleans, called Metairie. We stayed at his house just long enough for Pete to show us a painting one of his girlfriends had done. It showed him in his karate or judo outfit executing a kick. I'm pretty sure he had his black belt in karate before he ever joined the Marines."

Pitre had also been a boxer. He told his buddies that was where he got his broken nose. "The guy just loved to mix it up."

But Roland Pitre didn't marry his gorgeous girlfriend

Deb, and he wasn't faithful to her, either. He almost always had several women on the string at once. One of them may have been Cheryl, whom he eventually did marry. "We all traveled to Pennsylvania once," a buddy recalls. "Pete had a girlfriend there, too, who was a student nurse. I'm not sure what her name was. Her family lived on a farm just outside Union City."

They had another pleasant visit in that small town close to Lake Erie. Roland Pitre never seemed to mind that his buddies knew that he cheated on his women. Indeed, he seemed proud of it and counted on them not to say the wrong thing.

They also knew that Pete lied, but they suspected he did it to be funny, and he didn't hurt any of them; his fibs and outright lies were often hilarious. Early on, his closest Marine friend had his doubts about Pitre's truthfulness. They were assigned to the same training schools, beginning with seven months of avionics classes at a base just outside Memphis, Tennessee. Then they were transferred to the Marine Composite Reconnaissance Squadron 1 (VMCJ-1) for photo reconnaissance and electronic warfare operations at MCAS at Cherry Point, North Carolina. During their four months there, he and Pitre worked on two types of aircraft: the McDonnell Douglas RF-4B Phantom II and the Grumman Intruder. One of the planes was equipped to collect photographic intelligence; the other retrieved electronic intelligence and also jammed and garbled enemy radar. The young Marines worked principally on the jammers. Their training was given only to students with superior IQs and carried with it a lot of responsibility.

Roland Pitre had keen native intelligence, although he

had minimal formal schooling. He also had his rowdy and mischievous side. "Pete told me that he was working as a narc for the military police," his buddy says. "He would go out and smoke dope with his 'friends,' and then he would turn them in. He told me once he borrowed a car from one of his doper buddies and drove it to the MP station, revealing a substantial stash of marijuana. He then told the dopers that the MPs and a drug dog had busted him at the main gate."

Pitre never appeared to have any pangs of conscience about narcing on his friends, and he certainly never felt guilty about betraying the women in his life. He was 19 or 20 and romance was a game of conquest to him; he wasn't looking for any serious relationship.

When they graduated from ALQ-76, the Cherry Point school, Roland and his closest friends became lance corporals, and they celebrated at a bar in Morehead City. They were next transferred to Headquarters and Maintenance Squadron 14 in El Toro, California.

Seven of the highly trained Marines from Marine Corps Avionic School (MCAS) were soon notified that they had less than twenty-four hours to pack up and head overseas; they were ordered to travel in civilian clothing and board civilian airlines to Hiroshima, Japan. Once there, they changed into fatigue uniforms and flew in military aircraft to Cubi Point in the Philippines.

While the Marines were stationed in the Philippines, Pitre—who ignored the venereal disease warnings in the movies they were required to watch—contracted a painful dose of gonorrhea. Because he'd bragged so much about his success with women, his buddies were merciless as they tormented him. "We'd follow him to the latrine when he'd go to relieve himself, and we'd wait outside so we could listen to him whimpering in pain. Naturally, we'd either imitate him or just laugh our butts off."

Eventually the penicillin shots he received kicked in, and Pitre recovered. He'd pulled so many practical jokes on the other guys in his unit that nobody really felt sorry for him.

After that, Pitre slowed down on his dating by the numbers and became semimonogamous when he moved in with a Filipina whose nickname was "Baby."

"I particularly remember this," his buddy says, "because when we finally got back to the States, Pete tried to get off-base housing by telling the Marines that he had gotten married to Baby while we were in the Philippines. When he told me he had gotten married, I wrote to her to find out if that was in fact the case. I remembered her address because I had visited the house on occasion while I was there: 550 Santa Rita. By this time, I knew not to take Pete at his word on *anything*."

Baby wrote back, telling him that she had never married Roland Pitre, had never even considered it. "When I showed her letter to Pete, he was the typical kid caught with his hand in the cookie jar. Silly grin. No explanation."

The two Marines stayed in the same unit, waiting in El Toro for their next assignment. After a few months, they were transferred to Iwakuni, Japan. "We both found places to live off base," his long-ago friend says, noting that the base housing had two dozen men to a room "unless you were a sergeant. Pete was a regular at my house for parties or just to hang out. I don't recall any serious scams or activities that Pete was involved in at this time, but he did get involved in the streaking craze. People said he streaked the BX [Base Exchange] as well as an on-base softball game."

Pete Pitre may have run naked around the Japanese base to show off; anyone who ever knew him really well commented that he was exceptionally well-endowed.

The Marines were young men in their prime, all interested in having fun and partying. Although his buddy didn't trust the man he called Pete to tell him the truth or to be there for anything that counted, he liked him well enough.

In their off-duty hours, the young Marines threw parties. "We had a lot of parties at my place, so Pete spent a lot of time there, drinking, talking, just passing the time. Somewhere, I still have a tape of a time when Pete and I conspired to get another buddy of ours to sing a particularly risqué song. Of course, he didn't know he was being recorded!"

Roland Pitre had always had a short fuse, and he got in a little trouble when he punched a gunnery sergeant, but as always he talked his way out of big trouble. He did his job well in the Marines, and so he remained in the service even after some of his friends opted for civilian life. His best friend in the Corps was back at Cherry Point, awaiting his discharge, when Pitre came to see him.

"Pete's story was that he had been ordered back to the States to appear as a witness in a trial against some of his doper buddies. And, of course, he had to make it more interesting by telling me that someone had taken a shot at him—on base!"

That was not even vaguely believable, but that was

Roland Pitre, and all his friends knew it. He was a compulsive liar, but they were on to him. He wasn't a bad guy; you just couldn't believe what he said.

No one who knew him in the seventies expected Pitre to do anything criminal. Years later, when one of the other men they had been with all through the Marine Corps years wrote to Pitre's best friend to tell him that Pete had some "legal problems," he didn't believe it. "I thought he was pulling my leg."

The Pete he recalled was in his early twenties, a handsome guy who was a practical joker, at most a small-potatoes con man. Thirty years later, his closest service buddy, who has become a successful businessman, was stunned to learn all that happened to Roland Pitre Jr. after their paths diverged.

"Pete was bright, well-spoken, and talented. He was fun to be around. He made things happen. He was tough—a brown belt in judo and a black belt in karate— when I knew him. We worked side by side almost every day for nearly two years. He was a good Marine—most of the time—and a good electronics technician. And *funny!*

"When I think of what he could have accomplished and the life he could have had with just a little effort on his part, it depresses me."

6

Kept from the outside world in the McNeil Island Penitentiary, Roland Pitre had plenty of time to formulate careful plans for his future. He had been dishonorably discharged from the Marine Corps, of course, and he had no option of military service. He needed to make contacts that he thought would be helpful to him later.

His letters from prison to Cheryl and their daughter, Bébé, were masterpieces of persuasion, if not outright brainwashing. He'd assured Cheryl again and again that he wanted only to rescue their marriage and help her raise their daughter. They could start a new life together if only he could be free to be with her.

Cheryl took a huge chance. So they could be close to Roland, she left her family and the security they offered her as she and Bébé moved back to Washington in the mid-eighties. Now Cheryl could visit Roland in the McNeil Island prison. She found a tiny place to live near Bremerton, site of the huge Bremerton Naval Base. She immediately looked for a job and found one with a local car dealer, Bay Ford.

Cheryl began to attend a Seventh-Day Adventist

church and made friends. She was searching for the right church, and she read books and participated in Bible studies. Roland had been raised Catholic, but he hadn't practiced that religion for a long time.

One of the books that tremendously impressed Cheryl was a true story called *They're All Dead, Aren't They?* by Joy Swift. Swift wrote of her marriage to a man much older than she was and then becoming the mother of five, including three stepchildren, when she was still in her teens. Her family's lives were soon marked by terrible violence. Swift and her husband lost his two sons and the two little girls they had together to a teenaged mass murderer. Less than a year later, Joy's young stepdaughter died of cancer. Swift's book was a gripping and inspiring story about her struggle to find faith in the wake of incredible personal disasters. After studying the beliefs of many religions, Joy Swift found her answers in the Seventh-Day Adventists' doctrine.

The book helped Cheryl believe that she, too, could turn the tragedies in her own life into triumphs.

Cheryl had long since forgiven Roland for his affair with Maria. That was in the past. She also convinced herself that Roland would never have wanted to kill Maria's husband. She felt that if he had anything to do with Dennis Archer's death, it could only have been because he was hounded and manipulated into a situation that raged out of control. Cheryl blamed Maria. Now she was willing to wipe the slate clean and to look at her marriage as if it was just beginning. Somehow she would find a way to show the parole board in Washington that Roland wasn't dangerous and that he deserved to be free.

Cheryl Pitre was organized and precise, and she was a

whiz at math. She rapidly became a very valuable employee in the office at Bay Ford. In a few weeks, she knew everything there was to know about car contracts, title searches, simple and compound interest. It wasn't long before she was running the office and training new salesmen. Her bosses at Bay Ford were grateful to have her.

Greg Meakin, who later worked at the car dealer for over a year, recalls that Cheryl taught him "about paperwork and financing. She helped *everyone*. Cheryl was like—well, sort of like your favorite teacher in grade school. She was nice to everyone."

And she was. It didn't matter if it was the lot boy who washed the cars or one of the owners of Bay Ford, Cheryl went out of her way to help people.

Meakin remembers that it was obvious Cheryl didn't spend money on clothes or makeup for herself. She wore stretch pants and bargain knit tops. The dealership was very much laid-back and casual, and nobody cared that she didn't dress like a career woman.

"She was poor as a church mouse, and she lived in this tiny little house down in Port Orchard," Greg Meakin says. "She was pretty plain with long dark hair that had kind of a reddish tone to it," Meakin says. "She was only about five feet three, and she was a little chubby. But she had a completely angelic demeanor and beautiful light-blue eyes. Everybody at Bay liked her."

Between her job and her church, Cheryl Pitre had any number of friends. Some of them worried about her devotion to her convict husband, although she was careful to avoid telling anyone but Greg exactly why Roland was in prison. She wanted him to have a true fresh start when he was paroled.

Always seeing that Bébé had what she needed, Cheryl deprived herself of everything beyond necessities so that she could send Roland money for the prison canteen and put savings away for when he got out.

The dealer where Cheryl worked looked like a business frozen in time since the fifties or sixties. Bay Ford was owned by longtime Bremerton residents who knew almost everyone in Kitsap County. The office and the smaller cubicle rooms where car deals were made was a gathering place for a lot of Bremerton businessmen, who stopped by for a cup of coffee or a cigarette break or just to talk. Cheryl sat behind a counter in the large open space at the top of the stairs. Her desk was close to that of Bonnie Arter and that of the automobile title clerk.

Cheryl seemed always to be smiling, and customers and salesman alike enjoyed visiting with her. "She had a tremendous confidence in her own abilities," Greg Meakin recalls. "She was *completely* trustworthy. She was fun-loving, and she had a great dry sense of humor, but there was a romantic in her, too."

Because she took the time to listen, people shared their troubles and secrets with Cheryl. She wasn't a gossip and never betrayed their confidences. Meakin, who avoided talking about his personal life on the job, did talk to Cheryl. He had just proposed to his girlfriend—who lived on the other side of Puget Sound in the Federal Way area—and he was very happy that she had accepted, but he didn't want to talk about it with all the Bay Ford staff. Greg told only Cheryl, knowing that she would never tell anyone else.

And Cheryl talked to him about Roland. She was hoping to get him a job at Bay when he got out. Like her other friends, Meakin was worried that she might be in for a disappointment. Roland's track record for honesty and fidelity didn't sound promising. But Cheryl's optimism was pervasive. She was able to get a number of references from her church friends and prominent businessmen verifying that she had the resources to help her husband adjust to the world outside prison.

Her sincerity also came through to the Washington State Board of Prison Terms and Parole. She had established a good home and a solid place in the community and her church. She kept her small house spotless, and her credit record was excellent. And she had managed to arrange for a job for Roland at a branch of Bay Ford. He would start as a used-car salesman.

Cheryl blossomed with happiness when she learned Roland was coming home at last. She started wearing makeup, and she splurged on a haircut and styling at a beauty parlor. Her fellow employees at Bay Ford noticed when she wore a new sapphire blue dress to an office party. She had bought it especially for Roland. She was determined to be so attractive to him that he would never stray again.

On June 20, 1986, Cheryl waited for Roland when he walked through the gates of the McNeil Island prison. It was almost the first day of summer, and the sea air felt wonderful as they took the little ferry back to the mainland.

Their little girl, Bébé, was 8 then, and she was thrilled to have her father back in her life.

Roland Pitre was quietly paroled to his faithful wife after serving only six years of his thirty-five-year sentence. If there was any mention of his early release in the newspapers, it was only a short item in the back pages. Island County, where he was convicted of murder, was quite a distance away from Kitsap County, where he would be living. He settled into the Bremerton–Port Orchard area quickly. He went to work at the Subaru division of Bay Ford; Greg Meakin was his manager on the night shift.

To his surprise, Meakin found Roland less than the dynamic, handsome man Cheryl had described to him. "The first time I saw Roland was when he came to me with a car deal he was trying to make. He looked like a fish out of water. I remember he was wearing a 1960s-style plaid sport jacket and a really wide tie. His hair was very short—sandy-colored—and he wore really thick glasses."

Meakin was struck by Pitre's meek demeanor; he was nothing like the "killer convict" Greg had been worried about. "He spoke in a very soft voice, and he sure didn't look like the judo expert I'd heard about. But it was easy to see the 'sweet side' of him that Cheryl had told me about."

Cheryl seemed very happy to have Roland back in her life, and they were having a great time. She had always been a practical joker, a trait that balanced her angelic side. With Roland to assist in her elaborate plots, they often caught Cheryl's fellow employees off guard.

"She got me a couple of times," Meakin remembers. "I was brand-new the first time. In walks Cheryl with this 'cop.' It was Ed MacNamara, who was a civil deputy for Kitsap County. He told me he had a search warrant for my office for 'contraband from the other side of the water.' I was floored and shocked. Ed started searching my desk and all around my office. Then he pulls out a little bag of what looked like cocaine! I have never used drugs, and I didn't know how it got there."

While Meakin sputtered that he had never seen it before, he saw a big grin spread over Cheryl's face.

"April Fool!" she shouted, even though April was long past.

Roland helped Cheryl with her most intricate gag. A customer who was gay appeared to be very attracted to Greg Meakin, who was now the finance manager for Bay Ford, and the other salesmen loved to tease him about it. Philip* always asked for Greg when he came in to look at cars, and he called often to ask Greg questions. Finally, he signed a contract for a new car, and Greg figured he'd seen the last of him.

Apparently he hadn't.

"As the manager who closed the sales, I was the last one to talk to Philip," Greg says, "I knew Philip had a boyfriend named Ronnie,* who was very jealous. And all of a sudden, I started getting these phone calls from Ronnie, and he wasn't happy."

Meakin didn't notice that Cheryl was peeking around his office door and listening to his end of the phone calls. "So finally this Ronnie calls me, and he's mad. He said, 'I hear you were with Philip, and I don't like that. You'd better stay away from him—or you'll be sorry."

Ronnie was a big guy, and this sounded like a serious threat. Then Meakin looked up to see Cheryl giggling. She laughed as she admitted that it wasn't Philip's lover on the phone at all, it was Roland pretending to be Ronnie. Meakin's face was red as everyone in the office started to laugh, and then he laughed, too. None of Cheryl's practical jokes were mean, but she and Roland made quite a pair with their ability to catch someone off guard.

He didn't sell many used cars so Roland Pitre didn't last long at Bay Ford. After he left, he found work here and there. He worked for a while stuffing envelopes for the *Port Orchard Independent,* a biweekly newspaper in Kitsap County. It paid only minimum wage, but it was something. Although he had never shown any interest in a medical career before, Roland looked into nursing courses at the University of Washington and Olympic Community College in Bremerton. He told Cheryl that in two years he could get a degree as a licensed practical nurse, which would open up many job opportunities. He started the interviewing and paperwork process, saying that he hoped eventually to be an RN. He didn't feel that his criminal conviction was anyone's business, so he didn't mention it.

As always, Roland's charm with women helped him. Several supervisors reviewed his application and thought he would be ideal in the medical field, so he was not only admitted to the program but given a scholarship.

Roland made plans to teach judo classes again, an enterprise in which he had always succeeded. In the meantime, Cheryl worked two jobs: days at Bay Ford, and on weekends and some evenings she clerked at PJ's Market at Woods Road and Mile Hill Drive in Port Orchard. Sometimes when she worked the evening shift, then switched to days on Saturday and Sunday, she closed up PJ's at eleven and returned to open the store before seven in the morning. She also did the books for her boss. Cheryl had once taught math and was adept at bookkeeping and business matters.

With her careful budgeting and Roland's growing clientele of judo students, the Pitres were able to purchase their first home. It was a triple-wide mobile home on Westway in Port Orchard. Although it was about twenty years old, it had been kept up by the previous owners. It had wall-to-wall dark shag carpeting. They furnished their new home with pieces they picked up at yard sales or at bargain prices. Roland saw that the detached garage would make a perfect studio for his self-defense classes. He would have his own dojo.

"They looked like a normal suburban couple," Greg Meakin remembers. "My wife and I were very friendly with them, and a lot of the young people who took judo lessons from Roland looked upon their place as a second home."

Roland had contacted the local YMCA to arrange for a space where students of the art could meet. Judo was an offshoot of the much more violent jujitsu. Judo was the creation of Jigoro Kano, who visualized the graceful and powerful body movements as a sport, a nonviolent one. Kano, who died in 1938, was the ultimate master of judo, a holder of the highest degree of black belt. Pitre told students that Kano had inspired him and claimed to have attended the Kodokan Institute in Japan, the Yale or Harvard of judo instruction.

Pitre was very impressive and garnered a lot of attention in Kitsap County. The *Port Orchard Independent* published a two-page spread on his Port Orchard Judo Academy that featured photographs of Roland, his daughter Bébé, and several of his students.

Among his students were two brothers who met Roland when he was working as a salesman at Bay Ford.

He sold their parents a car and casually mentioned his classes to the boys. The teenagers had had some previous judo instruction and were excited about signing up at the Port Orchard Judo Academy.

"We took the foot ferry between Bremerton and Port Orchard," the younger brother, Isak Nelson,* remembers. "He was still teaching out of the Y at that point. Roland and Cheryl became like my family to me, even closer than my family for a while."

Isak was sixteen then, and Pitre rapidly became his hero. Looking back with the wisdom of an adult, he recalls things that didn't quite add up, but he didn't recognize deception at the time.

"I remember that Roland asked me to stay after class the first night, or maybe it was the second night I was there. He said that he and Cheryl needed to talk with me. But it was Roland who did the talking. He said, 'There's something I want you to know about me. I want to be honest with you.'"

Isak listened intently.

"I've done time," Pitre told him, "for stealing some money from a convenience store. I just wanted you to know so you can make up your mind about whether you still want to study with me."

Cheryl only nodded slightly as her husband explained his past to the teenager. It didn't seem so bad to Isak, who admits that he himself was something of a heller as a teenager. He had had to perform community service for a scrape he'd gotten into. Roland's honesty about being in prison only made him seem like a nicer guy to Isak. He didn't need any time to decide that he would stay with the judo academy.

"It was so rare for me to meet an adult that I could really talk to, who really seemed to understand me."

Isak and some of his other students helped Roland move mats into the garage. The dojo was a great place to hang out, to practice, to visit. "Classes were sporadic," Isak says. "Sometimes, Cheryl and Bébé practiced when I was there, and sometimes Roland taught regular classes."

For Isak, Cheryl and Roland were the perfect substitute parents. He was always welcome. He thought of Bébé as a little sister, and often babysat for her.

As for Cheryl, Isak recalls a wonderful woman. "She was just the nicest person you'd ever want to meet. She was so kind and giving. She taught me how to cook. When I had my first girlfriend, I brought her over for Cheryl's approval."

Isak believed as the Meakins did. "From the outside, they looked very happy," Greg said. "More so when Cheryl found out she was pregnant."

Cheryl didn't appear to mind the rough pace of her life, even with a new baby on the way, two jobs, and the responsibility of putting her husband through college. Roland had finished his prenursing classes at the University of Washington, where he'd had to commute by ferry between Bremerton and the docks in downtown Seattle, an hour's ride. It was easier to attend nursing classes at Olympic Community College in Bremerton. Cheryl was proud of him.

Perhaps she was unaware that he had become quite friendly with a number of female nursing students. Women still liked Roland, and he played on that. He had been unfaithful with Maria, but that was in the past. If Roland talked about other women, Cheryl resisted suspicion; if they were going to make it, she had to trust him.

Cheryl was delighted to be pregnant; she thought it would make her marriage more solid, and Roland seemed as happy as she was. He wanted a son. And she gave him one. In 1987, Cheryl gave birth to a baby boy, whom they named after his father. Just as he had nicknamed his daughter Bébé, a popular Cajun name, Roland gave his son a Cajun nickname. Everyone called him André.

The Meakins' older son, Tanner, took judo lessons from Roland, and he and Bébé were in the same class, wearing the traditional white pajama outfit and barefoot. They were working toward their yellow belts, the first level of achievement. They were too young to even have crushes on each other, but they were great pals. Bébé was a pretty little girl with straight blondish hair who could not pronounce her *r*'s.

Although Bébé and her mother had of necessity formed a very strong bond in the years they were alone, the little girl seemed happy to have her dad back in the family, and she was thrilled to have a baby brother. Whenever they could find the time, Bébé and Cheryl watched NFL football games, an interest they had shared since Bébé was little more than a baby.

Despite the odds against them and their chaotic history together, it looked as if Cheryl and Roland Pitre were going to make it after all. Many people who knew them were not aware of exactly what Roland had been to prison for. Seeing the clean-cut, athletic man who was so nice to his students, they couldn't imagine that it had been anything very serious.

Occasionally, though, even Isak had fleeting doubts

about what Roland had confided to him. "One time we were practicing iaido; that's the quick draw of removing the sword. I said something to Bébé about it, and she said, 'Daddy's not allowed to have swords anymore.' I didn't know what that meant, but it sounded funny. Why wouldn't he be allowed to have a sword? Just because he'd stolen a couple of things from a 7-Eleven?"

But the teenager soon forgot his doubts.

Isak remembers now that Cheryl was "subservient" to her husband. It was always Roland who made the decisions, but she didn't seem to mind that. She was a plain woman who moved in the shadow of her far more dynamic husband. *This* Roland was almost the exact opposite of the failed used-car salesman. He was in his element, in charge of his life and the center of admiring attention.

Roland drove to judo tournaments around the Northwest with his students. Isak recalls going to Spokane, a drive of more than three hundred miles from Port Orchard, and another time to Scio, Oregon. Greg Meakin's son Tanner often went on the trips.

"It was kind of funny, really, at one hotel we stayed at," Isak says. "One weekend in Oregon, the hotel where we stayed had two groups on their reader board: the judo tournament and a transvestite drag queen convention. Roland and Dave, another guy from the dojo, went to the bar to have a drink, and Dave came back to me and said he needed help getting a drunk and combative Roland out of the bar. I was too young to even go in the bar, but somehow we got him out of there and onto the elevator."

Roland was very confrontational with three of the transvestites who were dressed in their full regalia with wigs and makeup. In the elevator, he turned around and tried to stare them down. Towering over him in their four-inch heels, they asked him what his problem was.

"I have no problem," he said. "You do."

"We got him off the elevator," Isak recalls. "Without a fight."

Even though he was sometimes moody or surly, it didn't really matter how Roland Pitre acted; his teenage students saw him as almost perfect. His skill and grace were unmatched by anyone they had ever seen. His marriage was happy and serene, and they loved to hang out in the Pitres' mobile home. It wasn't that their parents weren't good to them; it was that Roland treated them like they were adults. He valued their opinions, and they were happy to help him with any chores he requested. They cleaned the dojo, folded the mats, carried groceries, and babysat for André.

It was in the late spring and early summer of 1988 when the first narrow fissures snaked through the perfect marriage. The solid foundation of the Pitres' home crumbled as Roland's students watched, disbelieving.

Just as observers had become absolutely convinced that Cheryl and Roland and their children were blessed, a faint shadow hovered over their happiness. Apparently the picture of health, Roland told Cheryl about some subtle symptoms that worried him. He said he'd been having strange rashes, slight episodes of fever, and growing fatigue.

He had always been so strong, and he still looked healthy, but he told Cheryl he was afraid. After she questioned him closely, he finally admitted to her that he feared his exposure to Agent Orange in Vietnam might have predisposed him to cancer. He'd heard from other guys in his old unit who had it.

It was only a week or two later when Roland sadly told Cheryl that he had been to a doctor. His fears were confirmed; at the age of 37, he was diagnosed with terminal cancer. As Cheryl started to cry, he vowed to fight it with everything he had. Still, he was very concerned about what Cheryl and their two children would do if he lost the fight. How could they survive if he died? Or— not nearly as likely—what would *he* do to care for Bébé and André if she should die? They were being shown how unpredictable life could be. He stressed that they had responsibilities, especially to their children.

His arguments made sense to Cheryl, and she agreed that they should each take out an insurance policy for $125,000, naming the other as beneficiary. She suggested that he contact Frank Haberlach, a popular fixture in the Bremerton insurance business. Haberlach was a regular at the coffee hour in Cheryl's office at Bay Ford.

Cheryl wasn't sure that Roland could even get insurance in his condition. He said at his age, no physical examination was required. He told her that their policies with the Lutheran Brotherhood Company in Minneapolis would go into effect in June 1988. Whether Roland *ever* got a policy on himself is unclear.

When one looks at the insurance transactions Roland arranged, there is a jarring note. Was he really dying? If he ever actually served in Vietnam, it isn't documented. No one who knew him in the Marines can validate it. According to his Marine friends, he was deployed to the Philippines and Japan, never to Vietnam. But then he was assigned to secret spy missions, so it was possible.

Despite his supposed terminal illness, Roland kept going to nursing school and continued to teach his judo classes. He didn't look or act sick. Cheryl watched him anxiously, waiting for the more serious symptoms that surely must come.

But they never did, and she was grateful that her prayers had been answered. Their marriage, however, was ailing. Although it had only been two years since she helped him get out of prison, and he had his own dojo, his college studies, a baby son, and a wife who worked constantly to help support him, Roland was restless. He had always planned to live better than they were living. The mobile home wasn't his idea of luxury, and Cheryl had put on some weight after her pregnancy with André. She no longer satisfied him.

He wanted to be rich, he wanted excitement, and he wanted, as always, more sexual adventures than he could find in a monogamous marriage.

Cheryl could no longer deny that Roland was cheating on her. He had far too many women in his life for a faithful married man. At first she had tried to believe that he was making friends with women because he was one of the few males in the nursing classes he attended. But she knew in her heart that he hadn't really changed at all. When she questioned him, he made excuses. Then by full summer he didn't even bother to explain why he came home late or why he was at local restaurants with women.

She was heartsick as she wondered if she had only been expedient for him, only a vehicle to facilitate his way out of prison. Still, whatever doubts she had, she kept them to herself, hoping he would come back to her.

But even Isak, who had come to idolize Roland, had begun to notice an undercurrent that made him uneasy. "Something seemed awkward, wrong somehow. But I was too young to figure it out."

Isak noticed that Roland and Cheryl were having fights. "They were verbal—not physical—and they were very mild, but I remember thinking, 'Oh, no! Like Mom and Dad are having a fight again.'"

Their arguments became more frequent, and it wasn't nearly as much fun at their house.

7

Despite all she had done to stand beside Roland to give him a second chance, Cheryl realized that her marriage was the same sham it had always been, a facade that he no longer needed. He had at least one girlfriend he met in nursing school. Cheryl confronted him, and they fought about it openly. Their relationship was stormy. Increasingly, Cheryl caught Roland in lies. He had been so wonderful to her when he wrote from prison, and she had believed everything he told her. She had even been convinced that Roland was the innocent person in the Archer murder, set up as a patsy by Maria to serve time for something he had not done.

Now she wondered about almost everything he said. Was it true or was it a lie? She learned that he didn't have terminal cancer; he didn't have cancer at all and never had. She was glad that he wasn't dying because a big part of her still loved him, but she had to wonder why he hadn't told her the truth. Maybe it was the insurance policies. He hadn't needed to do that; she would have agreed to buy insurance.

In midsummer 1988, Roland left Cheryl and moved in with his new mistress. There wasn't even an interim period. His judo students helped him move his belongings to his new address.

"I was still pretty naive," Isak remembers. "When we carried stuff into her house for him, Roland introduced his girlfriend as 'just a friend.' It was like he was renting a room there, and we bought it. It didn't really occur to us that he could leave Cheryl and move in with another woman."

She was a fairly attractive woman with blond hair and a good figure. Her name was Della Roslyn,* and she was 39, five years older than Cheryl. Just as Cheryl suspected, Roland had met Della when they were fellow students in the nursing program at Olympic Community College. Della had two children from a former marriage, a daughter, Amy Nash,* 17, and a son, Tim Nash,* 14. Della wasn't prettier than Cheryl, but she seemed to contribute something to Roland's life that his wife could not.

It's quite possible that Della was simply different, more of a challenge for a man who grew bored easily.

Cheryl gave up their mobile home; there was no way she could keep up the payments without help from Roland. With Bébé and André, she moved into a small rambler house that was close to PJ's. The street where they moved had been the scene of a violent crime only a year or so before; almost directly across from Cheryl's rental, a teenager had shot and killed his father in an ambush, then set off to shoot his mother, too. Fortunately, he was captured before he could kill his mother.

Cheryl wasn't nervous, but she adopted a German shepherd and kept it in the yard, just in case there were prowlers. She had learned to live alone while Roland was in prison.

Her marriage seemed to be over, but there was no true resolution of their relationship. Roland couldn't quite make up his mind. He didn't push for a divorce. He lived with Della, but he still saw Cheryl occasionally. They spent a weekend together in July on Vancover Island in Victoria, B.C., traveling in Cheryl's 1984 Mercury Topaz. They went to the Washington State fair in Puyallup together in September. Roland often took Bébé and André on weekends. He wasn't living with Cheryl, but he was good to their children, and he called her sporadically and talked about getting together, essentially being just kind enough to Cheryl to keep a little flicker of hope alive.

But she knew that he wasn't coming back to her, and she tried to embark on a social life of her own. At a friend's suggestion, she joined Parents Without Partners. On Thursday, October 13, 1988, Cheryl attended a small group meeting in a home in Port Orchard. It took courage for her to do that. She had no sponsor or friend to go with her. There were six women and three men at the PWP meeting, and they spent the evening drinking coffee and eating the desserts some of the women brought. As far as anyone can recall, Cheryl didn't make dates with any of the men who attended.

She was very busy as always, still working two jobs. If Roland didn't have the children when she worked at

PJ's, Isak Nelson was glad to sit with them. She had moved to within easy walking distance of where he lived. He still admired Cheryl, and he felt sorry for her after Roland left her. He was beginning to see that his hero had feet of clay.

The Port Orchard Judo Academy folded; Roland no longer had a place to hold classes. Where Roland had always been available to his students before, now they were rarely able to reach him, either by phone or in person. It was as if Roland had closed down one phase of his life and stepped through a door with a whole new cast of characters.

The weekend of October 15 and 16 was typical for autumn in the Northwest. The sun shone brightly, but the nights were growing chilly. The vine maples were turning bright coral, and the big leaf maples soft yellow. The University of Washington Huskies had a game on Saturday, but Roland Pitre was far more interested in Sunday's NFL game at the Kingdome in Seattle. The Seahawks were playing the New Orleans Saints. He told everyone he was going to root for his hometown team: the Saints.

Roland had a visitation with Bébé and André on that weekend. The 10-year-old Bébé got along well with Della's children. She was too young to really understand that her father and mother had broken up, and Della was nice to her. André was only a year old and wasn't aware of much of anything.

Cheryl was relieved to have Roland babysit with their children that weekend. She was scheduled to work on Saturday night until eleven, and then she had to start the

Sunday day shift by seven. She wouldn't have to worry about the kids. If they weren't with Roland, he would pay Della's daughter to babysit them. He told her he planned to take Bébé and Amy roller-skating on Saturday afternoon.

Although it made Cheryl sad to see her husband with another woman, she agreed to have Roland pick up Bébé and André and take them to Della's house on Friday evening, promising to pick them up after she finished work at PJ's on Sunday afternoon.

Cheryl worked until eleven Saturday night. A number of regular customers would remember chatting with her as she rang up their groceries. She sat in her usual spot, on a stool near the door. She had also talked with a young college woman, Nita Soames,* who was temporarily staying in her father's apartment. The small unit shared space with the market, and its entry door was close to where Cheryl sat. Nita could sit on her couch and chat comfortably with Cheryl. She had come home shortly after ten, and she told Cheryl she was moving into a new apartment but didn't have much furniture.

"I have some things you could use," Cheryl offered. "I'll bring them to work with me tomorrow morning." That was like Cheryl; she went out of her way to help people. She liked Nita.

Nothing untoward happened at PJ's that evening. As far as anyone could remember, Cheryl was dressed in her usual blue jeans, a blouse or a T-shirt, and she seemed to be in a good mood. She complained a little that she was going to have to "sleep fast" as she'd barely have time to get home, sleep, and come back to the store early the next morning.

After she totaled the day's sales, Cheryl put the receipts into the safe and called her boss. Nita locked the door on the east side of the building behind her. Cheryl drove off in her silver Topaz. Sometimes she stopped at the Subway sandwich shop to buy something for a late supper, but later, no one recalled if she had or not. The guy at the counter was new and didn't know her.

Nita recalled that Cheryl certainly hadn't mentioned any plans to meet someone after work. "If she had a date, she would have told me."

Because it was late as she headed home and Cheryl's neighbors were either out or asleep, there were no witnesses who could say if she had actually arrived at her little house safely.

And Cheryl Pitre would be gone a long time before anyone ever saw her again.

8

Roland Pitre had no particular reason to check on his estranged wife. He was living with Della Roslyn. As far as Della remembered, October 15 and 16, 1988, was a normal weekend. She got up at five Saturday morning to study for a test in her nursing course at Olympic Community College. Roland awakened an hour later and left the house. "He wanted to photograph the sunrise," she recalled.

But the weather hadn't cooperated, and the bright colors of dawn were obscured by low clouds. A few hours later, Roland called her to say that the battery on his car was dead, but he'd found someone to jump-start it. It was sometime between nine and ten when he arrived back at her house. As he had promised, he then took Amy and Bébé roller-skating for a few hours. They were all home by about four.

None of them went out that night. Instead, Della, Roland, and their children watched television together until nine. Della was tired and went to bed, leaving Roland to play Monopoly with Bébé and Della's son Tim.

At 11:30, just about the time Cheryl Pitre drove away

from PJ's Market, Roland came up to the bedroom he shared with Della. Then he changed his mind and told Della he was going back downstairs to watch wrestling with Bébé and Tim. Della was positive that she saw Roland at 11:30, but he didn't stay in the bedroom long.

By the time Roland finally did come to bed, Della had dozed off. But she glanced at the clock as he reached out and turned her toward him. It was half an hour past midnight. They made love, and Della fell asleep again. She didn't waken until about five. When she did, she saw that he was asleep beside her.

Sometime during those dark hours, Cheryl had gone missing. No alarm was sounded until the next morning when she didn't show up for work at PJ's. Early customers found the doors locked.

There are several routes between Port Orchard, Bremerton, and Seattle. Most commuters choose between a number of ferries. And it's relatively easy to drive to Tacoma and around the many waterways that branch off from Puget Sound. Many travelers do drive around, and if it isn't rush hour and there's no traffic to fight, it's a pleasant trip. But the ferry ride is more relaxing and scenic. As the seagull flies— or as the ferryboats cross Puget Sound and Elliott Bay—to downtown Seattle, only about ten miles separate the land masses. Both the ferries and the drive take about an hour.

As close together as the east and west shores of Puget Sound look on a map, most Olympic Peninsula residents who don't actually work in Seattle usually spend their lives in Bremerton and Port Orchard. Cheryl Pitre did; her world was the Ford dealer, PJ's, and her church. It was a rare thing for her to leave.

But on Sunday it appeared that she had left. She didn't show up for work or to pick up her children or appear at any of the places she was expected to be. Not on Sunday. Or Monday—or any day after.

Just as New York City has its Central Park, Seattle has its lakes. Lake Union is one of several lakes located providentially in the middle of the city of Seattle. The "Emerald City" is defined by water. Its vegetation is green and lush, both from the rain that falls in all but the warmest summer season and because it is bound on its eastern borders by Lake Washington and on the west by Elliott Bay. Lake Union begins just north of downtown and extends several miles to the Lake Washington Ship Canal near the University District. Its shore provides space and mooring for restaurants, Coast Guard ships, condominiums, tour boats and, especially, to scores of floating homes.

The houseboat neighborhoods that became familiar in the movie *Sleepless in Seattle* line private docks that extend into Lake Union like charms on a necklace. Some are lavish and worth millions; others harken back to the early days when houseboats were mostly little square wood cabins kept afloat by logs.

For nine months out of the year, flowers and vegetables flourish in containers on the docks and the houseboat porches. Residents in the most desirable end-of-the-dock locations can tie up their boats to their front porches. There is a feeling of security in the houseboat community. Everybody knows everyone else, and a stranger on the dock is carefully scrutinized. Neighbors know who belongs there, and they watch out for one another. It is a small town dropped into the middle of a big city and a wonderful place to live except, perhaps, when a rare blizzard dumps a heavy snow load onto rooftops and some houseboats begin to sink. Even then, neighbors are there to shovel frantically.

But this was not Cheryl Pitre's world. As far as anyone knew, she had never visited anyone along the rows of houseboats on Fairview Avenue East.

Cheryl's fellow employees at Bay Ford were worried sick about her, and so were her coworkers at PJ's Market. They had been worried since Sunday morning. When they called her house from the market, they got only Cheryl's voice on her answering machine. As the days passed and Cheryl didn't come to work at Bay Ford, they all had a sense of dread.

Greg Meakin received a call from Roland Pitre at eleven on Monday morning. He sounded very concerned, "Greg," he said, "have you seen Cheryl? She didn't come home last night."

Greg hadn't heard from Cheryl all weekend, and her regular post at the counter of the dealership looked empty without her.

"I was instantly concerned," Meakin recalls. "That wasn't like Cheryl. I hate to say it, but right away several of our employees suspected that Roland had done something to her."

Ron Trogdon, a Kitsap County deputy, was dispatched to check Cheryl's small house. From the exterior he could see no sign of a disturbance. Her car was gone, and the doors were locked.

When Monday and Tuesday passed with no word from Cheryl, everyone who knew her feared the worst. Their one hope was that neither she nor her car had been located. There was always the possibility that she had finally had enough of Roland's womanizing. It would be understandable; she had worked tirelessly to get him out of prison and continued to work while he went to nursing school only to have all her dreams explode. No one would have blamed her if she'd just opted out of her life and started driving, putting her disappointment behind her.

Some of those who knew Cheryl had darker thoughts. She had been through so much disappointment in the year just past. If she had given in to depression, it was possible that she had committed suicide.

"But that wasn't Cheryl. We knew she wouldn't leave her kids," Greg Meakin said. "Not if she had a choice. That was what scared us the most."

Roland insisted that he had no idea where Cheryl might have gone, but he acted as if she wasn't going to come home. He made arrangements for her family to come to Washington from Pennsylvania and take Bébé and André back home with them. He couldn't go to college and be responsible for the children, too. Della's days in nursing school were as full as his were.

Cheryl had been gone four days by Wednesday, October 19, and no one had seen or heard from her. Then some men walking toward their motorboat moored near the houseboat docks along the 1600 block of Fairview Avenue East were startled to see a woman's purse, a wallet, and some papers floating in the shallows of Lake Union. After they fished them out of the lake, they looked for a name or some ID.

They saw that several items bore the name Cheryl Pitre. Her address showed that she lived in Port Orchard. They called the sheriff's office and learned that

Cheryl Pitre's name was very familiar to Kitsap County sheriff's detectives. She had been reported as a missing person in their jurisdiction, and this was the first solid information that they had received.

Detectives Doug Hudson and Jim Harris went to the area where Cheryl's purse had drifted in the lake. They didn't really expect to find her there, but it was a place to start. Parking was at a premium along the narrow street; it was jammed with cars belonging to houseboat residents, visitors, and delivery people. The two men moved slowly north from the 1600 block to the 2200 block, looking for Cheryl's 1984 Mercury Topaz. They doubted that her car would be there. If she had killed herself, it would likely have been by jumping off the University Bridge or the Aurora Bridge, and for that the drift pattern for her purse and wallet was all wrong; those soaring bridges were a long way away. If someone had killed Cheryl and had any cunning at all, he wouldn't have left her car so close to her identifying belongings.

As the Kitsap County detectives got closer to Pete's Market and to a luxury condominium whose units were actually built on piers out over the water, they spotted a silver Topaz parked in a very dimly lighted area. The license plate read WHA-414. The plate frame said Port Orchard on the top and had the Bay Ford logo, too. There was no question that this was Cheryl's vehicle.

Hudson and Harris contacted the Seattle Police Department's Harbor Unit and requested divers. Cheryl had been gone for almost ninety-six hours; they were afraid that her body might be caught up under a houseboat or one of the docks.

The divers arrived and spent hours searching beneath

the surface but found no body. It was possible that someone had encountered Cheryl in Port Orchard as she left PJ's late Saturday night and had stolen her purse and her car. Alive or dead, she herself could be anywhere between Port Orchard and Lake Union.

A cursory look into the car revealed nothing to indicate violence. The transmission was still in drive, which suggested that whoever had left the vehicle was in a hurry. There were no car keys.

Sergeant Joe Sanford and Detective Hank Gruber from the Seattle Police Department's Homicide Unit responded to the Lake Union site and agreed to have Cheryl Pitre's car taken to the Seattle department's property room garage. It was too dark where the car had been abandoned to search for clues and, without the keys, difficult to check the trunk without damaging the vehicle. The lighting in the property/evidence area was far superior, and they would be less likely to miss something of evidentiary value.

It was a matter of which department had jurisdiction. There was no body. If there had been a crime, it almost certainly had occurred on the other side of Puget Sound and would be a Kitsap County case. Cheryl's vanishing was still officially a missing persons case, Kitsap County—Number 88-14014. Sergeant Sanford assured the detectives working it that the Seattle Homicide Unit would assist them in any way they could.

At eleven PM the truck driver who had towed in Cheryl's car called the Seattle detectives to let them know he had just impounded another vehicle a few parking spaces away from the silver Topaz.

"It's an old Ford van," the driver said to Hank Gruber. "It's got a Kitsap County Fire Department sticker on its windshield, and I know you've been looking for a woman missing from over there."

Shortly before midnight, Sanford and Gruber went to look at the van in the tow yard. They saw that it was dirty and full of litter: beer cans and garbage. It appeared that someone had been sleeping, possibly even living, in it. Beyond the fire department sticker, there were no other signs that it had any connection to Kitsap County. They ran the license number and the VIN (vehicle identification number) through computers, but there were no hits for the battered van. It wasn't stolen or even listed as being registered.

The silver Topaz remained in the property room until the Kitsap County sheriff's detectives in Port Orchard decided to have it towed aboard a ferry and returned to the area where Cheryl Pitre had vanished. Sergeant Sanford and Detective Gruber conferred with Doug Hudson and Jim Harris, and the quartet decided the car should be checked out more thoroughly before it left the Seattle Police property room.

Gruber, Doug Wright (another Kitsap County detective), and Jim Harris walked carefully around the car. It appeared to be well cared for, and they didn't see any dents that might indicate it had been in an accident or forced off the road. Three of the tires were in good shape, but the right front tire was nearly bald.

The car was unlocked, and Gruber opened it carefully and examined the interior. In the bright light, he could now see what looked like blood smears, long dried. There were dark brownish-red smears in and around the ignition slot, and on the inside of the driver's door on the armrest, the door itself, and the latch. His trained eyes saw small spots of blood on the back of the driver's seat and on the gearshift box between the front seats and tiny globules spattered in many locations on the driver's side. Even the passenger seat's seat belt retractor was bloody.

The smears on the steering wheel might still hold fingerprints—that would be the best evidence possible—but Gruber doubted that clear ridges had survived.

Other than the blood that appeared now in the glow of bright lights, the interior looked like the vehicle of any housewife. An infant's car seat was attached as recommended to the rear seat, and there was a jumble of papers in the car. Between the driver's seat and the passenger seat, they found a single key on an orange fob. It was marked "Do Not Duplicate." (Doug Wright and Jim Harris later established that this was a key to PJ's Market.)

The detectives said little as they moved around the Topaz, but they were all thinking the same thing. Something terrible must have happened to the missing 33-year-old woman, and it had probably begun as she sat behind the steering wheel.

"We decided to pop the trunk forcibly," Gruber remembers, "to see what else might have been left in the car."

Using a screwdriver and a hammer, Hank Gruber eased open the locked trunk lid. As it lifted, the four investigators were shocked. None of them had detected the odor of a decomposing body, so they weren't prepared for the sight before them. A woman lay there, wedged in. They couldn't see her face because it was covered by a paper bag and magazines and books—as if whoever had put her there didn't want her dead eyes to look at him.

They couldn't say for sure, but they were fairly certain that they had found Cheryl Pitre.

9

The woman in the trunk lay on her back, her shoulders and head toward the passenger side of the vehicle. She wore blue jeans with the left front pocket pulled inside out, an aqua T-shirt with a humorous logo, and a shiny red waterproof jacket. Her arms were hidden beneath her. The white lining of her jeans pocket bore blood stains, probably from the killer's hand. A child's folding stroller lay beside her. Her own car had been a hiding place for her body, and it might even be the scene of the crime.

The book that covered her face was entitled *They're All Dead, Aren't They?* It looked like a typical mystery novel; they didn't know that this was the true story of a devout mother and her battle back from losing five children to murder and to cancer, the book that Cheryl had found inspiring. Joy Swift's survival and renewed faith in the Seventh-Day Adventist church had helped Cheryl keep going when her world with her husband had shattered. What bleak irony that particular book should be used to hide her terribly battered face.

The fact that her face *was* covered made the detec-

93

tives suspect that whoever killed her had had a personal relationship with her. Even with such violence, the killer apparently hadn't been able to leave her body in the trunk without some attempt to hide his gruesome handiwork. Maybe, as he slammed down the trunk lid, he hadn't wanted to think that her empty eyes were watching him.

The detectives couldn't be sure who this female victim was yet, though they assumed it was Cheryl Pitre. The dead woman wore no shoes, but she did have either panty hose or knee-highs on, their bottoms shredded as if she had been walking on a rough surface.

Before the investigators removed the books and magazines from the victim's face, they called the King County Medical Examiner's office. An ME investigator, Kevin Gow, responded and assisted the detectives as they carefully uncovered the dead woman's face.

Even if they had known her in life, they wouldn't have been able to identify her. She had severe facial injuries. She had been battered repeatedly with something heavy and, possibly, with the trunk lid. Damaged tissue decomposes more rapidly than normal tissue, and the body's head was unrecognizable. Blood and tissue were sprayed throughout the trunk area.

It looked as if she might have tried to fight her way out of the trunk, only to be struck again and again until the trunk lid was slammed on her, crushing her face. The detectives retrieved and bagged several of her teeth and pieces of bones.

"There was blood spatter on the inside of the trunk lid," Hank Gruber wrote in his follow-up report.

Dr. Greg Schmunk, an ME's deputy, and Kevin Gow took possession of the body, teeth, and bony chips. An autopsy should show exactly how this woman had died and when. It was doubtful that she had been raped. She was fully clothed, with her undergarments in place.

As they lifted her corpse from the trunk, the investigators saw that her hands were bound behind her, tightly secured with strapping tape. Her shoes, athletic running shoes, were in the trunk, too.

The two detective teams—one from the Seattle Homicide Unit and the other from the Kitsap County Sheriff's Office—worked into the night, bagging tiny fragments of possible evidence that had been hidden by the body. Maybe some of it would help; maybe none of it would.

There was a bank envelope with seven dollars in cash inside, a receipt for a hamburger and fries from Friday, October 14, a red button, a single earring for pierced ears, a ballpoint pen. They found a small leather pouch that held a driver's license for Cheryl Pitre and a receipt from a veterinarian. Both important items in the victim's life and the detritus everyone collects were left in Cheryl's car.

The detectives found hair fragments in six spots in the trunk and on the rear bumper, and they located more swaths of blood from the trunk and its lid. They took the dimensions of the trunk and photographed the exterior of the Topaz. Finally, they sealed the car and roped it off until they and expert crime-scene technicians could process the vehicle inch by inch.

The murder of Cheryl Pitre had just become a Seattle case—because her body was found within the Seattle city limits—but Detectives Doug Wright, Doug Hudson, and Jim Harris would continue to work on it. They were inclined to believe that she had been killed in Kitsap County and disposed of in Seattle to delay the discovery of her body and throw roadblocks in the path of the men who investigated it.

Homicide investigators always look first at those who have been closest to the victim: relatives, friends, work associates. And even after their separation, Roland Pitre was probably the person Cheryl had been closest to. On Saturday morning, October 22—one week after Cheryl disappeared—Sergeant Joe Sanford and Detective Hank Gruber went to the Port Orchard offices of Detectives Doug Wright and Jim Harris. Roland Pitre and his new girlfriend, Della Roslyn, had been asked to come into the sheriff's office at eleven. They had not yet been informed about the discovery of Cheryl's body.

Joe Sanford and Jim Harris would interview Della, and Hank Gruber and Doug Wright would talk to Pitre.

Pitre and his girlfriend arrived fifteen minutes early. Neither of them appeared unduly nervous.

Alone now with Hank Gruber and Jim Harris, Pitre nodded as Gruber read him his rights under Miranda. He had heard them before, and he didn't question why he had been warned as a suspect. "A suspect involving *what?*" most men would have asked, but Pitre didn't. He signed the form.

"We found your ex-wife's body in the trunk of her car," Gruber said, studying Pitre's face. The man before him was very quiet when he heard this news, but he didn't seem overwhelmed or emotional.

"When did you see Cheryl last?" Gruber asked.

"In person?"

"Yes."

"That would have been last Sunday—the ninth. I had dinner with her." Pitre added that Cheryl was at work on Friday when he picked Bébé and André up from day care for their weekend with him. "So I didn't see her."

"Do you remember the last time you spoke to her?"

"That Saturday night. She was working at PJ's, and I called her there to talk about getting our children back to her on Sunday. I was going to the Seahawks game—to cheer for the Saints—so I told her I might be a little late getting the kids back."

Gruber already knew that Pitre had been to the football game on Sunday, October 16. The Kitsap County detectives had listened to the messages on Cheryl's telephone answering machine. Roland Pitre had called her after the game, and he was joking because the Saints had won.

When he was asked about his activities on the weekend Cheryl disappeared, Pitre had ready answers. He recalled being with Della and her family along with his own children on Saturday.

"On Sunday?"

"Well, Della's an early riser, and she always does her exercises each morning. Every Sunday I get up and go out to get the *Tacoma News Tribune* from a machine outside the Mile Hill Thriftway store. And then I fill up the gas tank of my Chevette at the Texaco station there because I have a credit card for it."

Pitre recalled that it was still dark when he left on Sunday morning, but Della was up. He wasn't sure how long he'd been gone. "However long it takes," he said offhandedly. "I didn't go anywhere else. I came home, read the sports section, and got ready to go to the football game in Seattle. Della, her sister, her brother-in-law, and I left for the game about nine. We drove to the ferry in Della's car and parked it on the Bremerton side."

When they returned from the Kingdome, Pitre said, he called Cheryl to see if she was coming over to Della's to pick up Bébé and the baby or if she wanted him to drop them off. "She didn't answer, so I left a message for her to call me if she wasn't already on her way over."

"What time was that?"

"About six-thirty." Pitre said that about an hour later he learned that Cheryl hadn't even gone to work at PJ's that morning. "I began to worry," he said earnestly. He'd had no idea where Cheryl might have gone, and he had called Bay Ford and other people she knew, but no one had seen her.

The investigators knew about Roland Pitre's record and that he had gone to prison for his involvement in another murder only eight years before. And now here he was, looking only slightly upset, and acting mystified about his ex-wife's fate.

He insisted that, of course, he was in no way involved in Cheryl's death. He was eager to do anything he could to help find her killer. He willingly signed a consent-to-search form for the detectives to search Della's home. Her recall of the prior Saturday and Sunday agreed with Roland's.

The four detectives followed Roland and Della to Della's house. Pitre showed them the two cars he routinely drove: a 1979 red Chevrolet Chevette, registered to him, and a silver 1980 Chevette, registered to Della. There was also a full-size Chevy pickup truck on the property, which was on loan to them.

Hank Gruber was known for his meticulous attention to detail in almost everything he did. He was a record keeper, an artist, a genius at scale drawings, and relentless when he processed rooms or vehicles for possible evidence. It was Gruber who introduced the idea of charting all Seattle homicides in any given year, noting address, date, victim's name, manner of death and, hopefully, the date of arrest and the murderer's name. He did all the diagramming of crime scenes. With his Bronx accent and his easygoing manner, he usually set suspects at ease, and they ended up telling him more than they intended to.

Now Gruber set about searching one of Roland Pitre's vehicles. He noted the roll of strapping tape beneath the hatchback window of the red Chevette. He asked Pitre if he could take it, and Roland nodded, hastening to explain that he had used it a few days before to tape a note for Della to his door. Gruber slipped it into an evidence bag, noting that there were some hairs and fragments of something stuck to the side of the roll.

Doug Wright and Jim Harris found nothing of interest in the pickup truck, but Della's silver car had what might be blood spots. The car was a little dirty inside, but the interior was light-colored so that they could easily see a tiny spot of what might be dried blood on the dashboard to the left of the steering wheel. With a swab dipped in a saline solution, they lifted the spot and sealed it for testing.

Gruber and Sanford searched the garage, noting that the overhead door was operated with a yellow nylon pulley rope. It was similar to a rope they had found in Cheryl's car but of a smaller diameter, and this rope was old and dirty; the rope in the trunk with Cheryl's body was new. A lot of people had yellow rope.

Joe Sanford helped the Kitsap County detectives gather dirt samples from the Roslyn property for comparison with dirt and debris found on the undercarriage of Cheryl's Topaz.

Inside Della's house, the investigators found blue jeans with red stains that could be either paint or blood. One of a pair of Adidas athletic shoes had hair and dried debris stuck to the bottom in dried liquid that might be blood. Pitre said those items belonged to him; he was very calm.

He wasn't perturbed until Doug Wright noticed a very small dot of dark red on the glasses that the very nearsighted Pitre wore. It looked to Wright like back spatter from either a high-velocity or medium-velocity spray of blood, possibly from a gunshot wound or a bludgeoning weapon swung with great force.

"He just about collapsed," Wright would recall, "when we saw that spot on his glasses."

Wright lifted the spot with a swab and noted that Pitre's hand was trembling slightly as he held out the glasses.

"I think it was blood," Wright says, "but there wasn't enough to test—not at that time—and it got diluted by the saline solution, so we couldn't say absolutely that it was Cheryl's."

As suspicious as the detectives were of Roland Pitre, they had no probable cause to arrest him. Testing in the Western Washington State Crime Lab might match some of the stains to Cheryl's blood type. It was 1988, though, and the science of DNA was in its infancy. Testers needed large samples because much of the substance to be examined would be destroyed by the tests themselves. Today, that tiny dried speck of blood on Pitre's glasses could be multiplied infinitely, but in 1988 it was not enough.

Della Roslyn and Roland Pitre watched as the detectives drove away. They may have wondered what would come next, but Della believed totally in Roland, just as Cheryl had. He had shed no tears for the woman who had saved him from years in prison, the woman who had borne him two children.

At four PM, the four detectives drove to the small 1960s rambler where Cheryl lived after her marriage broke up. Doug Hudson had already searched it thoroughly and found no sign that violence had occurred there. The garage was so full of miscellaneous furniture and stored items that no one could park a car inside it. If she had been attacked at home and forced into the trunk of her car, it would have to have been in full view of a number of her neighbors. Yet no one had seen or heard anything unusual.

It was far more likely that she had been waylaid on her way home from PJ's. She hadn't been in an accident. Her car wasn't damaged at all, not even a scratch, so that probably ruled out another vehicle's having forced her off the road. For some reason, she had pulled her car over. Her killer would have to have been someone she knew and trusted or someone with a carefully planned ruse to get her to stop willingly. That could have happened anywhere along her usual route home, a road little-traveled near midnight. Once Cheryl was alone on the dark road, someone had abducted her in her own car, possibly beating her into unconsciousness before she could cry out for help.

"She never got home at all," Hank Gruber said. "And I don't think she was conscious on the trip to Seattle where he, or they, left her car."

10

A postmortem examination of Cheryl Pitre's body was set for 9:30 on Monday morning, October 24. Detectives Wright and Hudson from Kitsap County and Hank Gruber observed as Deputy Medical Examiner Dr. Schmunk began.

"Autopsy" means, literally, "to see for one's self." Someone had intercepted Cheryl as she headed home ten days earlier, quite probably unaware of danger. The investigators were still unsure of how she had died.

Her jeans, blue T-shirt, and undergarments had been removed from her body, and so had the strapping tape that bound her hands behind her. Gruber noted that it did not resemble the tape he removed from Roland Pitre's vehicle.

The critical wounds had all been to Cheryl's head. There were many of them.

"This might have looked like a single, massive wound," Dr. Schmunk said, "but there were multiple blows."

There were no stab wounds and no indications that she had been shot. Someone had beaten her to death by striking her skull and face again and again. She might have been choked, too, but her neck area was decomposed so much that they could not be certain. The hyoid bone in the back of her throat was not cracked as it often is in cases of strangulation.

She had probably fought her killer; there were many bruises on her knees and legs. But she had not been raped, nor had she recently had intercourse.

A forensic technician collected a number of hairs from the victim's hair and ear and pointed out the dirt that clung to her body. It was very fine and appeared to be either beach sand or the soil found on road shoulders.

That wasn't much of a clue. Fine sand like that could be found in hundreds of locations in Kitsap County.

Harris, Hudson, Wright, and Gruber hoped that there might be something in Cheryl's car that the killer had left behind. They would see that it was processed with the utmost care so that no minute bit of physical evidence would be lost.

Bill Haglund, the Chief Investigator of the King County Medical Examiner's Office, who had great expertise in forensic odontology, called them to say that six front teeth were missing from the victim's jaw and asked them to search for them when they processed her car. Shortly after noon, the detectives met at the Seattle Police Processing Room with George Chan from the Western Washington Crime Lab, Don McDowell from the Photo Lab, and Donna West, an ID technician. They discussed the best way to process the Topaz. First they took blood swab samples for testing and cross-matching. Since the interior had many obvious blood smears, they hoped that there might be fingerprint ridges hidden in the swirls. To isolate fingerprints, Chan suggested that they use Super Glue to enhance any ridges but only after the inside of Cheryl's car was photographed to preserve blood spatter patterns.

If Roland Pitre should emerge as the prime suspect, finding his fingerprints in blood would be tremendously valuable, absolutely irrefutable evidence that he had been present when Cheryl was dying. That would place him at the murder as it happened. Merely finding his fingerprints in Cheryl's car wouldn't help much. Intrafamily murders—when a family member kills another—are extremely difficult to prove. Obviously, their blood, sweat, hair, fibers, etc., will be found in their homes and their cars, and there is little a criminalist can do to mark the time this potential evidence was deposited. Historically, the best physical evidence to be found is a clear fingerprint with numerous matching points pressed into the life's blood of a victim.

A button found in the trunk with Cheryl's body might have been important, but it turned out to be from her own jacket. The detectives bagged possible evidence from the car. With a vacuum, Gruber carefully recovered hair, dirt, and fibers from the driver's seat and floor, the passenger seat, the trunk liner, and the bed liner beneath it.

They removed a length of nylon rope, an orange throw rug, and miscellaneous items in a plastic bag near where the victim's feet had rested: a first aid kit, a window scraper, paper towels.

When they removed the bottom liner of the trunk they found something interesting. The wire that led to the taillights on the driver's side was completely free of its socket. Disconnected, neither the taillights nor the brake lights would have worked. Somehow, Cheryl Pitre might have either kicked the wire loose or managed to rip it free before her hands were taped behind her, probably in the vain hope that a police officer would pull her car over for a "no taillights" violation.

Sadly, on the Saturday night she disappeared, there hadn't been a cop around to notice.

George Chan and Don McDowell began assessing the blood spatter patterns on the silver Topaz early the next morning. Chan noted two small indentations on the trunk's opening frame between the hinges. He remarked that they appeared to have been made by a tire iron but could not say for sure. Mikrosil castings were made of the marks, and paint samples were removed from that area, too.

The rear bumper and the exterior of the trunk deck had been wiped clean, but a spray with leucomalachite green proved that a thin sheen of blood, invisible to the naked eye, remained, as it later proved to be in many areas inside the car.

The next morning, Hank Gruber assisted ID Technician Donna West in preparing Cheryl's car for the Super Glue method. First, she dusted the exterior doors and the trunk lid with black fingerprint powder to ensure they wouldn't accidentally destroy any prints as they moved in and out of the car.

Would they find any unidentified prints, perhaps unknowingly left by a stranger who had killed her? Even if they did, it might be several days before Donna West could have those prints transferred to a card and even longer to have prints of the victim and any suspects for comparison.

The Super Glue fumer was sealed into the Topaz at two PM on October 25. The fumes would make fingerprints appear as if they were stenciled on the car's interior. Hank Gruber returned three hours later to remove it. Next, Donna West would do her part in lifting the prints that had surfaced.

They desperately needed either prints that matched known suspects' prints or an eyewitness.

Still no one came forward with a story about seeing a woman struggling with someone, not in Kitsap County, not in Seattle. As unlikely as it seemed, whoever abducted Cheryl Pitre had done it without so much as raising any suspicion, silently and swiftly in the dark near midnight.

Chan turned to Hank Gruber to say what he believed had occurred. "I would say that the attack positively took place while the victim was actually inside the trunk," he said. "Her head must have been above the height of the trunk opening when the blows were struck. She was probably in a semi-seated position with her feet extended to the driver's side."

But the driver's seat had been in a far-forward position when the vehicle was found. Was it possible that Cheryl herself might have been forced to drive her car to the site where it was found, only to be bludgeoned there? The Seattle investigators searched for a female detective who was about the same height as Cheryl. Sara Springer was five feet four and half and about the same weight. She eased into the driver's seat and said she felt "perfectly comfortable" there.

When a male detective who was five ten and a half tried the seat, he couldn't fit; his legs were too long.

There were many questions they could not answer definitively. Either Cheryl herself or someone less than five feet five inches tall was the last driver of the Topaz. Or maybe someone had deliberately pushed the seat forward to leave that impression.

After the glue fuming, Donna West lifted twelve cards of prints, but she was not encouraged by the quality of those she isolated from the bloodstained area.

The investigators agreed that Cheryl Pitre had almost certainly been bound—but alive—when she was forced into the trunk of her car. How far she was taken before the trunk lid was opened and her killer had struck her fatally with the tire iron or some other implement would be impossible to establish unless they found witnesses. Maybe she was forced to get into the trunk at the houseboat docks. *Where* she was when she was put into the trunk was unknown. They suspected it might have been close to PJ's Market. If they could somehow find that location, they might also find the victim's six missing teeth and the spot where Cheryl's stocking bottoms were shredded by gravel and rocks.

That was a very big *if.* Searches near PJ's and around where her car was left yielded none of that information.

11

Cheryl's funeral was held in her church, and many of her friends were in attendance. Isak Nelson and his brother and some of the other regulars at the Port Orchard Judo Academy were there, as were, of course, most of her fellow employees at Bay Ford. So was Roland, who appeared to be stunned with grief.

"The pastor who conducted the service didn't know Cheryl," Isak recalled with some bitterness. "It was a horrible eulogy because he said he was just getting to know her. Maybe he was just awkward at choosing his words, but he kept describing Cheryl as a 'comfortable' person, comparing her to an 'old shoe.' She was easy to be with and she made you feel safe and accepted, but she was only in her thirties. She wasn't an 'old shoe' at all."

Roland came to the elder Nelsons' house after the funeral service was over, something he rarely—if ever—had done before.

"He was crying real tears, and he appeared to be grief-stricken," Isak remembers. "Roland talked at great length to my dad. He had all these theories of what might have happened to Cheryl. He said he'd found books in her house about how someone could change their identity. He said he'd told the police that a young kid had been stalking Cheryl and that the person following her was driving a white convertible.

"The thing was that I believed him at the time. I was in shock. You have to remember that I'd had to go to court to testify against these guys I knew who had shot their father not too long before Cheryl was killed. And they practically lived across the street from Cheryl. It was all too much for me to absorb at that age.

"Everything Roland said seemed plausible. He just kept spinning out these possibilities about Cheryl's murder. He'd never talked that much to my dad before, but he stayed at our house for hours."

Later, Isak Nelson wondered if Roland had been crying "crocodile tears" or if he were trying to foist suspicion onto someone else. It had never occurred to Isak, as it had to Cheryl's coworkers at Bay Ford, that Roland could have hurt Cheryl. But then he had never imagined that the couple he admired so much would ever break up and talk about divorce, either.

Despite his mourning, Roland took care of business. As her beneficiary, he filed a claim with the insurance company that had issued Cheryl the $125,000 policy just a few months before, and he applied for Social Security survivors' benefits for André and Bébé under Cheryl's account.

12

The investigators from Kitsap County and the Seattle Police Department continued to divide up the case. Officially now Cheryl's murder was a Seattle case, 88-551006, because her body was found there. But they all suspected that her abduction and the initial attack had occurred near Port Orchard. She would have had no reason to drive to Seattle late at night.

Hank Gruber contacted Roland Pitre's parole officer at the Washington State Department of Corrections. She had no trouble remembering him. Because his wife stood so firmly behind him and because he was a model prisoner, he had been released far sooner than most convicts with that long a sentence. His parole officer verified that he had first been enrolled at the University of Washington and had commuted there by ferry several times a week. The location near the houseboats where Cheryl's car was parked was a few miles south of the university and only a block off Eastlake Avenue, a popular route for those who preferred to avoid the I-5 freeway. Roland would have been familiar with the area.

As standard procedure, Pitre's parole officer had

talked with a number of people he interacted with as a free man. She was surprised to hear one of the administrators at Olympic Community College rave about Roland. "She went way overboard in describing what a wonderful person he was and spoke of him almost as if he was the greatest student she had ever encountered. She helped him to become student body president and seemed entranced with him. I began to wonder if there was more going on than the usual student-teacher relationship."

Although parolees are urged—sometimes ordered— not to spend time with other recently released prisoners, Roland Pitre had seen his prison friends and even returned to visit some of those still locked up. The parole officer furnished Gruber with the names and addresses of a half-dozen convicts and parolees Roland had associated with since he walked out of prison in 1986. Since there was still the suspicion that he had not acted alone in the murder of Dennis Archer in 1980, the Seattle detective wondered about his more recent felon friends. All of them had convictions for sexual crimes, some including rape. One man, Olaf Svenson,* had gone to prison for rape and "promoting a suicide." He was reporting to a parole office in Olympia. The others were scattered from the south end of King County down to Vancouver, Washington.

Detectives located and talked to them about their whereabouts on the night of October 15.

On October 28, six detectives from three jurisdictions attended a summit meeting on Roland Pitre. Doug Wright, Jim Harris, and their Chief of Detectives, Dave Morgan, were there from Port Orchard; Hank Gruber and

Joe Sanford represented Seattle; and Ron Edwards, who had investigated the Archer murder in Oak Harbor eight years before, gathered to discuss Pitre. Edwards brought the bulging file he'd put together on his case. He had certainly not expected Pitre to be walking free so soon.

Still frustrated by not knowing where the murder had taken place, all six returned to Lake Union, where they fanned out. It was a bright sunlit day and they covered every inch of the ground where Cheryl's car ended up. They were looking for Cheryl Pitre's six missing teeth. They didn't find them. They got little satisfaction from gathering dirt samples from the lake bank and the parking area to save for possible comparisons down the road.

This killer had been clumsy and sloppy, leaving a welter of blood and dozens of smudged prints, and he should have been easy to track.

But he wasn't.

On Halloween, Hank Gruber pored over Sea-King (Seattle police and King County sheriff) files looking for any entries for Roland and Cheryl Pitre and Roland's new girlfriend, Della Roslyn. He hoped that he might find some link to the houseboat area. Seattle police records noted both complainants and suspects. He found absolutely nothing on any of the three, either in the city or in King County. Next, he ran the names of the parolees that Pitre's parole officer provided. There was nothing to link any of them to the vital neighborhood. He checked their license numbers. No contact with the King County sheriff or the Seattle police. He couldn't even find a parking ticket for any of them.

Gruber placed a phone call the next day to Roland Pitre. Della answered. She sounded suspicious and a little hostile at first. Reluctantly, she called Roland to the phone. Gruber asked him if they could arrange to get a full set of fingerprints from him. He agreed but said he would have to go through his attorney. His children were returning from the East Coast in a few days, he said, and he wanted to get into Cheryl's house to remove some of her possessions he expected that they—and he—might need.

"I'm not the one who decides that," Gruber said easily. "Over here, we'd seal that house up, but you'll have to ask the detectives at Kitsap County."

Sensing that Pitre was going to stall, Gruber called Ron Edwards in Island County and asked if they could send down a copy of Pitre's prints.

What should have been easy continued to get more difficult. Detective Myrle Carner of the Seattle Police Crime Stopper program agreed to prepare a television announcement asking for help from the public. Someone had to have seen Cheryl or her car between Kitsap County and Lake Union. All it would take would be one sighting.

An ignition key was made for Cheryl's car. The engine turned over immediately, and the fuel gauge showed that the gas tank was between one-half and two-thirds full.

There were no prints on the gas cap, none on the ignition. The Mikrosil tool marks test from the trunk were insufficient to identify exactly what had been used in the bludgeoning or its manufacturer. None of the forensic science evidence of the kind that was often truly helpful was panning out. Both the detectives and the criminalists came to the conclusion that the murderer knew that he or she had to be wary of leaving fingerprints; the prints that had been lifted showed patterns that were consistent with someone who wore rubber gloves. Anyone who wore rubber gloves to carry out an abduction and a murder had to have carefully planned it all out.

In the end, despite the dozens and dozens of items of possible physical evidence the detectives had gathered, they had to admit that they were out of luck. Hairs, fibers, blood, buttons, smeared prints, keys, papers, books, tool marks, rope, strapping tape, and more: all of it useless as far as bringing them any closer to the person who had so callously bludgeoned Cheryl Pitre.

The circumstantial evidence didn't make them any more optimistic. If Della Roslyn was telling the truth, Roland Pitre could not have been the person Cheryl encountered as she left PJ's on the last night of her life. Della and her teenage children and his 10-year-old daughter had apparently seen him all that Saturday evening and at the very time Cheryl was believed to have encountered her killer.

Doug Wright and Jim Harris had searched her home thoroughly. They found absolutely no indication that Cheryl had ever come home that night. Although none of her friends who had seen her while she worked at PJ's remembered exactly what she was wearing that night, they agreed that it was jeans and a blouse or T-shirt of some sort. And that was what she was wearing when she was found: jeans and an aqua T-shirt.

Hank Gruber and his partner, Rudy Sutlovich, took another ferry ride to Port Orchard to confer with Harris and Wright, and they picked up evidence the Kitsap County detectives had preserved: Cheryl's purse and its contents, dried out now; a knapsack that held papers and records connected to her job at Bay Ford; and the answering ma-

WORTH MORE DEAD

Roland Pitre, 22, a U.S. Marine stationed in Iwakuni, Japan, 1974. He was a joker and something of a liar, but his buddies liked him well enough. He was already skilled at martial arts.

Maria Archer spent hours on the witness stand in her own defense, recalling her passionate affair with her judo instructor, Marine Corps sergeant Roland Pitre, and the way it ended. She was both demure and emotional as she denied any guilt whatsoever in the tragic murder of her navy lieutenant husband, Dennis. *(Leslie Rule)*

Maria's attorney, Gil Mullen, a former Seattle police officer, gives her a hug at the end of her trial. *(Leslie Rule)*

Maria Archer on trial for the murder of her husband, Dennis, in 1980. She testified most emphatically in her own defense, denying any knowledge of a plan to kill him. *(Leslie Rule)*

Steven Guidry sits at the defense table during the joint murder trial for himself and Maria Archer, a woman he had never met, although she was his best friend's former lover. The jurors would decide that the person behind Dennis Archer's murder was not on trial. *(Leslie Rule)*

Detective R. L. Edwards of the Island County Sheriff's Office tracked down the man responsible for the murder of Lt. Dennis Archer in his home in 1980. He expected that his quarry would be in prison for thirty years, but he was surprised to find that wouldn't happen. *(Leslie Rule)*

Roland Pitre, 1987, out of prison and reunited with his loyal wife, Cheryl. He had decided to become a registered nurse, and he also taught very popular judo classes. His life was definitely on an upward swing, especially when he and Cheryl welcomed a new baby son.

Staff party at Bay Ford—just before Roland Pitre came home to Cheryl. Her friend Greg Meakin is in the center and Cheryl is on the right.

Kitsap County detective Doug Wright worked with Seattle homicide detectives to solve the baffling murder of Cheryl Pitre. Here, he is participating in a raid on a marijuana grower.

Kitsap County detective Jim Harris (right) who, with his partner, Doug Wright, investigated the murder of Cheryl Pitre in October 1988. It would take more than fifteen years before that mystery was finally solved.

To the casual observer, this looked like an ordinary bathroom. But behind the shower curtain was a cleverly designed and insulated prison, built to hide a teenage kidnap victim. This was only the latest of Roland Pitre's complicated plots to make money for himself.

The cell hidden behind the shower curtain was padded with thick insulation so a kidnap victim's cries for help wouldn't be heard. Pitre worked for days to build what was, essentially, a death chamber for a teenager.

Lt. Lewis Olan first met Roland Pitre when his safe was mysteriously stolen, and Pitre was beaten while trying to get family mementos back. Later, Olan investigated the attempted kidnapping of Pitre's stepson.

Seattle police homicide detective Hank Gruber in 1988. Gruber thought he was giving only a "courtesy assist" to detectives from Kitsap County in a missing person case. It wasn't long before he found that he was deeply immersed in a homicide case in his own jurisdiction. It was to be one of the most frustrating cases of his long career—but sixteen years later, though he was retired, he saw that justice was finally done.

Fred McKee on his way to court to be sentenced for the murder for hire of Cheryl Pitre. The person who hired him once declared ever-lasting love for her.

Roland Pitre in 2004 as he appeared in court. The charismatic ladies' man had lost much of his charm, and he heard his own family beg a judge to send him away for as long as possible.

chine they took from her home. They rewound the machine and listened as it played all the messages left after Cheryl had reset it before leaving for work on Saturday, October 15. There were calls on Sunday morning from PJ's, the manager and another clerk wondering why she hadn't come to work. There was a call from Roland at about 6:30 that evening. Just as he told detectives, he phoned to ask Cheryl if she was going to pick up Bébé and André or if he should bring them home.

"If you're not already on your way over," his voice said, "give me a call." He sounded calm; there was no hint of concern in his voice. Either he had no reason to be worried about Cheryl on Sunday evening or he wanted to leave that impression with anyone who might listen to his message after she disappeared

It was hard to tell.

Kitsap detective Doug Wright asked the local phone company for records of toll calls made from the phones belonging to Roland Pitre, Della Roslyn, and Cheryl Pitre.

They found two of particular interest: collect calls to Roland on October 15 at 10:23 PM (fifteen minutes) and on October 18 at 7:52 PM (seven minutes). They came from the prison on McNeil Island. The McNeil authorities were able to identify the numbers as having come from pay phones in the Olympic Hall cell area; which prisoner had made a particular call would be more difficult to determine. Records were kept, but it might take a long time to cross-reference the calls.

The next place to go for Doug Wright, Jim Harris, Hank Gruber, and Rudy Sutlovich—who had joined the investigation—was an intense scrutiny of the list of Roland Pitre's associates inside and outside prison. They soon found that he was popular in both circles. If Roland hadn't left his mistress's bed on Saturday night, perhaps it was because he had already arranged for someone else to kill Cheryl. It was an awful thought, but with his history, it was possible.

Few of the people who knew Roland Pitre well in the late eighties found it strange that Roland could have been with Cheryl at the beginning of the summer and then moved in with Della without missing a step, acclimating smoothly to a different woman and different children. For most of his life, he lived parallel lives in the same time frame. He was a chameleon: the powerful and commanding judo instructor, the contrite prisoner who only wanted his wife back, the timid and ineffective used-car salesman, the charismatic nursing student, the good father who took the children in his life skating and played board games with them, the unfaithful husband, the sexual and sensitive lover, the schemer, and the charmer.

His friends and associates came from all walks of life, from the professional people who were benevolent to their fellow man to the lowest conniving and violent psychopath.

The latter seemed like the most fertile field for investigators to turn over. Roland Pitre's friend and fellow convict, Bud Halser,* had been out of prison only briefly: from May 1986, when he was sent to a work-release program, to December 1987, when he was returned to prison. Halser and Pitre were housed in the Olympic Hall cell area for six months just before Roland won his parole. They had evidently been in touch for some time inside and outside of prison. In fact, Roland asked to visit Halser on September 22, a little more than three weeks before

Cheryl was killed. That visit was denied by the prison.

Bud Halser could not have killed Cheryl; he was locked up tight on McNeil Island. But he might have served as an intermediary to connect Pitre to someone who was on the outside.

Although Halser had been in prison during the vital time period, Hank Gruber thought there still might be some connection to him. He learned that Halser's sister, Sally, had occasionally visited Roland in prison. She lived in West Seattle. When he knocked at her door, she answered carrying a newborn baby boy. She would have been eight and a half months pregnant when Cheryl was killed, hardly in any condition to participate in either an abduction or a murder.

"I knew Cheryl and Roland," she said. "But only because I went to McNeil to visit my brother, Bud."

"You didn't visit them in Port Orchard or Bremerton?" Gruber asked.

"I've never been to either of those towns."

"When was the last time you saw Roland?"

"I never knew him well, so I was kind of surprised last June when he came by my house with his kids and asked me to go to lunch. I was busy and told him no. And then he called me in July or maybe early August. He said he just wanted to see how I was doing. That was the last time I ever talked to him."

Sally Halser seemed truthful and eager to help the detectives, but she really didn't know much about Roland Pitre or anyone else in Seattle he might know. She wasn't sure if he had been coming on to her or if he was only genuinely concerned about her. But she had a boyfriend, and he had no reason to worry about her.

Gruber hooked up with Doug Wright again, and they went to McNeil Island to talk to Bud Halser. Halser realized right away that Hank Gruber was the detective who had talked to his sister. But the Seattle detective made small talk for about seven minutes until he explained that he and Wright were there investigating Cheryl Pitre's murder.

Halser stood up so rapidly that he might have been stung by a bee. "I have nothing further to say to you," he said gruffly. "I want to talk to my attorney." And he stomped out of the interview room.

A few minutes later, he came back but only to request the detectives' business cards to give to his lawyer. Gruber said that they might be back as the investigation was proceeding.

They had no shortage of suspects. And they still weren't convinced that Roland Pitre and Bud Halser hadn't figured out a way to bring someone who was on the outside in mid-October into a common plan.

As the holidays approached, the Pitre family underwent what might be called a reorganization. Christmas in 1987 had been happy for Cheryl; she and Roland had their new baby and a new house, and the future looked promising. Now Cheryl was dead and their children were almost three thousand miles away.

But Roland planned to rectify that. He arranged to have Bébé and André return from their maternal aunt's home in Pennsylvania. They would soon have a stepmother to help care for them: He and Della Roslyn planned to get married on New Year's Eve of 1988, ten weeks after Cheryl's murder. It was as if she had been erased from Roland's life and someone else quickly penciled in.

Frank Haberlach, the insurance agent who sold the Pitres their individual $125,000 policies, got a call from Roland requesting payment on Cheryl's death. Haberlach explained that the company would have to follow procedure and that it might have to go to the underwriters since the criminal case was still open.

King County Deputy Prosecutor Jeff Baird had been evaluating the efficacy of bringing charges against Roland and calling possible witnesses to appear before an inquiry judge. As with a grand jury, what is said before an inquiry judge is secret. Should Della become the next Mrs. Roland Pitre, she could invoke marital privilege and refuse to answer questions that might serve to incriminate him.

Baird subpoenaed Della to appear before Judge Charles Johnson on December 29. She was still single on that date. What she said behind closed doors was not revealed.

On New Year's Eve, Della and Roland were married. He became stepfather to her children, Amy and Tim, and Della, stepmother to Bébé and André. She loved them and knew they needed a mother badly, and she legally adopted them. Although Bébé, particularly, would never forget her own mother, Della wanted to be as close to a real mother for them as she could. Their lives went well at first, despite the stress of the murder investigation.

At 14, Tim was at a difficult age to accept another man into the household, and he and Roland soon had problems. He always felt that Roland was putting him down.

And soon there was no question that his new stepfather detested him.

13

The detectives were a long way from giving up. With the new year, Doug Wright and Jim Harris and Hank Gruber and Rudy Sutlovich continued their search for Cheryl's killer. It had been a hard-luck case so far. Then, on February 13, 1989, they received information that moved the probe in an entirely different direction.

Gruber and Sutlovich got a phone call from a man who identified himself as Creg Darby, a reporter for the *Bremerton Sun*. He said that someone had phoned him, asking for him by name.

"He told me that he was the person who killed Cheryl Pitre," Darby reported. "He said he killed her because she told him he was too young for her."

Darby said the anonymous caller went into specifics, saying that he first tried to strangle Cheryl but was unsuccessful. Next, he hit her with a pipe, then with a rock. The caller, who did sound like a young male in his late teens or early twenties, said he took Cheryl to Lake

120

Union in Seattle about two on Sunday morning and left her in her car there.

"She didn't want me," he said in what seemed a contrite voice. "I'm too young. I'm sorry."

This information galvanized the investigators. Maybe they had been focusing on the wrong suspect. The caller had his facts right about the manner of death, and his time line matched what they knew, too.

Darby said he had tried his best to get the caller's name. "He wouldn't tell me that, but he said he would call back. He wanted my home phone number, but I wouldn't give him that. He was very suspicious that his call was being recorded, and I had to reassure him about that. Of course, it wasn't being recorded."

But as any good reporter would, Darby took notes during the call, and he readily agreed to give a taped statement to Hank Gruber. He mentioned that the unknown caller had a very soft voice.

Darby and his editors agreed to have a trap put on his phone in case the man did call back. Rudy Sutlovich arranged with US West's telephone security department to have a pen register put in place on Creg Darby's office phone. It would be there for two weeks and would note the date, time, and phone number of the caller.

Sixteen years later, the phone trap sounds antiquated, but there was no caller ID in 1989, and the pen register was state of the art as it mechanically wrote down phone numbers.

Hank Gruber went to Bremerton and met with Creg Darby and his fellow reporter Gene Yoachum. Darby thought it was strange that the caller had asked for him because it was Yoachum who was tracking Cheryl's murder investigation. His byline had appeared above the Pitre article. Gruber asked if it might be possible to run another article, one designed to lure the caller out of the shadows. "Maybe it could be something like this," he suggested. "You could write that you weren't sure that the call wasn't a hoax, and you needed something more to prove it was the real guy"

The reporters were receptive to the idea, but they didn't want to go so far as entrap the caller.

"You wouldn't have to," Gruber explained. "You would write the truth and say that you had revealed his call to the police. He'd expect you to do that because you'd be obligated to report that kind of information."

Their editor agreed that an article would be appropriate as long as it was truthful and not misleading.

It was decided that Darby would write a short piece about the stranger's call that would run in the *Bremerton Sun* on February 16.

In the meantime, the investigators decided to contact Cheryl's associates and friends to see if they knew of any teenager or young man in her life who might have been obsessed with her. They didn't have to do that because the article sparked the memory of one of Cheryl's bosses at Bay Ford. He said that several of the dealer's staff had read it and agreed that the younger man might be a former lot boy who had worked for them doing chores, washing cars, bringing cars around for prospective buyers.

"His name is Alby Brotzweller,*" the caller said.

The car dealer didn't have an address for him. Jim Harris ran a background check on Brotzweller and found he was 20 years old, and had no prior record. He had a father, 43, and a brother, 17, in the area. Detective

Ed Striedinger of the Seattle Police Department ran "Brotzweller" through records and found a woman named Patsy Brotzweller, 37, who lived in the north end of Seattle and had an old address in Bremerton.

Hank Gruber and Jim Harris went to Bay Ford to ask Cheryl's fellow employees about Brotzweller. They learned he was a loner.

"He wasn't very good at relating to women," one salesman said. "The kind of kid you knew wanted to have a girlfriend but just didn't seem to know how to start anything going with them."

Alby had talked about getting a job as a dental technician; he'd done that in the army. Cheryl had told him she would help him compose a short résumé. She had helped him once before when he had car trouble. "He called her for a ride and she picked him up, but she never mentioned anything about his asking her for a date or coming on to her."

Cheryl said she would help Alby, but she was firm with him, telling him that she would type his résumés, but only if he put some effort into it, too. He would have to find the names and locations of dentists and address the envelopes. "You have to show some effort," she chided him. "To prove you really want to get this job."

Alby Brotzweller was showing more and more promise as a suspect. But the anonymous caller didn't bite on the article about his call.

Records at Bay Ford showed that Alby left work early on Friday, October 14—the day before Cheryl's murder—and never came back. "He called in on Monday and said he was resigning from his job as a lot boy," a representative said. "We ran into him later that week, and he had this big bandage on his hand covering a finger and part of his palm. It looked professionally done, like maybe a doctor had put it on."

When the detectives asked more about Brotzweller, his bosses said that he had a difficult time accepting criticism. "If he did something wrong or failed to get it done, he'd be really apologetic. He had a problem handling stress, like he wouldn't know what to say, get very upset, almost to the point of trembling."

"Was he ever violent?" Gruber asked.

"We never saw that, but everything in the article in the paper fit him perfectly."

In addition, Brotzweller's father lived at Long Lake, which was only a short distance from PJ's Market. Detectives Jim Harris and Hank Gruber drove the route between the father's house and Cheryl's home; they clocked it at 3.6 miles, and it took six minutes. They then drove from the Brotzwellers' to PJ's and found it was only eight-tenths of a mile, driving time: one minute. Furthermore, the most direct route for Cheryl to have taken from PJ's Market was past where Alby lived.

The elder Brotzweller had once been under investigation for a homicide, although charges were never filed.

The detectives went to his house to talk with him, and he met them in his yard. He was polite but evasive. He told them his son had moved out sometime in October. "I don't know where he's at, and I haven't heard from him in a long time."

Cal Brotzweller* had no idea who Alby's friends were or where the investigators might check to find them or him.

"What about his mother?" Gruber asked. "Could he be with her?"

Cal spat on the ground. "We don't have anything to do with her. We both hate his mother. She lives someplace in Seattle, I hear."

"Do you know how he hurt his hand?" Jim Harris asked.

"He cut it fishing."

"When was that?"

"Right about the time he moved out."

That was all the information they got from Alby's father. They left with the impression that Alby was no longer living with his father but were pretty sure that Cal Brotzweller knew exactly where to find him if he wanted to. He had been lying to protect his son even though he believed they were there to see Alby over a DWI (driving while intoxicated) warrant.

Harris radioed the Kitsap County Sheriff's Office and asked them to do a search on a current DWI involving Alby Brotzweller. That netted a possible current address for him: his grandparents' home in Bremerton. When they drove there, Gruber and Harris found a very run-down tri-level house. No one answered their knocks, and there was no car on the property, although there were fresh tracks in the mud of the carport. And then, just as they started to drive away, a car pulled in. Three men carrying grocery bags headed for the house.

The detectives approached one of the men and asked if Alby Brotzweller was there. At first, he said "No" but then admitted that the young man in the back seat of the car was Alby. Alby agreed to talk with Harris and Gruber and willingly got into their car.

"We're here about Cheryl," Gruber told him. "We've been talking to everyone who works at Bay Ford."

Alby nodded. "I read the article in the paper about that guy who called."

Asked if he would accompany them to the sheriff's office, the suspect—and he *was* a suspect—said that would be fine. There Alby was advised of his rights and he gave a detailed statement. He denied having anything to do with Cheryl Pitre's death and insisted he was not the person who had called the *Bremerton Sun*. "I've never called them for any reason."

"You go to Seattle much?" Harris asked.

"I don't like it there," he said. "I only went there one time with my grandparents to visit my mother. She lives in an apartment on someplace called Queen Anne Hill."

"Is that near Lake Union?" Gruber asked casually, knowing that the area was a mile or so from the lake.

"I don't know. I don't know where that is."

He was either stonewalling them or telling the truth or, perhaps, the partial truth. Alby said he'd never called Cheryl when he had car trouble, never asked her for help, didn't know she worked part time at PJ's.

Gruber didn't change expression, but he wasn't buying Alby's story. He wouldn't have been surprised if Alby even denied knowing where PJ's was. He certainly wasn't admitting to having any thoughts about dating Cheryl.

Alby's alibis all sounded contrived. He told them that Friday, October 14, had been a bad day for him. He had an accident with his car on his lunch hour and spent the rest of the afternoon trying to get that straightened out. He quit his job that day, too.

"On Saturday?" Harris asked. "What did you do on Saturday?"

"I was with my friend, Jer, until about ten PM, and then I went home to my dad's house about 10:30. He was asleep, but my brother was there listening to music."

As for Sunday, Alby said he'd gone fishing with Jer about eleven AM. "I cut my hand that night trying to fillet a flounder. I had to go to the hospital to get it stitched up. Jer and his father were there when I cut myself."

If that was true—and there were, indeed, witnesses to his injury—that would make Alby Brotzweller look far less guilty. Even so, there was the possibility that he might have deliberately cut himself to hide any injuries he suffered when Cheryl was bludgeoned the night before.

This was a case where detectives had felt sure they knew who killed Cheryl. That was her husband, Roland Pitre. Yet more and more suspects kept popping up, suspects they would have been glad to find under other circumstances. They were all veteran investigators and knew the dangers of tunnel vision, so they shoved their gut instincts aside and pursued every lead that came in.

Hank Gruber and Rudy Sutlovich met with Jim Harris and the reporter Creg Darby. They brought along audiotapes of Alby Brotzweller's and Roland Pitre's voices for Darby to listen to.

Darby shook his head when he heard Pitre's voice. "I'm pretty certain it wasn't him."

He was even more sure that he had never heard Alby's voice.

At the time, none of the detectives knew that Pitre was spreading a rumor that some younger man had been stalking Cheryl only days before her death.

14

A Port Orchard woman had been wrestling with her conscience for several months. She believed that her ex-boyfriend might be the one who killed Cheryl, but because she herself had been beaten by him so many times she was afraid to report him. In late February 1989, she finally called the police. His name was Jack Short,* and he had a long rap sheet filled with charges for assault and rape. He was also an associate of a wealthy man who once had a financial interest in PJ's Market.

Short had been imprisoned on McNeil Island, too, and was paroled in December 1987. Once more, Hank Gruber talked to the security staff at McNeil. He learned that though Short and Roland Pitre were never housed in the same unit, they had worked in prison shops that adjoined each other. There was a good possibility that they had known each other in prison.

But an intensive check of phone records in and out of the block where Jack Short served time failed to bring up any connections. Detectives were able to establish that Jack Short and Martin O'Brian,* a former owner of

PJ's, were well acquainted. The ex-con with a reputation for hurting and sexually attacking women and the wealthy man who tried countless times to set him on the straight path were both familiar faces at PJ's Market.

When detectives talked to O'Brian in his opulent and well-kept home, they asked him about both Cheryl Pitre and Jack Short. O'Brian said he'd known Jack since they were kids when they'd been friends, but they'd taken different paths. He said Short had an "explosive personality" and was "scary" when he was drinking. Even so he had tried to help him. "I gave him jobs," O'Brian said. "I even set up a work-release job for him, but the past few years he's just been bad news."

He said he'd given up on helping Jack Short because he no longer trusted him.

"Do you know if he knew Cheryl Pitre?" Hudson asked.

"I don't know. He might have seen her at the market."

O'Brian had nothing but good things to say about Cheryl. He'd always found her to be an excellent employee and said he'd been planning to ask her to do his bookkeeping for him in his various business ventures.

"When she worked for me," he continued, "it was standard procedure for her to call me when she was locking up the store. She'd tell me what the day's receipts were and assure me that she was okay and ready to leave. I may have been the last person to talk to her. She called me at 11:15 that last night. Everything was fine."

O'Brian was able to account for his whereabouts that night. Telephone records verified that account.

The wild card in the deck was still Alby Brotzweller. His reluctance to cooperate with the investigators made him look guilty. Detective Jim Harris set up an appointment for Alby to take a polygraph test, telling him that that was one way to clear himself. He reluctantly agreed; then, on the March day when he was to be transported to Seattle for the lie detector test, he was nowhere to be found. When Harris called the house where he had been staying, someone who said his name was Harry said Brotzweller wasn't there. Harris called again. The person who answered the phone said "Wrong number" and hung up. It sounded to Harris just like Alby's voice.

Irritated, the Kitsap County detectives drove to the address. The residents said he wasn't there; he had moved again. "He's back at his dad's place, and he don't want to take that lie detector test anymore."

Jim Harris spoke with Alby's friend Jer. To Harris's surprise, Jer said that Alby had indeed cut his hand on a very sharp fish knife. He himself had taken him to a hospital emergency room to get it sewed up. His mother said she was there when it happened. "He was new to fishing, and that was his first clumsy try at cleaning fish."

Her description of the incident was identical in detail to what Alby told the detectives.

Beginning on March 13, 1989, Hank Gruber and Rudy Sutlovich literally moved to Kitsap County to begin an intensive probe of Cheryl Pitre's murder. They intended to talk to every suspect and every witness and to join in searches of homes and vehicles, anything that might tip the scales and cause a single suspect to emerge as Cheryl's killer.

Detectives Harris and Hudson searched Alby Brotzweller's car, which had been wrecked on the afternoon of October 14 and stored in an impound lot ever since. The front window was broken out, and there was a lot of interior water damage caused by winter snowstorms. They removed a tire iron and the steering wheel cover and had them tested for signs of blood. There were none.

Interestingly, they found a professionally typed résumé for Brotzweller in the car. This seemed to war with his statement that he had never gotten a résumé from Cheryl. They checked the tape of his statement, and their memories were correct. They had asked him: "Was Cheryl going to do a work résumé for you?"

"She was. She was going to help me out with a job or work résumé for the dental field but due to my procrastination, we never got around to completing that or even getting started on it."

Yet here was a complete résumé! Had they caught Alby in a lie? They compared the font on the papers in Brotzweller's car with all the typewriters at Bay Ford. None of them matched.

Now they checked again with the source at the dealer who told them that Cheryl had picked the young lot boy up when his car broke down. Rumors were like the childhood game of "telephone." They changed slightly when each person repeated them. Cheryl had told a friend of a friend about receiving a call at three AM from someone who needed help, but it hadn't been from Alby Brotzweller at all. Rather, she said it was a friend of Roland's who called. And Roland's statement that his car had broken down the day before Cheryl was killed might even mean that he was the one who had attempted to lure her out of her house.

Jim Harris received an angry phone call from Alby Brotzweller. He was upset because the investigators were still asking questions about him. "I didn't kill the bitch!" he said vehemently.

"Then why didn't you take your polygraph?"

"It was snowing and I couldn't make it. I talked to people who told me not to take a lie detector test in a police station. They said the police would just hold me there and pin that murder on me because you don't know who did it. Those police lie detector guys can make the test come out any way they want them to."

Asked about the résumés found in his car at the impound yard, Alby Brotzweller said he'd had that done four or five days after he quit Bay Ford. "They did it for me at the JPTA job training place in Bremerton. Cheryl didn't have anything to do with those."

It was the truth. The youth employment agency put detectives in touch with the typist who prepared the résumés. Alby Brotzweller caused himself a lot of trouble with his attitude, and he could have been cleared of suspicion a lot sooner. The investigators now believed he had nothing to do with Cheryl's murder.

Jack Short was the next suspect for the detectives either to close in on or to eliminate. It was quite likely that he had at least seen Cheryl working at PJ's Market since he had been friends with the store's owner. Whether he knew her as anyone beyond a clerk no one knew. And there was his record of violence against women to consider. At the investigators' invitation, he sauntered into the Kitsap County Sheriff's Office. He explained to Jim Harris and Hank Gruber that his official address was with his brother, but he was presently staying with a "female friend" in Port Orchard.

He was a very relaxed interviewee, apparently not in the least upset to be questioned about a brutal murder. Shown photos of both Roland and Cheryl, he said he didn't know either of them.

"You never saw her at PJ's?"

"Don't remember her. I go there to charge stuff and cash checks sometimes, but I don't remember her face at all."

"You were housed close to Roland Pitre during the same time period at McNeil Island," Gruber said.

"Naw, I was on D Block. Never met the guy. I was in a whole different place. I was a meat cutter there."

"You keep in touch with the guys you knew there?"

"Nope. I don't have any contact with them. No mail. Nothing. My mom won't pass on mail or messages from anyone wanting to talk to me if they're from McNeil. She doesn't want me seeing that old gang."

Gruber and Harris noted that Short talked a lot but didn't say much that was useful to them. His demeanor was so confident that they felt he had no guilty knowledge of Cheryl Pitre's death.

Perhaps the most peculiar suspects yet in this totally frustrating investigation were the men who had found Cheryl's purse floating in Lake Union way back in October near where her body lay hidden in the trunk of her own car. They were Native Americans who actually lived in Suquamish, which is in Kitsap County north of Bremerton, not that far from where Cheryl lived and worked. That they should be the ones who spotted her belongings so far from where they—and she—lived could serve to implicate them in the crime. Initially, detectives didn't know that the men who called to report the purse were not Seattle residents.

But then this case was becoming infamous for the number of slam-dunk "has to be a connection" suspects, none of whom had panned out.

And this one didn't either. Hank Gruber talked to Sant D'Eagle,* who owned a funky and popular antique store in Suquamish. D'Eagle said that he and a male friend had indeed found the things that belonged to Cheryl Pitre drifting near the houseboats as they walked along Fairview Avenue East.

"What were you doing way over there?" Gruber asked.

"We went over to see a game on TV. See, we scout out different places around Puget Sound, checking to see which taverns have the biggest TV sets. And Bogie's has the biggest screen—ten feet diagonally—and the best food. We've got a boat with a canopy, and we just take an excursion . . ."

"You cross the sound in a small boat to get to a tavern?" Gruber asked incredulously.

"Sure do. It only takes us about half an hour to get to Seattle and then some more time to get through the locks in Ballard."

Apparently D'Eagle and his pals considered taking such an unorthodox shortcut to Seattle, even in bad weather or rough seas, an adventure.

"We're going to Camano Island next weekend," he added.

It seemed like a long way around to watch a televised game in a tavern, but Gruber had been a detective for years and he'd seen stranger things. He went to the address D'Eagle had given him for another of the Native Americans who made it a point to find the best taverns on Puget Sound via the sea route. Asked if they really did travel that far in a small craft, the man gave the same details D'Eagle had. They didn't see any need to take the ferries. Cost too much and took too long.

Neither man had the slightest connection to Roland or Cheryl Pitre (beyond finding her sodden purse near where her body was left) or to Alby Brotzweller, Jack Short, or Bud Halser.

Although leads continued to trickle in through the spring of 1989, their possible worth in identifying Cheryl Pitre's murderer diminished steadily.

One man, a truck driver, said he stopped at PJ's every morning to buy a cup of coffee, a newspaper, and a pack of cigarettes and sometimes talked to Cheryl there when she worked a rare morning shift. He said he also knew Roland. Like so many others, he had met Roland in prison.

"Last time I talked to Cheryl was about three weeks before she got killed," he said. "At the time, there was some guy and a bunch of kids in the parking lot, and I asked her what that was all about. She said she thought the guy was selling drugs."

"Can you describe him?" Sergeant Joe Sanford asked.

The witness shrugged his shoulders. "All I remember is he was older than the kids."

"What kind of car was he driving?"

"I can't remember."

He offered his opinion. "You know, toward the end,

Cheryl was having mood swings," he said. "She was going over the deep end. She was dating some guy from Seattle."

"That's from your own knowledge or did Roland tell you that?" Sanford asked.

The man mumbled something that was hard to understand. The investigators knew that Roland Pitre had a number of observations about Cheryl that he was quite willing to share. Most of them were different scenarios about who might have killed her: stalkers, men she might have dated. But Cheryl hadn't really had time to date. When she wasn't working, she was looking after André and Bébé or in church. Her foray into the Parents Without Partners coffee group was the most adventuresome thing she'd done since Roland left her.

The Kitsap County and Seattle detectives still had the same problem: they had not come up with enough physical or circumstantial evidence to arrest Roland Pitre for her murder.

Nevertheless Roland was getting impatient. It was May, seven months after Cheryl's death, and the Lutheran Brotherhood Insurance Company had not yet paid off on the policy he purchased on her life. When the company called Joe Sanford to ask if the police investigation was over, Sanford told them that the active investigation was still alive. "Roland Pitre has not been eliminated."

Hank Gruber and Rudy Sutlovich had to end their full-court press on the other side of the sound from Seattle and move back home. With Jim Harris, Doug Wright, and Doug Hudson, they had given the Pitre murder investigation everything they had for several weeks, talked to dozens of people, followed innumerable leads—no matter how far-fetched—and were left with unanswerable questions.

Cheryl's murder looked as though it might be headed for the cold-case files. It galled them, but there it was. If anything new turned up, they would of course check it out. But there were other homicides to work in Seattle and in Port Orchard. Nobody forgot Cheryl Pitre, the young mother who had fought so hard to have a happy family only to be savagely beaten to death.

Sadly, no one knew how long it would be before Cheryl would have some kind of justice.

15

Roland Pitre moved swiftly on to his next marriage. He and Della Pitre graduated from Olympic College and applied for their registered nurse licenses. Della became an RN, but Roland ran into trouble. When the Washington State Nursing Board checked his background and found that he had been convicted of murder and a number of lesser crimes and that he "was a prime suspect in his ex-wife's murder," they denied him a nursing license. Della became the main financial support of the family, often working double shifts at Harrison Hospital in Bremerton and Tacoma General Hospital while Roland stayed home to take care of the children.

In a sense he contributed to the family income: Cheryl's children, Bébé and André, received Social Security payments from their dead mother's account. These payments went to their father, of course.

Later, Roland tried again to get a nursing license. With some sleight of hand, he apparently became a certified nursing assistant (CNA). He had learned not to use his own name, however. He used the identity and the Social Security number of his long-dead brother, Wade, who was only two when he died.

Roland's marriage to Della was troubled from the beginning. Try as she might, Della couldn't make Roland accept her son, Tim, or Tim accept Roland. They were always wrangling about something. Initially, she believed her new husband when he told her that Tim was sneaky, told lies, and stole things. She began to look at her son with suspicion.

Tim later recalled his mother's marriage to Roland and their family life as "an absolute living hell." His mother was always at work, and he felt that Roland was constantly criticizing him and making him look bad. In Roland's eyes, nothing Tim did was right. André was only 3 and he could barely remember his mother, but Bébé, at 12, mourned for her mother and wanted to believe in her father. When he was nice, he was really fun to be around. But Bébé was also afraid of him; his temperament was volatile and she never knew how he was going to act. Sometimes he slapped her for no reason at all. Della was good to her, but Della wasn't her real mother.

Della and Roland had frequent arguments, and they separated in October 1990. They hadn't been married even a year. They got back together after several months, but there was no feeling of permanency in their family.

Roland eventually got a job as a CNA at a nursing home in Poulsbo, although Della still made about double the salary he did.

Frank Haberlach, the insurance agent who had sold

Roland the policies back in 1988, stopped in at Bay Ford and spoke to Greg Meakin.

"He looked glum," Meakin recalled. "He had this check from the insurance policy. He said, 'It just kills me to give this to Pitre.' He said it was one time he wasn't happy to present a payoff . . ."

As it turned out, except for about ten thousand dollars—which he spent right away—the money didn't go to Roland Pitre; it was put in a trust by the Court for Bébé and André to have when they were old enough to go to college. Cheryl had apparently realized that her husband wasn't trustworthy with money and had taken steps to protect her children. André wasn't old enough to know anything about trust funds. As Bébé grew older, her father told her repeatedly that the money wasn't hers—it was his—and that she would have to sign it over to him as soon as she got it.

Roland played with Bébé's mind a lot. He had always manipulated people around him; he was skilled at making them believe what he wanted them to believe. It didn't matter to him whether they were strangers, friends, or members of his family. A little girl was an easy target.

Bébé was confused about the sequence of events on the night that her mother died. She and André were living with her mother, but her father had visitation rights every other week. "One week, he came to pick me up," Bébé said, "and after that night, I never saw her again."

Bébé recalled going skating on that Saturday afternoon, but the evening was hazy. She had been very tired and couldn't remember staying up late to watch wrestling on TV with her father and Tim. That would have been around midnight or one. She was pretty sure that she watched only a few minutes of TV before she went to bed and was therefore sound asleep at that time, but her father had told her she should tell the police that she was watching TV with him all that time. And she had done what he told her to do.

But Bébé was a very bright girl. She had a vague feeling that it was her father who killed her mother or at least that he had had something to do with it.

While Roland's judo students and her mother's church friends believed that her parents had had a perfect marriage, she had seen the dark side. One night after André was born, she had wakened to the sound of her mother's screams. She had tiptoed out of bed and seen her father holding her mother's arms "real tight, and squeezing and shaking her."

The next morning, her mother had big purplish bruises on her upper arms.

Bébé Pitre was about 13 when she met Bud Halser. He became a fixture around their house after he was released from prison. He and Roland were really good friends. She was told to call him Uncle Bud, although she didn't think he was her real uncle. Bébé had long since learned to tiptoe around her father because she knew what he was capable of. She was afraid of him and knew that money meant everything to him.

On the night of July 14, 1991, while Della Roslyn was at the hospital working a night shift, Bébé was the only one at home when her father and Bud Halser drove up in Bud's van. She watched as they removed a safe from a closet and carried it to the van. Tim came home unexpectedly, and Bud hid in the back of his van with the safe until Tim left.

Afraid of her father, Bébé never told anyone what she saw. All Della knew was that the safe had been stolen sometime between 6:30 PM, when she left for work, and 7:40 the next morning, when she got home. Officer Moon of the Bremerton Police Department took the burglary report and noted that Della said their house had a security alarm that should have been activated that night. Moon was unable to find any sign of forced entry, and the Pitres' next-door neighbors had neither seen nor heard anything unusual during the night.

Although the safe itself was arguably Roland's possession, it was filled with sentimental items belonging to Della Roslyn Pitre: two dozen pieces of her jewelry and important documents. She was distraught when she realized that they were gone. She told Moon that she suspected her husband because they were once again on the brink of divorce.

Roland said he had no idea who might have taken the safe; he had been away from home the night it disappeared. He said he'd taken Bébé and André to Panther Lake at 7:30 and hadn't returned until the next day. As he thought now about the contents of the safe, he recalled that there had been some of his own jewelry in a jewelry box inside it. He added seven items to the inventory that Della had made of twenty-five pieces of her jewelry. Not counting the sentimental value of family keepsakes, the loss of the contents of the safe—almost all of it Della's property—was well over $10,000.

As he often had, Roland Pitre submitted yet another insurance claim, this time for the stolen safe, to the

American States Insurance Company. He soon received payment in the amount of only $1,715. The company said that the policy did not cover jewelry. The check didn't begin to cover the value of Della's rings and necklaces or the sentimental value of the family mementos she had lost.

Two months later, on August 23, Roland went to the emergency room at Harrison Hospital to be treated for what he called "slashing cuts" he said he sustained when someone assaulted him. He wasn't badly hurt. He told Greg Rawlins, a Bremerton policeman, and Gary Crane, a Mason County detective, that he had set up a meeting with "some people" he suspected of stealing his family's safe by pretending he had drugs to trade for Della's jewelry. He had packaged up some powdered sugar to make it look like cocaine.

"I met these four males who were driving a yellow car. They showed me a bag with some of our things in it," he said. "I grabbed the bag and pulled it inside my van. But then I was either shot or hit with a club or something . . ."

Roland said he somehow managed to struggle free and drive himself to Harrison Hospital's emergency room. He showed the investigators the bag he allegedly wrested from his mysterious attackers. He gave the police the bag of costume jewelry. They noted that it contained only the inexpensive pieces Della listed as missing.

In February 1992, Roland Pitre allegedly suffered a stroke, although he seemed to have no lingering effects beyond what he termed "seizures." These often occurred when he was in the Social Security Administration offices, filling out forms to apply for Supplemental Social

Security benefits. He claimed to be 100 percent disabled. He was so convincing that he received payments of $600 a month for his disability. Among the perks resulting from his stroke were license plates that allowed him to park in spots reserved for the disabled.

The once-powerful judo instructor and Marine Corps staff sergeant said he could no longer work as a CNA at the nursing home. Instead, he again enrolled as a full-time student at Olympic College, this time majoring in accounting.

With his marriage to Della crumbling, Roland turned to religion, or seemed to. He began to attend the Church of Abundant Life, a fundamentalist congregation. He became so devout that he even went to Bible study classes at the home of Duane and Beth Bixler,* a couple he met in church.

"Everyone in our group felt sorry for him," Beth Bixler said. "He told us that he had been framed for murder and sent to prison for the death of his wife. And he was very unhappy in his current marriage."

Again, Roland Pitre had shaded the truth, combining his earlier crimes and rearranging them to make his story better. He had *not* been convicted of murdering his wife; Cheryl's murder case was still open and unsolved. He sensed—correctly—that the facts about the murder of his mistress's husband wouldn't garner as much sympathy if he told them that that was why he went to prison. To the naive churchgoers, his troubles seemed overwhelming. The tears is his eyes appeared genuine, the grief of a martyr. The Bible study group soon spent as much time discussing Roland's misfortunes and trying to help him as they did examining Bible passages.

"We were supposed to support and pray for each other," Beth Bixler explained, "and in that particular environment everyone showed compassion and sympathy."

No one in the congregation knew that Roland Pitre's estranged wife, her children, and his own children lived in fear of what he might do next. He had always been able to morph from a seemingly meek man to a swaggering martial arts expert and then to a charismatic ladies' man.

By February 1993, Della Pitre could see clear to the center of who her husband really was. She found herself in the same position that Cheryl was in when Roland cheated with Della. At first, Della believed him when he said her son Tim was the liar and had probably stolen their safe.

As she lost her trust in Roland, it slowly dawned on Della that her son was the innocent one and that she had made his life worse by doubting him. Although she couldn't prove it, she suspected that Roland was behind the disappearance of the safe.

She also speculated that her husband was being unfaithful to her despite his protestations when she questioned him. Finally, Della asked Roland to move out of their home and filed for divorce. This time she meant it, and no amount of sweet talking from him changed her mind. His children remained with her; Della had adopted them, she loved them, and she feared for them if they were alone with Roland. By 1993, Della's son Tim was 18, Bébé was 15, and André was 5. Although he had not lived with the family for a month, Roland came over often to visit his children, his eyes filling with tears as he tried to tell Della how lonesome he was without her.

He made a big show of being a concerned father, particularly when Bébé began to date. Her boyfriend, Mike, was just an awkward, "cocky, pretending to be invulnerable" kid, and their dates were innocent. "I was close to Bébé from September 1992 through June 1995," Mike recalled. "After Roland's separation from Della, he invited Bébé and me over for dinner. He made a very good manicotti and he entertained us with stories from his Marine Corps drill instructor days as I was considering [enlisting], which I did after graduating. After dinner, Bébé excused herself to go to the bathroom. Roland stepped right up in my face, playing the role of the all-American father, saying, 'If you ever hurt my daughter, I will kill you, and believe me, I know *how*.'

"I just looked him back in the eye and told him I would never hurt her."

Mike remembered Roland as a man of contrasts, as one who desperately wanted the affection and loyalty of his family but was also quite willing to hurt them deeply. And, even though he had tried to intimidate Bébé's young boyfriend, Roland came to his wrestling matches, taught him techniques, and cheered for him.

In truth, Roland was not heartbroken over the end of his second marriage, and he wasn't lonely. He had someone to talk to. Beth Bixler, who along with her husband had been among his most sympathetic church friends, was there for him. The two began to meet outside of the Bible study meetings, and Beth didn't bring her husband along. They consummated their passion on Valentine's Day 1993. Della Pitre's suspicions were accurate.

Not surprisingly, Beth's marriage soon became shaky. By March 1993, she and Duane separated.

She later admitted that she had become more and more attracted to Roland Pitre. They began to see each other regularly. Although he later denied they had a sexual relationship, Beth admitted that they did. Beyond her infatuation with him, Beth turned to Roland with *her* problems. She owned a large house, but as a single woman, her finances became a problem. She'd had no idea how much it cost to maintain a house: mortgage payments, taxes, utilities, general upkeep. Without her estranged husband's help, Beth soon found herself wallowing in debt.

She counted on Roland's considerable wisdom to help her with her financial quandary. He promised her that everything would be all right. She didn't even consider one of his suggestions, thinking that he could not be serious even though she was aware of at least part of his criminal past. After they discussed her marital problems, he suggested that he could arrange for her estranged husband to be killed.

"How much insurance does he have?" Roland asked her bluntly.

"I don't know," she answered, hesitantly. "Maybe $100,000 or $150,000."

"Well . . ."

That conversational thread ended abruptly. Beth would never dream of having her husband hurt or killed. Besides, she figured Roland hadn't really meant it. He must have been making a bad joke.

Sometime later, Roland suggested that she consider renting out part of her house. That would bring in income, and she agreed it was a feasible possibility.

He told Beth that he knew of "an individual" who

was looking for what Roland called "a safe house" for about six weeks.

"You can make $3,000 in rent in that short a time," he promised her, and he calmed her fears that having a complete stranger with some kind of secret in her house might be dangerous. "It's perfectly safe," he assured her. "I wouldn't do anything to place you in danger—you know that—and I don't see that you have any other choice right now."

Beth Bixler nodded hesitantly. Everything was happening so fast. It had been such a short time since she was a happily married, churchgoing young wife. Now she was with another man, and neither of them was officially divorced.

But she did depend on Roland Pitre. She totally believed in him, unknowingly stepping into the next vacancy in a long line of women who had felt the same way only to regret it mightily later.

Roland had a plan for Beth Bixler.

16

Tim Nash drew his first easy breath in a long time when he realized that his mother was serious this time when she kicked Roland out and filed for divorce. Even though his stepfather still came by the house to visit with André and Bébé, Tim could make himself scarce and avoid him. To have his mother believe in him again meant a lot to Tim, and he began to regain a lot of his self-respect.

The next step up a ladder of disturbing events in the Pitre family took place at a time when crime is usually at an ebb. It was a rainy Sunday evening, March 21, 1993—the first day of spring—when a Bremerton Police radio operator received a call from a man who sounded hysterical. It took a while for the dispatcher to understand his words. He was able to make out the address and understood that there was a burglary or robbery going on there, but not much else. The call for help came in shortly before 8:30.

149

Officer Steve Emm was dispatched to the residence. There he found a young male who was still unable to control his emotions. In fact, he looked scared to death. Patiently, Emm got the complainant to calm down to a point where he could get information from him.

He said his name was Tim Nash and that he lived there with his mother and a younger stepbrother and stepsister. His older sister had moved out, and so had his stepfather.

Tim had a bizarre story to tell. He was all alone in the house when he received a phone call about half an hour earlier from a woman who called him by name. From background noises, it seemed to him that the call was coming from a phone booth. The woman sounded young and incredibly sexy. He thought it might have been some girl he knew at high school making a prank phone call.

"She asked me if I knew who she was, and I said no, but she seemed to know who I was," Tim told Emm. "She was kind of flirting with me and teasing me and making me guess her name. She finally said if I really wanted to find out about her I should come up to the Pancake House and meet her. So I said I would."

Tim said that the restaurant wasn't far away. Tantalized, he hopped on his motor scooter and rode to the Pancake House. He checked out the restaurant for familiar faces, expecting to spot some girl he knew. There weren't many people in the place at the time, and he didn't recognize anyone there. Nobody waved at him or signaled to him in any way.

Next, Tim checked out the parking lot for a vehicle he might recognize. But none of the cars parked there looked familiar. He waited for a while at the edge of the lot, thinking the woman must have called him from a phone booth located someplace else. He watched the area for five minutes or so, but no car pulled in.

Tim told the investigators that he figured he had fallen for some dumb practical joke, so he left and went back home.

He was sure he had armed their alarm system before he left and locked the front door. That was the rule in his family. Upon his return, he used his key to get back in and immediately disarmed the system.

What happened next is the stuff of most people's nightmares. As he would explain first to Officers Emm and Bogen, who had pulled up just behind the first squad car, and the next day to Detective Lewis Olan, Tim said he'd had the eerie sense that he was not alone in the house. It was quiet enough, but he still felt the hairs stand up on the back of his neck. He wasn't sure why.

Suddenly he heard a sound that seemed to be coming from his upstairs bedroom and recognized it as the slight rustling of venetian blinds. It was as if something or someone had just brushed against them. Of course, it could have been the wind.

His mother was working, as she always did on Sunday nights, and his stepsister and stepbrother, Bébé and André, were supposed to be having a visitation weekend with their father. There shouldn't have been anyone else in the house.

Tim recalled that he tried to turn on the light on the staircase that led up to the bedroom landing, but it was burned out. He walked slowly up the stairs. When he got to the top, he pulled aside a curtain that covered his bedroom doorway and at the same time reached in to click on the light in his room.

That light didn't go on, either. He went in anyway, wondering a little at the coincidence of two bulbs burning out at the same time.

"As I walked in," he said, "a guy wearing a ski mask stepped out and stuck a rifle up against my throat."

He froze, panicked, his heart beating loudly in his ears. Tim remembered that he looked into the dimness of his bedroom, lit only by a street light outside, and saw a second figure who also wore a mask. It was a woman. He couldn't see her face, but she had full breasts that were obvious under her tight black pullover.

She mumbled something, and he instantly recognized her voice. It was the same woman who had called him and persuaded him to come to the Pancake House to meet her.

Although Tim didn't know what was happening or who these wraithlike figures were, he believed he was in terrible danger and that the gun at his neck might go off at any moment. A scream burst from his throat. "Help! Help!" he called out frantically. "I'm being robbed."

He had no reason to think that, but why else would anyone be hiding in his room? It was just the first thing that came to his mind. The Roslyn family owned a small apartment that was connected to their house at the first-floor level. He hoped desperately that the couple who lived there were home and would hear him. His house had a large window at the bottom of the stairs that offered a view right into one of the apartment's windows. If he could manage to get downstairs and their drapes weren't drawn, they would be able to see him.

No one responded at first to his screaming. And then one of the tenants shouted something. At least they were home and aware that he was in trouble. His knees buckled under him and he went limp, still calling out for help.

"Shut the fuck up," the man in black growled.

"Shut up," the woman hissed. "Just shut up."

It was her all right. Tim couldn't mistake that voice, but he had no idea who she was. The man ran down the stairs, but Tim, still lying on the floor, blocked the woman, so she nudged him aside and followed.

Unable to stand up because he was so frightened, the teenager prayed that they were leaving, but he expected them to come back upstairs and kill him.

He waited, the sound of his hoarse breathing seeming to fill the room. Then he realized that the house was silent. The two masked strangers appeared to be gone. Trembling, he made his way to a phone and called the Bremerton police emergency number. Next, he called his mother. She said she would come right home.

Then Tim grabbed a kitchen knife and put it his pocket. He locked all the doors and wedged a chair under the front doorknob. Although he doubted it would do any good, he reactivated the alarm system. It was odd. He had armed it when he left to meet the mysterious woman, but somehow she and the man had gotten in anyway without setting it off.

When Officer Emm arrived, he saw several faces peering out the window at him, trying to see who was knocking on the door. The neighbors had joined Tim. They were all frightened, but Tim was the most afraid since he was the only person who had actually encountered the strangers in black.

None of them knew who might have been in their house or why. They were not wealthy. They didn't own anything worth a home-invasion burglary.

Emm and Bogen searched the house and checked the exterior doors. They found no sign of forced entry. Indeed, they couldn't even be sure what the point of entry into the house was. They did discover why the lights on the stairs and in Tim's room hadn't responded when he hit the switch: someone had carefully unscrewed the bulbs.

They also found an empty gun case in Tim's bedroom.

Della arrived home shortly after the police left. She was instantly suspicious. She had her own idea of who had attacked Tim. That was strengthened by Bébé's call to Della from Beth Bixler's house, where she was babysitting. The teenager was nervous because she kept getting phone calls. The caller hung up as soon as she answered. And she told Della that Roland phoned her late in the evening to tell her that he'd suffered a blackout and couldn't remember what he had done for several hours. He had had blackouts and "spells" before, which he attributed to his stroke; nevertheless, Della found this sudden loss of memory a little too convenient.

Roland had been late picking Bébé up earlier in the day, arriving at noon rather than at 10:30 as he'd promised. They hadn't spent very much time together. He told her then that he promised she would babysit for Beth Bixler's children.

When Bébé got home late Sunday night, she found the house in an uproar. Of course, it wasn't the first time she experienced some kind of emergency in her family. Over the years she had known any number of traumatic times: she witnessed her parents' violent fights, her mother's fear, her parents' divorce, and her mother's disappearance, which proved to be her kidnapping and murder. There was the theft of the family safe, the time her father said he'd been beaten so badly he had to go to the hospital, his fights with Tim, and all the times Della and Roland broke up.

Rather than becoming accustomed to unexpected events, it was natural that Bébé was sensitized to danger and particularly fearful. In the month since her father had been out of the house, it had been almost serene, at least compared with what it was like when he lived there.

Now everyone in his family tried to reassure Tim that he didn't need to worry anymore. The police knew what had happened, the family was all together now (with the exception of Roland), and the doors were locked. Eventually Tim calmed down and Bébé headed upstairs.

She was startled to see that there were two carryall bags in Tim's room. She recognized them. One belonged to her. It was a white canvas bag with "Slumberjack" printed on the side and her name written in pen in small letters. She had kept her old sleeping bag in it, but lately she used it to carry things to school. The other was a blue nylon bag with "Mum's" embroidered on the side with red thread. It was a laundry bag from a local firm. Both bags had been around for a long time, a familiar sight in the household.

But Bébé had seen those bags earlier in the day, and they weren't in her adoptive mother's home at that time. They had been in Roland's green van when he picked her up at noon. She was positive of that. Her dad's van was cluttered with a whole bunch of stuff, and she had moved the bags out of the way to make room for her little brother, André, to sit down.

Now, here they were back in the house, in Tim's bedroom. They were full of items, but she didn't check to see what was inside. When Bébé told Della what she had found, Della called the police and asked that the officers return. "I want to report a suspect, too," she said.

She told the police officers that her estranged husband, Roland, was quite capable of either committing or orchestrating a crime like burglarizing his family's home and threatening her son. She also showed them the two bags, explaining that Bébé had seen those bags in Roland's van earlier in the day. She believed that he must have brought them back into her house at the time her son was assaulted. He knew the alarm code, she said; she hadn't bothered to change it. She allowed him to do his laundry in her house, and he still came to visit André. Still, even though she knew Roland to be a liar and a cheat, she hadn't considered him a real danger to any of them. Now she wasn't so sure.

Bogen and Emm took the suspect bags and logged them into evidence.

Bébé Pitre had a really bad feeling. Her father had acted out of character all day. After he picked her up at noon, he actually asked her how Tim was doing and made a number of positive comments about her stepbrother. He never said anything nice about Tim. She knew that her father and Tim hadn't gotten along for years, and it was weird that all of a sudden her dad talked about Tim in such a solicitous and complimentary way.

"How's Tim doing?" Roland had asked her. "I'd like to spend more time with him, sit down and talk with him and become pals."

That caught her off guard. The two had hated each other for as far back as she could remember. Why was her father suddenly doing this about-face?

Bébé Pitre was 15, a very intelligent 15, and she was no longer the easily manipulated little girl who always did what her father wanted her to do. Questions kept popping up in her mind. She even began to explore her doubts about her mother's murder. Cheryl Pitre's death remained a mystery five years after it occurred, and Bébé could no longer deny her sixth sense that her father might have had something to do with it. She didn't want that to be true. It was hard enough to have her mother gone. She didn't even want to think that her father had done something as bad as that.

Secrets she had been forced to keep for a long time bubbled up to the surface of her consciousness, demanding that she tell someone. Part of her still loved her father, but she was afraid of him. After what had happened to Tim, they were all afraid of Roland and what he might do next.

Bébé made up her mind to tell the police investigators about her doubts.

17

On Monday, March 22, 1993, Bremerton detective Lewis Olan was officially assigned to the investigation of the attack or attempted kidnapping or burglary—whatever it was—of Tim Nash and his home. Olan had encountered Roland Pitre, Tim's stepfather, two years earlier. He was one of the detectives who investigated the theft of the Pitre family safe. That investigation was never successfully concluded, although Roland had recovered some of the jewelry reported to be missing in the murky incident in which he said he was beaten and cut by someone never identified. That had been a strange case. This alleged burglary was even more peculiar.

Tim Nash appeared to be terribly frightened, but he wasn't hurt. There was always the possibility that he'd made up the whole thing to get attention. Any experienced detective knows that people give false reports of crimes for all kinds of reasons. With no sign of tool marks or broken windows signaling a forced entry and no one tripping the security system, it was natural to wonder if the kid had done it. Nothing was missing.

But when Olan talked to both the victim and family

members, taping their statements, they told him essentially the same things they told Officers Emm and Bogen the night before. None of them even suggested that Tim Nash might have made it all up. How would he have had access to Roland Pitre's van and the two bags later found in his bedroom? That didn't compute at all.

Tim made a very believable witness. According to all reports, he was a good kid. Olan pursued his investigation on the assumption that someone had indeed lured him away from the house just long enough for the couple in black to sneak in. And he suspected what the Pitre family suspected: that for some reason Pitre himself had crept into his onetime home and threatened his stepson.

Next, the Bremerton detective searched the two bags that Bébé Pitre had seen in her father's van at noon on Sunday, then in Tim's bedroom that night.

The blue nylon bag, now marked Number One, held a hundred-foot reel of white nylon rope, an open roll of duct tape, two rolls of duct tape still sealed in a package, several large plastic bags, a diver's knife in a black rubber sheath, foam earplugs, a plastic sack from a Kmart store with a box half full of .44 Magnum bullets, and a receipt dated March 10, 1993.

Curious, Olan opened another, smaller, Kmart bag. It held a full box of earplugs and more than a dozen greeting cards. There were five more cards in another sack, a package of utility knife blades, and a white handkerchief.

So far, with the possible exception of the .44 rounds, there wasn't anything really ominous about the contents of the blue bag. There could be dozens of legitimate reasons for having rope, duct tape, and greeting cards. Even the earplugs and the diver's knife weren't suspicious; there were hundreds of people in the Puget Sound area who dove beneath its surface for sport.

Olan turned next to the Slumberjack bag. Inside he found a bag from a PayLess store. It held three packages of five-by-eight-inch cards. One was open, and several of the cards had printing on them, done with a black felt-tip pen.

They seemed to be cue cards, meant for someone to read or perhaps to memorize or simply say aloud. It was apparent that Tim was the one who was supposed to read them.

Basically, the message was the same. Tim's voice—probably in a phone call—would say he was in some kind of trouble and that the only one who could help him was Roland Pitre.

One read, "Hi, Mom, this is Tim. I moved out of the house." Another said, "I'm in trouble this time. I need Roland's help. I don't know if he'll help me because I switched his medication and then I put, I think, arsenic in his chewing . . ." (Olan couldn't tell whether the blurred next word was "gum" or "tobacco.") The writing ended abruptly.

Why would Tim need cue cards? Why couldn't he just call up his mother and talk to her?

Detective Olan asked Bébé Pitre to look at the cards to see if she could identify the writing on them. She could. It was her father's. For some reason, Roland Pitre had written a script for Tim to read.

There were more papers in the white canvas bag. Della Roslyn recognized them, even though she hadn't seen them for almost two years. They were the documents that had been in her stolen safe. Stuffed in a paper bag were marriage and birth certificates, passports, insurance policies, and legal documents. Roland's marriage certificate with Cheryl was there, as were birth certificates for some members of Della's and Roland's combined family. There were the adoption papers from when she had adopted Bébé and André. And there was a handful of newspaper clippings about Cheryl Pitre's homicide in Kitsap County and even newspaper accounts of the trial after the murder of Dennis Archer on Whidbey Island and Roland's conviction on conspiracy to commit that murder.

Lewis Olan had never believed that Roland wasn't involved in the theft of the safe back in 1991, but he hadn't been able to prove his complicity. Now in this bag was proof that he had undoubtedly kept the fruits of that theft while collecting insurance for the loss. The only documents that ever surfaced were papers that Roland needed. All of Della's, Bébé's, André's, Tim's, and Amy's important papers were gone, but Roland managed to keep his birth certificate and that of his dead brother, Wade Pitre.

Olan tended to believe Della Pitre when she said that Roland Pitre was connected to the incident with his stepson, Tim.

But why? Surely he wouldn't have gone to all this trouble just to terrorize a kid he didn't like. Motive is a vital part in an investigation, and so far it was as obscure as a gray ship cruising on Puget Sound in a pea-soup fog.

One older mystery was solved, however: Bébé Pitre had identified her father's handwriting on the cue cards and also said that the handkerchief in the Slumberjack bag belonged to Roland; now she was finally ready to reveal a secret he had made her keep since she was 13. She cleared up the question of who had stolen the safe from her house in 1991.

Bébé admitted that she had watched her father and Bud Halser carry the safe out. She explained, to her stepmother's shock, that at her father's insistence she accompanied them as they drove to an isolated spot near Panther Lake, Washington.

She told Lewis Olan and Della Roslyn that she saw the two men remove the contents of the safe before they attempted to bury it near an old outhouse. As they began to dig, they disturbed a nest of angry hornets. They abandoned that plan and drove instead to Renton, Washington, where she thought they left the safe with some relative of "Uncle Bud's."

Roland had warned Bébé that she must never tell that she saw him and Uncle Bud take the safe and bury it. His warning had been very effective; she was so frightened that she hadn't told the story until now.

But Roland apparently hadn't been able to restrain himself from bragging to his daughter about how clever he was. Bébé also told Olan that she knew her father used another name to get his certified nursing assistant's license from the State of Louisiana. He used Wade Pitre's name and Social Security number, and he finagled a way to use the Louisiana CNA credits to gain employment in Washington State. Wade had been dead for almost half a century, and apparently no one checked on the authenticity of Roland's stolen identity.

Bébé's admissions were a huge relief to her and proved that Roland Pitre was a liar and a thief, though that wasn't a surprise to the investigating detective or Roland's latest estranged wife. But the question of motive—*if* he was involved in the attack on Tim Nash—remained.

When Olan looked into the murders of Lieutenant Commander Dennis Archer and Cheryl Pitre, he learned that Roland Pitre had had an alibi in each case. He was far more likely to be a conspirator in a crime than the one who actually committed it. Maybe "Uncle Bud" was the man in black in the mask?

Olan located the man Bébé called Uncle only to find that Bud Halser had the best alibi of all. He was once again behind prison bars, and there was no way he could have been free to commit any kind of crime on the night of March 21.

It wasn't Halser, and the woman's identity was even more difficult to puzzle out. All Tim could describe about her was that she had a good figure and that her voice sounded young.

That woman soon returned to Tim's life.

18

On March 24, three days after the home invasion, the Bremerton Police Department had an unexpected visitor. A nervous woman appeared, saying that she wanted to confess to a robbery.

Her name was Beth Bixler. She had red hair and pale skin dusted with freckles. She was undoubtedly paler than usual now but was pretty in a quiet way. She looked like the sort of young woman who should be teaching Sunday school rather than turning herself in as a felon.

She was quickly escorted to an interview room, where Lewis Olan and Detective Doug Wright listened with fascination to her story. They heard yet another woman go to bat for Roland Pitre.

Beth Bixler told them that she had conspired with Tim Nash to work out a plan to fake his own kidnapping.

Beth recalled that she had met Roland, Tim's stepfather, at her church three years before and had participated in many church activities with him. She admitted that she recently found herself in love with him. Her husband accused her of having an affair with Roland, and her marriage completely collapsed. But her love for

Roland Pitre was so compelling that she had accepted that she was headed for divorce.

According to Beth, Tim called her and told her that Roland was trying to get back with his mother, Della. Tim didn't want that to happen; he hated Roland and wanted him to stay away forever. Beth said she didn't want the Pitres to reconcile, either. She loved Roland and wanted to be with him. So, she said, Tim had come up with a plan that would make Roland look really bad to Della so that she would lose all respect for him and refuse to take him back.

The detectives stared at the woman who was confessing to what she called a complicated plot. They had seen Tim in the aftermath of the attack on him, and he certainly had not impressed them as the kind of mastermind who would suggest that Roland be framed to appear to be a monster. But that's what Beth Bixler was telling them. At this point her version of the crime began to falter. She said Tim told her that if the two of them planted items that had obviously been in Roland's custody—specifically, the two bags—in Della's house, Della would be furious. That didn't seem to be a particularly terrible thing for Roland to do: the investigators knew that Della allowed him to do his laundry there. She hinted that it was Tim's idea to make up a story about the couple in black who threatened him, knowing that Della would immediately suspect Roland.

When Wright and Olan questioned Beth Bixler about the details of the plot, her answers became increasingly vague. But she continued to insist that Roland had done nothing wrong; that he wasn't even in Della's house on Sunday night and had no knowledge of the plan she and

Tim had formulated. She told them that it had basically been Tim's plot to get rid of a stepfather he hated. He was so persuasive that she went along with it in the hope that Della would be angry and reject Roland and then she would have him to herself.

Beth said she filled the two carryall bags that were supposed to be given to Tim to put in his bedroom and that a "female and a male were there," but her description of the evidence didn't match what the detectives knew. She inadvertently put herself into the crime, slipping up and admitting that she was the female involved.

"The police were not supposed to be involved," she stammered. "Somehow, everything got messed up."

It didn't take much adept questioning by the detectives to shred Beth Bixler's story. Doug Wright told her frankly that the statement they had just taped was obviously false.

"After a brief discussion that we did not believe her story," Lewis Olan told a Superior Court judge, "at which time she was given the choice to tell the truth—and decided not to—she was arrested and charged with first-degree burglary, conspiracy, attempted kidnapping, and conspiracy to commit murder."

"When was she arrested?" the judge asked.

"She was arrested yesterday: March 24, 1993."

Beth Bixler was stunned when Doug Wright placed her under arrest. She had probably been duped, just as Roland Pitre had duped so many other people, many of them women who—at least initially—were in love with him. At this point, her feelings were ambivalent. She still felt a very strong attraction to him, but she said that she had also come to be afraid of him. He had told her that he believed in revenge and that he knew people who owed him favors.

Shaken, Beth was booked into jail.

It took only a few hours for Beth Bixler to send word to Wright through the jail staff that she wanted to talk to him. It was ten minutes after ten that Wednesday night when Wright called Olan and then walked over to the jail. At Wright's request, the jail staff advised Beth Bixler of her rights under Miranda and asked her if she wanted to have an attorney present.

She shook her head. "I want to talk to the detectives," she said. "I want to tell them the truth and confess."

Even though the two detectives hadn't believed her original recitation of events, the real story was nevertheless a surprise.

The winsome, churchgoing mother said that she was desperate for money, and the $3,000 in rent money that Roland promised her never materialized, even though she kept asking him where the renter who needed a safe house was. She was ready to listen to any solution he could offer her.

Finally Roland told her that he had developed another plan, one that would bring them a lot more money. He explained to her how much he disliked his stepson, Tim. "He was responsible for the failure of my marriage to Della," Pitre said. "And now, he's going to be involved in my new plan."

While Beth listened, both shocked and mesmerized, Roland laid out the specifics of his scenario. First, he and his good friend, Bud Halser, planned to kidnap Tim and hold him for $250,000 ransom. Currently in jail,

Bud would have been out in plenty of time to help Roland.

When Beth opened her mouth to protest, Roland jumped ahead. "We won't *really* kidnap him," he promised her. "I know I can convince Tim to go along with the plan. See, I'm going to pay him $50,000 and buy him a plane ticket to Hawaii."

She wondered where the $250,000 was going to come from. Surely Della didn't have that kind of money. Roland said that was true, but Della's parents had a large and expensive home. Tim would be instructed to tell his mother that he had been abducted by people to whom he owed money. Then Della would persuade her parents to take out a second mortgage on their house. They were very respectable citizens with good credit, and they loved their grandchildren. Roland was positive they would agree to do that, anything to save Tim from his kidnappers. They would be told to leave the $250,000 somewhere where Roland or Bud could retrieve it without being seen. Subsequently Tim would be released.

Nobody would be hurt, Roland had promised her. The police would never even know about any of it.

It was a wild idea, a scheme rife with holes and things that could go wrong. What if Tim wouldn't go along with it? How long would it take to get a house refinanced? What if his grandparents refused to go into debt for a quarter of a million dollars? What if somebody called the FBI?

Roland waved away all of Beth Bixler's questions, telling her that she lacked the "ability to think big." He assured her that he had never had a plan go wrong, that he always won because he was a detail man with a great talent for predicting what people would do. It was all a matter of pushing the right buttons, and he knew where those buttons were.

She was entranced with him, passionately in love with him. She had already betrayed her husband for him, shocked her church, and put her family in jeopardy. And she was about to lose her house because she couldn't pay her bills.

Beth asked Roland what her part of the project would be.

"Hardly anything," he said easily. "All we need is your house, just the basement of your house, actually. We have to have someplace to hide Tim."

She wondered about that. If Tim was cooperating and would get a ticket to Hawaii, why would they have to hide him? But Roland said they needed him at first. Tim would have to be available to make phone calls to his mother. If he were in Hawaii, there would be long-distance phone bills that could be traced, and there was also the matter of controlling Tim. Roland wanted to be right there with him to be sure he said the right things at the right time.

One element of the perfect caper went awry early on. Bud Halser, who was to be Roland's wing man, was arrested for the umpteenth time and sent back to prison. He was no longer available to help Roland "kidnap" Tim.

That wasn't a real problem, Roland told his new girlfriend. She could take Bud's place. It wouldn't require any particular strength. All she had to do was follow his instructions.

First they had to do some construction in the basement

of Beth's house. She became caught up in the plotting, each step tumbling after the other until it seemed to make some crazy kind of sense, and the deeper she was pulled in, the more difficult it was for her to back out. Roland convinced her that they had to build a little room within a room that had to be soundproof so that no one inside or outside the house would know where Tim was staying.

The bathroom in Beth's basement was fairly good-sized, and Roland built a tiny room inside. By removing the shelves in a large closet in the bathroom, he constructed a space that was approximately two feet by three and a half feet. He built a false wall that hid the entrance to the room within a room. He added thick layers of insulation to deaden any sounds coming from the cramped chamber. Then he pulled the flowered shower curtain over his handiwork so that no one could detect that this was anything but a basement bathroom.

Beth went on with her confession. The earplugs in the two bags accidentally left behind after the failed kidnapping had a purpose. Tim Nash was supposed to be tied up and taped to a chair in the hidden room. Then the earplugs would be inserted into his ears so he wouldn't be able to hear whether anyone was home in the house.

Essentially, had the kidnapping been a success, Tim would have been held captive and deprived of most of his senses. He would not have been able to move, to see, to hear. If he called out for help, no one would be able to hear him outside the soundproofed walls.

By this time, Beth said, she was terrified by Roland. She felt she had to continue with the plot. "I was afraid of not doing it, and I just didn't say no."

He instructed her to get a gun. She borrowed one from

a coworker, telling him that she was afraid to be alone and needed a gun for protection. Roland told her to buy a box of bullets and some greeting cards. They were to be used as letters that Tim would periodically send to various relatives. Beth said she wore brown gloves whenever she purchased the things on Roland's list at Kmart so she wouldn't leave any fingerprints behind.

Roland prepared the script that Tim was to follow and printed the words carefully on the five-by-eight-inch lined cards she bought. When Tim called his mother, he would be forced to stick to the words written on the cue cards. Roland's scenario called for Tim to tell his mother that he hated her and that she was responsible for making his life miserable and for his disappearance. Further, the script called for Tim to say that Roland was not to be blamed for leaving, that instead Della should notify Roland that Tim desperately needed his help.

This woman, who never expected to see the inside of a jail, said she was completely trapped at this point and could find no way out of her lover's scheme. Beth said Roland's scenario moved along with a life of its own. Whether the detectives were buying her whole story was questionable, although it was apparent that she didn't have a strong personality: they could see how someone like Pitre could have dominated her.

Doug Wright asked her what she and Roland had worn when they went to his former home to confront Tim Nash.

"Roland was wearing black pants and either a black turtleneck or sweatshirt; I can't remember which right now. He had a black leather fanny pack and a black pair of shoes."

On his instruction, Beth said, she also wore black clothing, and they both wore dark ski masks.

Actually, they had been geared up to kidnap Tim a week earlier than when they carried it out. Roland said they should do it on a Sunday night since he could be sure that Tim would be alone. They'd gotten dressed in black on March 14, but for some reason Roland had a bad feeling and put it off for a week.

Roland had it worked out to the tiniest detail. He had Bud Halser's girlfriend, Bobbi,* babysitting for André at his apartment. Bobbi would also serve as an alibi for Roland, swearing that he had been home all evening.

Bébé would be sitting for Beth's children so her father could be sure she wasn't in the house with Tim.

Beth told Doug Wright that she was the female who called Tim. "On the way to the house, we stopped at the R and H Market on Kitsap Way. I disguised my voice and called Tim and coaxed him to come to the Pancake House."

After Roland and Beth were sure Tim had left his home, they went to Della Pitre's house, parked in the back, and entered the house through the garage. "Roland still had a key to the door. He turned off the alarm system and then unscrewed the lightbulbs over the stairs and in Tim's room."

Beth said that when Tim returned, the alarm had temporarily activated, which spooked her, but Tim quickly turned it off.

"I was in a state of shock at this point," she said. "When the light didn't go on over the stairs, he walked up anyway. When he reached the landing, Roland pointed the gun at him and said, 'Shut the fuck up!'"

Everything had started to collapse. She said Tim began to scream wildly, and someone in the apartment yelled and asked what was the matter. Beth said she and Roland ran to the bottom of the stairs and then ran from the house. "Roland was driving like a maniac when we left, and he was telling me I had to get rid of our masks and the gun, just dump them somewhere.

"We didn't notice that we'd left those bags behind until we were driving away in the car. Roland asked me where they were, and I told him they were still in the house, and he said, 'We're fucked!'"

It certainly seemed that they were. After they managed to lure Tim away from the house and were able to enter without a problem, nothing went as Roland planned. They weren't even able to accomplish the kidnapping, much less go forward with his foolproof plan to keep Tim tied up in Beth's basement until his grandparents came up with the $250,000 ransom.

What would he have done with Tim at that point if Roland's scenario had worked? The answer was obvious: Roland could never have let Tim go free. Tim surely would have figured out who was holding him captive, even if the amateurish soundproof prison actually blocked out all sound and Roland and Beth managed to change their voices enough to fool him when they checked on him. Tim would have become a major threat. Any reasonable person would deduce that Tim Nash—alive—could and probably would report Roland Pitre to the police.

Tim Nash, like others less lucky, would have been worth more dead to Roland Pitre.

19

At **4:10** PM on March 24, Superior Court Judge Karen B. Conoley issued an arrest warrant for Pitre, not for kidnapping or conspiracy—which were still under intense investigation—but for burglary stemming from the theft on July 13, 1991, of the family safe, which was still missing. That would be enough to take him off the street and give his family a measure of relief that he would not be sneaking back into their house. Just to be sure, Della Roslyn obtained a restraining order that barred Roland from any contact whatsoever with his terrified family.

Tim had believed his stepfather had wanted to kill him for a long time, and the rest of the Pitre family, including his daughter and estranged wife, were deathly afraid of Roland. The charges were soon amended to include the attempted kidnapping and burglary. Christian Casad, Chief Criminal Deputy Prosecuting Attorney for Kitsap County, and Deputy Prosecutor Brian Moran were assigned to handle the State's case. Steve Sherman was appointed to represent Roland Pitre.

Held on $500,000 bail, Roland said he was shocked

that anyone could possibly deduce that he would hurt his family. He said that he suffered from such terrible feelings of loneliness and loss after Della asked him to move out and told him she was going ahead with a divorce that he had come up with all the reasons he could to go back to what had been his home. Why would Della have allowed him to keep his key to the garage if she didn't still need him? He said he tried to find small repairs to make and took his laundry there, making any excuse he could to stay close to her and his children.

As far as his having a sexual relationship with Beth Bixler, he laughed that off. He told detectives that he never considered sleeping with Beth and had no romantic feelings toward her. It was she, he insisted, who was the aggressor. She regularly came to his house, complaining about how miserable she was in her marriage, and they had commiserated with each other.

Roland said he was taken aback when Beth approached him and asked him to kill her husband, promising him a share of his $200,000 insurance policy.

"I told her immediately that I did not kill people," he protested, seeming to be appalled at the very thought of it.

But Beth had persisted in her demands that either Roland or someone he could hire would murder her husband. It was at that point, Roland said, that he realized that Beth might be just the kind of person who could help him create a false danger for his family. He thought he might be able to use her to work out a scenario that wouldn't truly be a menace to Della and the kids but one in which he could appear to be their savior.

Yes, he had told Beth Bixler a tall story of how Tim

would be kidnapped and held for ransom. But her own "greed" took over, he recalled, and she came up with ideas on how they could accomplish the kidnapping.

"The holding room, the cards, and most of the other ideas were all hers," Roland said quietly. "I just went along with several of her suggestions so she wouldn't guess my true intentions of pretending to rescue my family until the last minute."

Roland Pitre swore he never meant for the plan to go beyond frightening Tim. He assured the investigators that all he planned was for someone to get into the house, frighten Tim into believing he was about to be abducted, and then leave. At that point, Roland would come back home, and his family would realize they needed him to take care of them. His marriage would resume, and they would all live happily ever after.

But he knew that he couldn't do it himself. If he went into the house, Tim would recognize him. Beth was afraid to go in alone, so she found some young guy Roland did not know to pretend to be a kidnapper. It was she, he insisted, who said they needed a gun. "I asked her to please just get a BB or a pellet gun," he sighed. "Without my knowledge, she borrowed a .44 caliber gun from some coworker."

He added that Beth was having a sexual relationship with that man.

On March 21, Roland said, he and Beth picked up a young man at the Handy Mart on Marine Drive. Then she called Tim and flirted with him, luring him to the Pancake House. When they saw Tim riding by on his scooter, Roland drove to Della's house.

Yes, he parked in the back and provided them with a

key and the alarm system code, but he only waited in the car. Beth got out of his van, carrying the two bags of items she thought she needed, and the stranger carried the rifle case.

Roland said he took the young man aside to be sure he understood that no one was to be hurt. All he was supposed to do was frighten Tim, then leave. "No harm was to come to him; I told him that."

Beth and the other man came running out of the house a short time later, and Roland drove off with them. He left the stranger at the Handy Mart, and then Beth took over the driving and dropped Roland at his house.

As far as the theft of the safe holding Della's possessions, jewelry, and the family's documents, Roland admitted to that. But that had happened two years ago. He and Bud Halser had taken the safe to retaliate against Della for trying to divorce him a year before, sneakily filing papers when he was far away visiting in Louisiana. Insurance? Of course not, he said. He never even thought of insurance on the safe.

Roland maintained that Della was the one who filed the insurance claims and that the money received from the company was deposited in her personal bank account. After he managed to recover the jewelry, he said, he attempted to report that to the insurance company, but they weren't interested. "They told me the matter was closed and wasn't worth pursuing."

Roland's great and good friend, Bud Halser, presently in prison, was not charged in Tim's kidnapping attempt, but he was charged in the theft of the safe in 1991. As tight as the two men had been for years,

Halser's lawyer nevertheless set out immediately with motions to sever his case from Pitre's. Evidence showed that Halser's girlfriend was involved in the kidnapping plot, too. She placed several phone calls to Bébé, who was babysitting for Beth Bixler, in an effort to give Roland a backup alibi.

It was a matter of whom to believe, Beth Bixler or Roland Pitre. Their stories were diametrically opposed, each version rendering the other as entirely false. But if Beth Bixler was the brains behind the plot to kidnap Tim Nash, why had she come to the police in an attempt to take all the blame away from Roland? On the other hand, he had thrown her to the wolves quite easily. And Roland Pitre was the one who had a long rap sheet and a reputation for being a convincing liar. It wasn't that the investigators believed her just because she was a woman; they had seen a number of female felons. But Beth Bixler had no criminal past, and Roland had been tied to two homicides.

Roland lied as easily as he breathed. And he had a history of filing claims with insurance companies. He was a shoplifter and a faithless lover. Was he only a con man and a grifter, or was he far more dangerous than that? It certainly seemed so when one considered the escalation of his alleged crimes over the past twenty years. He had been close to the violent deaths of both Dennis Archer and Cheryl Pitre, although his actual whereabouts at the moment of their murders was still murky.

Even though she had come to fear him, Bébé Pitre clung to the hope that deep in his heart her father loved her and the family. That all crumbled when she and her boyfriend Mike were cleaning out Roland's rental house after his arrest for attempted kidnapping. As they made piles of things to keep and things to give to the Goodwill, they found the transcripts from the 1980 trial in which Roland testified against his mistress and his best friend. Reading them, Bébé suddenly came across the questions about Pitre's onetime plan to kill her for insurance money. To her shock and sadness, she finally comprehended just how little she meant to her father.

She was only 15 years old when she realized the danger she had been in at the tender age of 20 months. On page 102 of the transcript, she read that her father admitted to buying an insurance policy on her life. A page later, he spoke of thinking about ways to kill her.

"How did you plan on killing your daughter?" the defense attorney, Gil Mullen, asked him.

"I thought about making it look like she accidentally got into some drugs. I thought about making it look like she was kidnapped. I hadn't really come down to a final . . . the plan was that I was more leaning towards was her getting into the medicine cabinet. She was at the . . . she was always crawling around getting into things."

"Did you call anybody [Seattle's Poison Control Center] in reference to a drug overdose or anything in Seattle?"

"Yeah."

"What was that about?"

"Uh, I didn't know how much it would take. I called to see about how much it would take, how many. I couldn't get any prescription drugs. I was thinking about sleeping pills. I wanted to know how much it would take to kill somebody."

Mullen had questioned Roland about the details of his buying the insurance policies.

"Okay. Now let's talk about the times that you bought these policies. When did you buy those $20,000 policies?"

"I got the first policy during the first or second week I was there in Pennsylvania [when he was picking tiny Bébé up for a visit to Washington in 1980]."

"Before you thought of killing your daughter?"

"Yes."

"And the second $20,000 policy was purchased after you thought of killing your daughter?"

"Yes."

It is almost impossible to contemplate what reading these transcripts must have been like for a teenager. Now Bébé admitted to the prosecution team that she had always been afraid of her father and that he had continually tried to draw her into whatever his scheme of the moment was, but she had been much too fearful to tell anyone, even her adoptive mother, who was also frightened. With Roland shut away in jail, Bébé made copies of the court transcripts where her own murder was contemplated and gave them to the prosecutors and the investigators.

They didn't disagree with her when she told them that she was finally convinced that her father had killed her mother. That was the very worst truth she had to accept. She had loved him so much, but his latest attack had been just another of his sinister schemes, this time to take away the only family she had left. His lies and manipulations were obvious.

• • •

Della Roslyn Pitre talked to the investigators about her fear of Roland Pitre. He had been a very romantic boyfriend, but once they were married he soon became another person. She was shocked by the way he twisted the truth to suit his purposes. Her family had seen through him before she had—as families often do—but she had been bedazzled by him. That caused a rift between Della and her family, although she was working hard to mend it. Della had always enjoyed a good reputation, and she felt that her association with Roland had tainted her image and cost her promotions at work. Worst of all was how he had persuaded her to distrust her son. She regretted the pain that Tim had gone through and vowed to make it up to him if she could.

Della knew her children were all suffering from post-traumatic stress. To be at home with them during night-time hours, she resigned from her second-shift job at Tacoma General Hospital. She had been making about $70,000 a year; suddenly, her income had dropped to $24,000.

Like Bébé, Della came to believe that Roland was behind Cheryl Pitre's murder, even though she had been his main alibi witness. Five years earlier, he persuaded her that he had come to bed that Saturday night at almost exactly the time Cheryl locked up PJ's Market and headed for home. She had had no reason to doubt Roland at the time, but now Della wasn't so sure.

Everyone in the Pitre house was sleeping, either in bed or in front of the TV set, between 11:30 PM and 12:30 AM. Everyone but Roland. Roland told Della that it was 11:30 when he came to bed, but she hadn't checked. It was an hour later when they made love.

When Della awakened at five the next morning, he was there beside her. But had he really been there all night?

Bébé knew that she hadn't watched wrestling on television with her father that night because she had gotten so sleepy that she went to bed. But she was only 10 years old at the time, much too young to even understand what an alibi was.

Now she did.

20

Beth Bixler had plenty of time to think about what a fool she had been. She was the one who had taken almost all of the risks. The only thing Roland had done was to finally agree to go into the house with her to grab his stepson. She had borrowed the gun, bought all the items Roland needed, made the phone calls to Tim. And, afterward, when everything had gone wrong, Roland ordered her to get rid of the ski masks, the gloves, and the rifle. He even talked her into going to the police and telling lies meant to remove all suspicion from him.

Doug Wright asked Beth where she had disposed of the rifle and the other items. She told them, and their hearts sank. Anyone who thinks being a detective is all intrigue and excitement should know they often have to endure repugnant assignments that nobody would ever choose to perform. Beyond working a homicide crime scene with the corpse of the victim still present, searches for physical evidence too often lead them through garbage dumps or rat-infested hiding places under bridges and in sewers. Now the Bremerton and Kitsap County investigators had an even worse job ahead of them.

It was almost dark on March 24 when Beth Bixler

rode with Lewis Olan and Wright to a park near Port Ludlow, pointing out places where she had thrown away the ski masks and the two pairs of gloves worn during the abortive kidnapping.

It was two when they found the women's outhouses where Beth said she left the gloves and masks. They had come prepared—as much as they could be. "We had salmon-fishing poles with big hooks on them," Wright recalled. "And we were there all night long, fishing through the sewage."

Using high-powered flashlights to see, they dug through the human waste, and the trash, and garbage cans. They found one black racer-type glove with a white stripe on it in the filthy muck of an outhouse. The glove was just as Beth described.

The next morning, Olan, accompanied by Detectives Andy Oakley and D. Trudeau and Sergeant K. Long, returned to Port Ludlow to continue the search. After a long nauseating exploration in the privy, they found another glove, one of the brown gloves Beth wore when she purchased the bullets, greeting cards, and ski masks.

Olan went to the rock breakwater that held back the surging waters of Puget Sound. There he gazed down into the water trying to make out what seemed to be a rifle. Luckily the tide was out, and he could see a Winchester-type .44 Magnun rifle. The butt portion was sticking out of about three inches of water.

Beth Bixler's house was located in Kitsap County, and Doug Wright and Jim Harris prepared to search it to see if the outrageous plan Beth had outlined to Wright was really true.

"We went all out on that," Wright remembers. "If there was evidence of that kidnapping plan in her house, we were going to find it."

Armed with a search warrant, the detectives swarmed over both Beth Bixler's house and Roland Pitre's green Ford Econoline van with its handicap license plate. They particularly wanted to inspect the basement bathroom to see if there really was a hidden holding room there. There was.

The thought that a human being was to have been held in the near coffin-sized space was sobering. Had Tim Nash not managed to escape from Roland and Beth, he would have been imprisoned in this impossibly small, airless room, so tiny, it would make anyone claustrophobic. Gagged, Tim's voice would almost certainly have failed to carry through the walls that Roland had covered with thick insulation. Tied to a chair, his ability to hear shut off by earplugs, probably blindfolded, Tim's confinement would have been torturous.

The detectives took dozens of photos that would be exhibits at Pitre's trial. The pictures showed Beth Bixler's basement, the holding cell itself, the insulation, earphones, earplugs, a knife and rope, and numerous receipts from Costco, Home Depot, and Wal-Mart for the purchase of tools and the lumber used to build the silent chamber in Beth's basement.

The Bremerton detectives found that Roland hadn't even bothered to remove the leftover pieces of lumber from his van. There they also found the family records that had once been in the stolen safe, in good shape because for years they'd been kept in a plastic bag. The duct tape, cue cards, and ammunition certainly dovetailed with Beth Bixler's description of the kidnapping she said Roland had planned.

If there had ever been any romantic connection between Roland Pitre and Beth Bixler—and detectives believed there had—there no longer was one. Now they were both in jail, and Roland evinced shock that Beth had betrayed him. He insisted that she didn't know what she was talking about.

Yes, he had originally deceived her when he told her that they were going to "kidnap" Tim and hold him for ransom. And yes, he had built a holding cell for Tim in the basement of Beth's house. But that was all a false plot never meant to come to fruition

"I never intended to go through with it," he said. "I just wanted to scare my family. I just wanted to be around to foil the attempt so Della would feel the need to have me move back in the home to protect them."

He had wanted Della to understand the sense of loss that he felt when his marriage collapsed and he was banished to live alone.

When detectives asked him about the theft of the safe, Roland finally admitted that he had taken it from Della's house. "But I never received or cashed any insurance checks from that," he claimed once more, not very convincingly.

Trial dates for Roland Pitre were set and reset at the request of the defense for a delay.

As he had done after he was arrested for the murder of Lieutenant Commander Dennis Archer on Whidbey Island thirteen years earlier, Roland Pitre apparently suffered a mental collapse and made a halfhearted suicide attempt in the Kitsap County Jail. Judge Karlynn Haberly asked for a mental evaluation by a psychologist from the Washington State Department of Social and

Health Services. Dr. Gregg Gagliardi was appointed and met with Roland Pitre on April 8, 1993.

This time, there was no "Targan," the entity that Roland blamed for Archer's death in 1980. When Gagliardi said that he would like to review reports of Pitre's earlier breakdowns and his alleged stroke in 1991 and those of his outpatient counselor and the neurologist who verified the stroke's effects to the Social Security Administration, Roland looked at him and said that he could not sign permission slips because he wasn't Roland Pitre.

"I'm *Wade* Pitre," he said. "The records say I died when I was two, but I didn't really die. I was in a coma, and I didn't come out of it until 1988. You'll have to ask Roland's attorney to sign those permission slips for you."

Gagliardi stared at the man before him. Was he really looking at a dual personality, or was this a show put on just for him? He attempted to point out inconsistencies in Roland/Wade's premise. "Wade" denied that he had ever been in the Marine Corps, even after Gagliardi pointed out the large Marine Corps tattoo on his upper left arm.

He tended to think that Roland Pitre was malingering and that his performance was "exceedingly amateurish" and thoroughly unconvincing. Despite the prisoner's refusal to let him access his earlier psychiatric records, there was plenty of information on him on file in the corrections system of the State of Washington.

The psychologist knew the basics of Roland's family history. There was no evidence of psychiatric disorder in any of his family members. Roland had always tested above average in IQ tests, and he had a stellar service record. He was a model inmate on McNeil Island. He'd done very well in college courses, both in prison and after he was paroled.

But now Roland Pitre was acting psychotic. He seemed to know he was in Bremerton but thought the county was either "King" or "Kansas City." He couldn't—or wouldn't—remember even three objects shown to him and couldn't count backward by seven, yet in other intelligence tests Gagliardi gave him, Pitre scored slightly above average.

On one test, Pitre scored in the bottom 0.007 percentile of the relevant adult population.

"If the present mental status examination findings and test results were to be believed," Dr. Gagliardi wrote, "it would indicate that Mr. Pitre is not only suffering from multiple personality disorder, but also that the alter personality, 'Wade' Pitre, is moderately mentally retarded or moderately demented."

But Gagliardi didn't believe him for a minute. He'd talked to Pitre's family and to Beth Bixler, and he believed the patient was faking. He mixed up his symptoms in ways that warred with what—or who—he was attempting to portray.

The psychologist even doubted that Pitre had suffered a stroke that allegedly made him 100 percent disabled. There were no indications of it. He felt he was looking at a Class A imposter.

One of the mental evaluations of Roland Pitre was available to Dr. Gagliardi. He read about the 1980 case and mentioned it in his 1993 report. "While undergoing a forensic mental evaluation pursuant to charges of Second Degree Murder, Mr. Pitre malingered symptoms of psychosis."

Dr. Gagliardi made the following DSM-III-R (the "bible" used by psychologists and psychiatrists) diagnoses:

AXIS 1: 1) Malingering V65.20; 2) Alleged Adult
   Antisocial Behavior V71.01
AXIS II Antisocial Personality Disorder, by history
AXIS III Alleged Stroke resulting in 100%
   disability, March, 1991 (unconfirmed)

These terms are meaningful to professionals in mental health. According to this summary, Roland Pitre was much like any number of felons who make headlines.

Next, Dr. Gagliardi wrote a narrative that would hopefully help the Court decide what Roland Pitre's sentence should be for the crimes where he had chosen to take the Alford Plea—which stipulated that he denied guilt, but believed he would be found guilty in a trial. Roland had every reason to hope that he would get a short sentence. Hadn't he, after all, walked out of prison in only six years after his first conviction of murder? Surely, the simple theft of a safe and what he insisted was nothing more than a little scheme gone wrong wouldn't bring him even that much prison time.

Dr. Gagliardi was not of the same mind.

Forensic Psychological Opinions:

As the foregoing evaluation shows, Mr. Pitre is not suffering from a major mental disease or defect. Consequently, by statutory definition, he is competent to stand trial. Moreover, the available information suggests that at the time of the alleged burglary and the attempted kidnapping, Mr. Pitre was not suffering from symptoms of a mental disease or defect. The factual basis for my opinion is not only a clinical assessment of Mr. Pitre, but also the statements of witnesses (particularly Mrs. Beth Bixler) who knew the defendant well over a period of the alleged offenses. Since Mr. Pitre is not suffering from a major mental disease or defect, he would not qualify for an insanity defense.

By state law, I am obliged to render an opinion regarding the defendant's future dangerousness. If the information presented in the voluminous police discovery materials is, in fact, true, there can be little doubt that Mr. Pitre represents a particularly high risk of engaging in future felonious acts, jeopardizing public safety and security. If it is ultimately shown that Mr. Pitre did kill his first wife Cheryl, this, taken together with his past conviction for second-degree murder and the present allegations would indicate that Mr. Pitre is not only at high risk for engaging in future felonious offenses but also at high risk for engaging in future homicide. In view of the past allegations that the defendant is capable of engaging in extremely risky, self-injurious behavior as a means for achieving his personal goals, there is some risk that he could constitute a risk for harming himself in the Kitsap County Jail. . . .

Dr. Gagliardi was not sure that Roland would be a danger to himself, but he had certainly demonstrated he was a likely candidate to be a danger to others. He saw no reason to spend more time with Roland Pitre; it would only be a waste of the taxpayers' money because Roland was playing games. He wasn't cooperating, and he continued to pretend he was the resurrected Wade Pitre, not Roland Pitre at all.

• • •

The long summer of 1993 crawled by, and detectives from several jurisdictions continued to add evidence to the case against Roland Pitre. He had tested mostly below normal with Dr. Gagliardi and well above normal in his scholastic venues and in prison. But despite all his planning and preparation to carry out crimes, he had always had a certain "klutziness" about him. Maybe he underestimated those who tracked him; maybe he was only careless.

He assumed that his telephone conversations with a number of people involved in what was to have been a smooth caper to kidnap Tim Nash would be private. He had a private phone line, but he never learned how investigators could put traps on phones, obtain phone company records, or trace calls made from inside jails and prisons. As it happened, neither Pitre nor the police expected that someone unconnected to his ambitious scheme might listen in on his calls.

A man named Wally Ersker* lived next door to the house Roland had moved to after Della kicked him out. Four years earlier, Ersker had purchased a set of Realistic brand walkie-talkies to use when he was hiking or camping with friends. They were fairly powerful—49.83 megahertz—and Ersker discovered that he could easily pick up phone conversations in the house next door to his. Technically, it was illegal to monitor someone else's phone conversation, and some might well characterize Ersker as a busybody. Nevertheless, the conversations that came over his walkie-talkies were hard to ignore.

They were electrifying enough that Ersker felt he should report them to someone, especially after Roland Pitre and Beth Bixler were arrested. He called Detective

Andy Oakley and repeated what he had heard back in February and March.

Ersker said he hadn't recognized the voices he had heard at one AM on March 10, 1993. His ears perked up when he heard a discussion about leaving a van in a shopping mall parking lot with the keys in it in the hope that it would be stolen. In subsequent calls, he heard a man talking with a woman. They were discussing insurance fraud and car theft, getting a key to a side door somewhere, and obtaining a gun.

By this time, Ersker thought he knew the man's voice. It was that of his new neighbor, Roland Pitre. Pitre kept talking about someone named Tim, who was "screwing him over."

Apparently, this Tim would be sending postcards from his travels for a couple of weeks. The female voice reminded Pitre that they would have to take the tape off Tim's eyes so he could sign the cards.

"We'll have to disguise our voices around him," Pitre warned her.

The planning went on. Ersker wasn't sure what they meant to do, but it sounded pretty suspicious. The voice he was sure was Pitre's said that Tim would be sleeping upstairs. He said that he knew the code to the alarm system, and he and the woman talked a little about deactivating the system.

Wally Ersker took to watching Pitre's rental house to see if there was any strange activity over there. "About 3:00 PM on March 21," he told Oakley, "I saw Roland Pitre breaking out the passenger side wing window on a maroon van. Then he swept all the broken glass from the sidewalk."

Two hours later, as he listened on his walkie-talkies, Ersker heard a man named Bud start making collect phone calls to Roland. The calls were coming from the King County Jail. "This Bud guy was saying something about Roland taking the van and putting it on the Seattle–Bremerton ferry, and then Bud would have somebody pick it up and take it to Darrington, Washington, and hide it."

Bud talked about a woman named Bobbi and said that a woman named Beth could use her car. The man calling from jail also asked if he was going to make any kind of profit for helping Roland. "He asked about jewelry, gold, rifles or handguns, or anything that Roland would give to him. Roland said he could get Tim's school ring and give him that."

It appeared to Ersker that something big was going down on the third Sunday in March because the calls were coming closer together. Bud's next collect call to Pitre came in about 7:15 PM. This time, it was a female who accepted the call, but it wasn't the woman Ersker had come to recognize as Beth. There had been another call from the county jail at 8:10 PM. The woman next door laughed as she told Bud that Roland was showing off his "fashions in basic black."

He heard a male voice warn, "Don't say nothing to her what's happening."

Without Beth Bixler's confession, the myriad phone calls that Wally Ersker reported wouldn't have made much sense. But her details made it all clear. Bud Halser was, of course, Roland's friend who was to have been the co-kidnapper of Tim Nash. But Bud was stuck in jail in Seattle, so Beth had to help kidnap Tim. She had told Doug Wright that she had never met Bud but had talked to him on the phone on three occasions. She also heard Roland planning the crime with him during their phone calls.

Roland told her about a three-way call among himself, Bud, and Bud's girlfriend, Bobbi. On the night of the kidnapping, Bobbi would be at Roland's house, babysitting the 5-year-old André and also accepting collect calls from Bud. If anyone checked, phone records would prove that someone at Roland's house—presumably Roland himself—had accepted collect calls at the exact time Tim was being kidnapped. That was to be Roland's alibi.

"Roland told me that he and Bud had been planning for two and a half years to kidnap Tim," Beth told Wright. "He said that they stole the safe as the first part of that plan. That was just to set up Tim."

The van they used in the abortive kidnapping belonged to Beth. It was a year-old Chevy, and she was months behind in the payments. Bobbi, Bud's girlfriend, was supposed to drive it away after they locked Tim up in Beth's basement. But Bobbi lost her nerve, so, Beth said, she and Roland drove it up to Snohomish County, north of Seattle. With the wing window broken out, it would be easy for someone to steal it. It was probable that Pitre would then advise Beth to make an insurance claim so that her van would be paid off. She might even realize some profit.

On May 1, 1993, Bud Halser was charged with Willful Destruction of Insured Property. On June 15, his indictment was amended to include Conspiracy to Commit Kidnapping in the First Degree. Halser, always before a willing participant in Roland Pitre's schemes and his longtime close friend, no longer wanted to be associated with him. Through his lawyer, Halser petitioned to have the charges against him completely severed from any courtroom proceedings involving Pitre. Obviously, he had not participated in person in the clumsy kidnapping of Tim Nash; he was locked up tight in the King County Jail. As far as the theft of the Pitre family safe, Halser insisted that he was simply helping his good friend move a heavy item, much as any friend would help someone move. He said he had no idea the safe was stolen.

Roland was in a much more tenuous position than Bud. On September 9, 1993, faced with the multitudinous physical evidence and eyewitness testimony against him, Roland Pitre, who appeared to be fully restored to sanity, entered Alford Pleas to several charges against him before Judge Karlynn Haberly of the Kitsap County Superior Court. He was not admitting guilt: the Alford Plea mean that he was neither admitting nor denying guilt but that he believed he would be found guilty if his case went to trial.

There were indeed many charges against him, and Chris Casad, the prosecutor, intended to ask for exceptional sentences for each of them. Given Pitre's record and that he had taken advantage of the very people who should have had reason to trust him—his own family—made his alleged crimes particularly egregious.

Still feeling confident, Roland Pitre took the Alford Plea in Count I: First Degree Burglary; Count II: Conspiracy to Commit First Degree Kidnapping and to further charges, many evolving from the theft of the family's safe and its contents: Willful Destruction of Insured Property and Theft in the First Degree.

• • •

Sentencing would come later. In the meantime, Roland moved ahead to add luster to his reputation as a loving and caring man. Tears welled up in his eyes as he spoke about Cheryl Pitre's murder to a presentence investigator, a twenty-three-year veteran of the Flint Police Department in Michigan. The investigator had been a detective sergeant before he retired to do private work. He had had ample opportunity over the years to study human nature. He found Roland Pitre an interesting challenge.

Roland said he felt he was being singled out and punished again because people suspected that he had killed his first wife. And that simply wasn't true. "I didn't kill her," he sobbed. "I knew when she was murdered that I would be blamed for it. There's a time in a person's life when things like that can happen, and everything just goes downhill from then on. I knew I'd never get my nursing license after she died. I've never been able to recover from that or clear myself."

Even though he had semi-confessed to the current charges and was awaiting sentencing, Roland continued to try to improve his image by doing his own PR. He readily agreed to speak with a reporter for the *Independent,* Port Orchard's newspaper.

He had to share the front page with Beth Bixler, but Roland got more coverage. Beth helped the detectives after her first obviously false story of Tim's kidnapping, and she was prepared to testify against him if he had gone to trial.

Because she had no prior record and because the investigators and the judge believed she was telling the truth, Beth had been sentenced to only four years in prison. With "good time," she could hope to be back with her three children sooner than that.

Beth had lost her marriage, come close to bankruptcy, and was no longer a member in good standing of the Church of Abundant Life because of her obsession with Roland, but at least the Court gave her a break in her sentence.

"She was not the primary motivator behind the crime," Chris Casad told a staff writer, Verina Palmer. "It was obviously thought up by Pitre."

Roland Pitre, speaking in the Kitsap County Jail, told Verina Palmer that he was horrified at the prospect of receiving a twelve-year sentence, the exceptional sentence sought by the prosecutors Casad and Moran. That was unthinkable to a man who cried as he spoke of how much he truly loved his family.

Roland persisted in his version of what he considered a noncrime. He said that he saw himself as a hero, as only a simple man who tried his best to preserve his family. He had always been their protector, and he desperately needed to show them how very vulnerable they were without him.

To be sure they were all protected, Roland related that he often parked nearby and stared at their house, sometimes spending all night, his eyes burning from lack of sleep as he watched over them. He had to find some way to prove to Della that she needed him to come home. He had even fantasized about different ways he could rush into the house at just the right moment when they were having a problem or even foil a crime in progress. If a rapist or a voyeur threatened his vulnerable family, he would be the shining knight there to save them.

"I didn't even have any certain crime I was saving my family from; I would just fantasize being there for the emergency, being there when I was needed."

Maybe he felt this way because he hadn't been able to save Cheryl, he said. "I've always felt totally responsible for Cheryl Pitre's death. I feel that if we had not divorced she'd still be alive. I suppose I'll feel that way ad infinitum. The guilt is overbearing [*sic*]."

Roland said he probably deserved to go to prison for the unsuccessful kidnapping of Tim, but he didn't feel it should be for the twelve years that might lie ahead. "I was just trying to get back in my house to be part of a family."

Roland made sure that the *Independent*'s reporter saw the results of a private polygraph he had taken on September 11.

John L. Ketchum administered the lie detector test to Roland, hooking him up to the usual leads: blood pressure, galvanic skin response, respiration, heart rate, pulse.

Pitre's attorney conferred with Ketchum. They chose thirty-five questions, going back to 1980 when Lieutenant Commander Dennis Archer was murdered in Oak Harbor. Ketchum asked the questions and watched the pens on the polygraph move along the chart.

Q. Were you at your apartment with Maria Archer while Steven Guidry shot and killed Dennis Archer in the Archer home?

A. Yes.

Q. Did you and Steven Guidry conspire to kill Dennis Archer?

A. Yes.

Q. Did Maria Archer ask you to kill or have Dennis Archer killed?

A. No.

To questions about whether he had known about Dennis Archer's insurance policies, Pitre answered no. He also denied that he bought insurance on Bébé's life when she was a toddler for any reason other than because he was preparing for a custody battle with Cheryl.

Q. Was the last time you saw Cheryl Pitre on Sunday, October 9, 1988?

A. Yes.

Q. Did you leave your home on the morning of October 16, 1988, to purchase *The Tacoma News Tribune* and gasoline for your car?

A. Yes.

Q. Did you meet with anyone on the morning of October 16, 1988?

A. No.

Q. On the previous night—October 15, 1988—did your stepdaughter's conversation with Della delay your going to bed?

A. Yes.

It seemed odd that Ketchum did not ask if Roland killed Cheryl. Rather, he moved on quickly to queries about Beth Bixler.

Q. After your refusal to kill Duane Bixler, did Beth Bixler then offer that you and she could share in Duane Bixler's $200,000 life insurance?

A. Yes.

Q. Was your response . . . also no?

A. Yes.

The polygrapher asked Roland if Beth had told him she was romantically and sexually involved with a man other than her husband. He answered Yes.

Q. Did Beth Bixler approach you to have her van stolen for a sum of money to be given to her?
A. Yes.

The lie detector test ordered by Roland's defense lawyer resulted in Ketchum's belief that the subject had replied truthfully. At least, his physiological responses indicated no deception. There were several ways to react to these startling results. One was that Roland Pitre was an honest man, wrongly accused. Another was that the questions asked of him were carefully crafted to avoid those that would evoke the strongest response.

It was also possible that Pitre was a human completely without conscience, one who felt no guilt and no remorse. Without those emotions or any real apprehension about punishment, antisocial personalities often pass lie detector tests. Polygraphs are not foolproof; they depend upon the person who administers them, the emotional state of the subject, possible personality disorders in the subject, and a number of other factors. Unless both the prosecution and defense agree, lie-detector results are not admissible in a trial for those very reasons.

Verina Palmer wrote down what Roland told her. He seemed sure that those who read his version of the story would see that he was a much maligned innocent man and that the judge would feel the same way. Hadn't he proved that with his lie-detector results?

He had not.

21

In December 1993, Roland Pitre was to appear for sentencing for First Degree Burglary, Conspiracy to Commit First Degree Kidnapping, Willful Destruction of Insured Property, and First Degree Theft.

Chris Casad stated his reasons for believing that Pitre deserved an exceptional sentence. There were six factors to consider: abuse of trust; sophistication and planning; deliberate mental cruelty; lack of remorse; an especially culpable mental state; and, Casad stated, that Pitre's crimes were more "egregious and onerous" than typical crimes in the four classifications.

While it is difficult to say what makes a crime typical, it is true that most criminals don't confine their nefarious plots almost entirely to members of their own families. Roland Pitre had been a flimflam man to get relatively small amounts of money from strangers, colleges, and government agencies but his master plans involved his wives, children, and mistresses. He appeared to have loyalty to no one except himself and concern for only his own wants and needs.

Casad felt it was appropriate to impose a sentence of

fifty years in prison and an additional five years of postrelease supervision.

On December 17, 1993, Judge Haberly sentenced Roland Pitre to 240 months in prison (with credit for 268 days already served in the Kitsap County Jail) on Count I and 120 months (with credit for the 268 days) on Count II. It was less than Chris Casad had asked for but far more than Steve Sherman, the defense counsel, felt was called for. Roland Pitre had been afraid of getting twelve years in prison; now he faced more than twenty-five years of captivity. He was 41 years old, and would be 65 or more when he was paroled.

Pitre was also ordered never to have contact with his wife and children.

The prisoner's immediate family picked up the frayed strands of their lives, although the emotional damage they suffered would never really go away. They moved on, some of them changing their names (Living in constant fear leaves victims with a programmed panic reaction.)

And with it all, Cheryl Pitre's murder was still a cold case. Despite the genuine suspicions of dozens of investigators, they were still unable to link her ex-husband to the terrible beating that ended her life.

Years passed. Cheryl's children grew up, but they never forgot their mother, and their overwhelming need to bring her some measure of justice didn't go away.

22

In the decade since Roland Pitre's conviction in 1993, forensic science leapt ahead with remarkable techniques. Police departments across America established "Cold Case Squads." The Seattle Police Department was one of them. Gregg Mixsell and Richard Gagnon were the first Seattle homicide detectives assigned to read through cases that had gone unsolved for many years. Although Cheryl Pitre's life was centered in Bremerton and Port Orchard and most investigators had concluded that she probably died there, her body was found in Seattle proper. By 2003, cold case squads utilizing DNA matches were closing unsolved cases in mounting numbers. Mixsell and Gagnon had solved a dozen cold cases, and they continued to move forward, mowing them down one by one.

Hank Gruber, Rudy Sutlovich, and their sergeant, Joe Sanford, had retired from the Seattle Police Department by late 2003, although they never forgot the Pitre case.

Kitsap County detectives Doug Wright and Jim Harris had also retired. Cheryl's murder lingered in their minds, too, as unfinished business. But it was more than that for all the detectives, uniformed officers, and criminalists who had worked Cheryl's murder case; she had been a warm and loving woman, a young mother, a friend to dozens of people.

There is an unseen bond that links murder victims with the men and women who strive to find out exactly what happened to them and why. The investigators come to know the victims as well as—often better than—those who have known them in life. It is a heavy responsibility that doesn't go away when a case is over, and an unsolved case is never over.

Hank Gruber, who now works in courthouse security, has always kept in close touch with his former colleagues in the Homicide Unit, and he was one of the first to learn from Gregg Mixsell and Richard Gagnon that there might be a revitalized probe into Cheryl Pitre's murder, now fifteen years in the past.

He was elated, as were the other detectives who had hoped that this day would come.

There was someone who knew what had happened to Cheryl Pitre, someone other than the person or persons who had killed her. The knowledge had eaten away at his conscience for years, acid thoughts that disturbed his sleep and made him feel guilty, even though he had not participated in her death.

But he was in prison, and there are few more dangerous things to do while in prison than to tell other prisoners' secrets. "Snitches" don't last long in prison. They have unfortunate accidents or untimely deaths. Even those who do come forward lose some of their effectiveness because their identity has to be protected by the law enforcement agencies they contact. Not surprisingly, they rarely agree to testify in court.

Why do they come forward at all? Some prison informants do it because they have consciences. Some tell what they know out of the need for revenge; others hope they might get their own sentences shortened. A few of them are just natural-born tattletales and gossips.

Since Roland Pitre was well acquainted with the much shortened life spans of prison snitches, he may have assumed that no one on the wrong side of the bars would be a threat to him, especially since with his contrived charisma, he had always been popular in prison.

But there was at least one person who didn't like him at all. The vast majority of inmates are serving sentences for crimes that haven't physically hurt anyone. They have mothers and wives and children. They deplore sexual crimes and murder—particularly against female victims—just as much as anyone on the outside.

Cheryl Pitre hadn't had a chance, and that galled the man who managed to get a message out to the Seattle Police investigators. With all the names that had come to the original detectives working Cheryl's murder, the name this person put forward was new. Somehow he had never been mentioned in connection with her death. He wasn't a big-time felon at all, just a druggie, both a user and a pusher.

His name was Frederick James McKee. His mug shot showed a cadaverous man, pale and thin with haunted eyes. If he was a likely suspect, there was no tearing hurry to contact him; he wasn't going anywhere. In

2003, Fred McKee was in the Washington State Prison in Walla Walla, serving twelve years for manufacturing methamphetamine. Pitre, still in prison himself at the Washington State Reformatory in Monroe, couldn't even hope for a parole hearing until 2018. The cold case detectives had plenty of time to investigate.

McKee wasn't listed as one of Roland's close associates during his stint at McNeil Island in the eighties, but according to the prison informant, Roland had done fatal business with McKee.

A convict's accusing McKee of a fifteen-year-old murder wasn't enough to charge him. Gregg Mixsell and Dick Gagnon would have to find a way to connect him to Cheryl with physical evidence gleaned on the night of her murder.

McKee was 29 or 30 at the time of Cheryl's murder. Now he was 45. Roland was 51. It would be difficult to work back through the intricate connections among and between convicts who served parallel prison terms on McNeil Island in the eighties, their release dates, where they were while on supervised parole, and *their* associates. Roland had his close friends on the outside he'd kept up with, and he'd even tried to go back to prison to visit some of his tightest buddies, for instance, Bud Halser. Would it be possible to link Pitre and McKee? Or Pitre, Halser, and McKee?

Maybe it wouldn't be necessary to go that route. If Gagnon and Mixsell could tie McKee to some part of the direct physical evidence found in Cheryl's Topaz, they would have a strong case.

In 1988, DNA was a little-used forensic tool. It had been successful in closing a landmark homicide case in

England the year before, but this had involved taking DNA samples from every male in a small town, more than five thousand of them. When Cheryl was murdered, detectives and crime scene specialists had retrieved blood, body fluid, hair, and tissue samples in the hope that they could obtain DNA matches. However, at the time it took a large sample to test for DNA, one that was usually destroyed by the tests themselves. Moreover, there was no national registry then of known DNA comparisons, not like the millions of fingerprints available from the AFIS (Automated Fingerprint Identification Systems) computer system. But the early investigators hadn't been able to retrieve usable fingerprints. The cost of DNA testing was also prohibitive in the early days of forensic investigation.

Fortunately, Hank Gruber is an extremely precise man, and he had saved and labeled every scintilla of possible evidence he gleaned from Cheryl Pitre's car. Evidence from her autopsy had also been carefully preserved. Gruber had always believed that something that existed in that silver car on the night Cheryl's body was found would lead to her killer, despite the many blind alleys they went down in the intervening fifteen years.

Cheryl's wrists had been bound behind her with strapping tape, and that tape still existed in the Seattle Police Department's Evidence Room. The killer hadn't left his fingerprints, but was it possible that he left something else of himself on that tape?

Gregg Mixsell and Dick Gagnon obtained a search warrant to get Fred McKee's DNA samples so they could compare them with material isolated from the strapping tape.

And finally, after so many years, they learned that the crime scene processing done in October 1988 had come to fruition after all. It just happened to take more than fifteen years for forensic science to catch up with this unsolved murder.

Fred McKee's skin cells still clung to the tape he had used to bind Cheryl's hands.

He might as well have written his name in her blood on the night of October 15. What could have possessed him to carry out such a cruel assignment?

McKee admitted to Mixsell and Gagnon that he met Roland Pitre and the anonymous protected witness while they were all serving time in prison. He had harbored no ill feelings toward Cheryl; he didn't even know her. His motive was money. Roland Pitre promised him between $5,000 and $10,000 if he would kill Roland's wife. The money was there, according to Pitre; McKee would just have to wait for it awhile until her insurance paid off.

Roland was still in the reformatory in Monroe, a small town about twenty-five miles northeast of Seattle. The Seattle cold case detectives traveled there to talk to him.

He had a story to tell Mixsell and Gagnon. His version of the motive behind the attack on Cheryl might even have been convincing—if it weren't so familiar. The detectives had of course read over the Kitsap County and Bremerton Police Department files regarding the attempted kidnapping of Pitre's stepson ten years earlier. Pitre had insisted then that the kidnapping wasn't real; it was only an imitation of life, never meant to be carried out.

It was done, he had said, to win back the love of his second wife, Della, and the trust of his family.

Maybe Roland had forgotten what he told the authorities in Kitsap County, maybe he was confused and thrown off balance to find the two Seattle investigators waiting to talk with him about an old, old murder, or maybe his fertile brain had just run out of ideas.

Confronted with the evidence linking him to McKee and to Cheryl's murder fifteen years earlier, Roland admitted that he hired McKee to frighten his estranged wife. He even gave him a key to Cheryl's house, advised him of her work schedule for Saturday night, and drove him by the house to be sure he knew where she lived. Somewhat surprisingly, Cheryl wasn't supposed to be abducted along the road from PJ's Market as she headed for home. Instead, Roland wanted to have her surprised by a stranger in her own home. The time of the attack was set for midnight.

To be extra helpful, Roland even drove McKee to a hardware store to buy the rope and the duct tape he would need to render Cheryl immobile. Yes, he admitted he wanted her to be scared. "But he wasn't supposed to kill her," Pitre insisted. "I never intended for her to die."

As he had always done, Roland constructed a finely tuned plot. He was going to tell Della, his new girlfriend, that he was going out for popcorn. Then his intention was to race to Cheryl's house where he would storm in and thwart Fred McKee's assault. Roland said he hadn't planned to stay with Della; he wanted only to win back Cheryl's love, and he figured that saving her from a mysterious intruder in the middle of the night would prove to her that they were meant to be together.

He would be her hero.

Gagnon and Mixsell stared at him. This was virtually

the same scenario Roland had constructed to explain why he'd "pretended" to kidnap Tim Nash.

There was every indication that Cheryl Pitre was still in love with her estranged husband at the time of her death. She had been through so many challenges to get him released from prison and had done her best to support him emotionally and financially in the two years they lived together as man and wife after his parole. She had borne him a second child and worked double time while he attended college. And for most of those two years, he was cheating on her with other women, although she probably didn't suspect it until their last few weeks together.

Ever the optimist, Cheryl wouldn't have needed a staged rescue to convince her that she needed Roland. She knew she needed him.

Cheryl's and Della's roles in Roland's life were almost interchangeable. The only difference was that Della had caught on quicker, so she was still alive.

Yes, Roland conceded that he hired McKee but hadn't been able to stop him in time. During the late night of October 15, he had the terrible bad luck to suffer another one of his "blackouts," the spells he said he had most of his life. Those blurred places in his memory had occurred way back, even before he suffered a stroke. And he seemed brokenhearted now as he spoke to the cold case detectives that it had to happen just when he needed to rush to Cheryl's aid.

"I woke up the next morning," he said morosely, "and went about my day, and I suddenly realized that I forgot that I was supposed to rescue Cheryl."

"You *forgot?*" Gagnon asked.

"That happens when I get blackouts."

On January 20, 2004, Barbara Flemming, a King County deputy prosecuting attorney, filed charges of first-degree murder against Roland Pitre and Frederick McKee in the death of Cheryl Pitre. Both men were already in prison, but as a precaution the prosecutors asked for $2 million bail for Roland anyway. He had managed to stay free of the law for large chunks of time since his original arrest for murder twenty-four years earlier.

Roland Pitre and Frederick McKee would be arraigned on February 2. Despite intensified security in the King County Courthouse, the chance of escape is always highest when prisoners are being transported.

Even though the secret witness said that Fred McKee had admitted abducting Cheryl from her home, strangling her, and then beating her to death as she lay unconscious in the trunk of her car, McKee pled not guilty to the charges that he had murdered her.

Roland Pitre was predictable. Once again, he accepted an Alford Plea. "I did not intend to cause her [Cheryl's] death, but I believe a jury would find I did, given the evidence against me."

This time he did not feign insanity or seizures or blackouts. Perhaps even he realized he had come to the end of the road.

He had never really been on trial for any of the crimes he had committed, always choosing to cop a plea instead of facing a jury. Although he testified against his mistress, Maria Archer, and his boyhood friend, Steven Guidry, twenty-four years earlier, *he* wasn't the one on trial; he had already made his plea bargain and wasn't risking anything.

Just as he preferred not to actually participate in the crimes he planned, he seemed intimidated by the idea of facing his accusers, a judge, a jury, and a courtroom full of spectators.

Roland Pitre always schemed to be a behind-the-scenes man. He was forced to join Beth Bixler to kidnap Tim because Bud Halser was in jail. Detectives believed that he had been there with McKee when Cheryl died, too. That tiny speck of blood on his glasses might have been the connection if it had happened ten years later, but the speck dissolved on the damp swab.

He may even have been the person who shot Dennis Archer in 1980.

In a way, proving any of these things didn't matter. He was looking at a very, very long sentence.

23

2004

On March 11, 2004, Roland Pitre was led through the marble corridors of the King County Courthouse. He scarcely resembled the muscular young Marine whose high jinks and practical jokes once made his buddies laugh. Nor was he the slickly handsome judo instructor and ladies' man he was on Whidbey Island and later in Port Orchard in his first years on parole from prison. Rather he looked like an old man, far older than his fifty-one years. He was balding on top, and the rest of his hair was graying. It was long and tangled, and he had a beard. Headed for Superior Court Judge Paris Kallas's courtroom, Pitre wore the bright red coveralls of a high-risk prisoner, handcuffs, and leg shackles. He looked so scrawny next to the two husky corrections officers who flanked him that he seemed hardly a threat.

This man who had connived and schemed and planned to terrorize and kill the family who tried to love him no longer controlled anyone. He may not have expected to face the presence in the courtroom of those who had every right to judge him most derisively. But they were there. André was in high school, and Bébé was a brilliant law student. They had changed their names and moved on with their lives (their names have been changed in this book, too, to protect their privacy). Despite everything their father had done to them, despite losing their mother to murder, they were survivors who still needed the opportunity to face the man who had done so much to destroy the serenity of their childhood years, the man who had killed their mother.

Bébé was 25 now. She was a beautiful young woman, married, happy, and on her way to a successful career. Given an opportunity to speak, Bébé addressed Judge Kallas:

"I request [that] you sentence my father to the max sentence allowable under the law," she said firmly, describing him as a "dangerous psychopath" who hurt people because he was ultimately greedy. She said he had selfishly decided that a $125,000 life insurance payoff was worth more than her mother's life.

"My mother and I shared a tremendous bond of love, fun, and nurturing. I knew that I was her world."

She turned toward her father, boring her eyes into him as he sat slope-shouldered, head averted, at the defense table. He would not look at her, but she continued to say the things she had held back for so many years.

"You are a dangerous psychopath who cannot be a member of society, because you kill those around you . . . to attempt to fulfill your monetary greed," Bébé said, tears beginning to flow. She had sensed that her mother was never coming back. "I remember feeling this horrible rush on Saturday; I just knew . . . I think intuitively I just always had faith he would be brought to justice."

She told her father that she had learned of his plans to kill her, too, so he could collect on the insurance policies he held on her life. "The pain of knowing that you wanted me dead is so deep inside that when I think about it, my heart hurts. All I ever wanted to do was please you and have you love me the way I loved you.

"What's so sad is, I really thought I could get you to stop killing people, lying, stealing, and hurting people. For so many years, I wore this pain on my shoulders. . . . You have given me a lifetime of fear."

André, 16, didn't even remember his mother. At least Bébé had that to hold on to. He said he recalled only a punitive, angry father. He, too, turned to face the shrunken man in the red coveralls. "I came to you as a kid looking for comfort," he told Roland Pitre, as others in the courtroom fought to hold back tears. "Instead, you beat me. I came for guidance; instead, you terrorized me."

Della, Roland's second wife, told him what she hoped for his future: "You have used and abused people all your life. I will never forgive you. Or myself, for bringing you into our home. I wish you loneliness and pain the rest of your life, and even that is too good. I wish you were dead."

Undeterred, Roland Pitre chose to address the Court and those gathered there. He seemed to still believe that he could explain and temper the harshness of what he had done. He had always been able to use words effectively. He had taken the Alford Plea, he said, only to spare his family the ugliness of a trial. He recalled some nostalgic times with Cheryl, whom he claimed he had loved, and spoke of happy memories with Bébé and André. He apologized to his children and his ex-wife for the pain, fear, and embarrassment they had endured because of his actions.

"I'm a different person from the one you last saw," he explained. "May the Lord smile on you and grant you peace."

How different? In what way? The question begs an answer. Only a few months before, Roland Pitre had told Gregg Mixsell and Richard Gagnon the same old tired story of his wish to be a knight on a white horse who would ride in and save André and Bébé's mother, his wife who had done the best she could for him. But he had *forgotten* to rescue her.

He will have many years to ponder the new Roland Pitre. Perhaps he has seen the error of his ways, although it seems unlikely.

Judge Kallas sentenced him to forty years in prison. And those forty years will not even begin until he has completed serving the twelve years he still owes the state for his unsuccessful attempt to kidnap Tim Nash.

In fifty-two years, Roland Pitre will be 104 years old.

Seven months after Pitre was sentenced to life in prison, in October 2004, Frederick McKee stopped protesting that he had no guilty knowledge of Cheryl Pitre's murder and pled guilty to second-degree murder. On November 19, 2004, Judge Robert Alsdorf of King County Superior Court sentenced him to twenty years in prison, four more years than the sixteen-year sentence the prosecutors recommended. He will be well into his seventies when he comes up for parole consideration.

Roland Pitre's closest friend in the Marine Corps in the early seventies shakes his head in disbelief when he remembers Roland as he was then. He was a rascal and a chronic liar, yes, but there were also many periods when Pitre sailed smoothly, using all of his considerable intelligence to turn what he dreamed of into reality. He maintained a successful career in the service for a dozen years, moving up through the ranks. His onetime Marine buddy, now a successful, middle-aged businessman, says he was absolutely astounded to learn that the man he knew as Pete had gone to prison not once—but twice—on murder charges.

"You know, he could have been anything he wanted and done anything he set his mind to. I guess the one thing that surprised me is that his criminal career was so shot-through with mistakes and missteps."

In the end, it was a matter of pure greed over intelligence.

And Pitre chose greed.

"It's Really Weird Looking at My Own Grave"

Almost everyone has felt a sudden, unexplainable shiver, that feeling that someone or some ghostly presence is running cold fingers up and down your spine.

I can remember my grandmother saying, "A rabbit just ran over my grave." I couldn't understand what that meant. How could she know where her grave would be?

She explained to me that was just an expression, something people said when they got that shivery feeling. In this case, it was much more than a strange, scary feeling.

Very few victims of violent sexual assaults want to return to the place where they were attacked. Some of them can't return because they didn't survive the attacks. One of the teenage girls in this case, whose quick thinking saved her life, went back to the frightening and lonely place, so far from anyone who could have res-

cued her from a madman. She knew just how close she had come to dying, and she breathed the words more to herself than to the detective who accompanied her: "It's really weird looking at my own grave."

Knowing that she was dead was extremely important to the murderer whose story follows. He didn't kill for money or insurance or revenge or out of jealousy. He didn't even know most of his victims until shortly before he attacked them. They were worth more dead to him because alive they could take away his precious freedom, perhaps even send him to the execution chamber.

And he had every intention of shutting them up.

Forever.

It was close to five on the afternoon of September 25, 1979, when a resident of the Timberlane area east of Kent, Washington, drove slowly down a familiar rutted logging road near his home. It was seldom traveled by anyone other than loggers or residents of the neighborhood. He glanced idly over the vegetation that crept up to the road, much of it just beginning to take on the tinge of fall color. The underbrush was thick as it grew over deadfall logs with tangles of blackberry vines, Oregon grape, salal, and sword ferns. Suddenly, he spotted something light-colored that seemed out of place, and he backed his four-wheel-drive vehicle up and got out to get a better look. The only sounds in the lonely area were his boots crunching through the brush and the cries of crows and hawks. Then he sharply drew in his breath, shocked by what he found.

A skull that was almost certainly that of a human being lay about twelve feet from the road. He paused long enough to see that there were some tattered fragments of clothing, a few swatches of blondish-brown hair, and then he ran back to his rig and drove rapidly to his house, where he could use his phone.

When he reached the King County Police radio dispatcher, he blurted, "I just found a skull and some bones! They're located approximately one mile northeast of SE 259th and 199th SE. I think that's just outside the Kent city line. I'll wait here at my house until you can send a car out."

Patrol Officer Phillip Orwig was the first deputy to respond to the radio call to investigate "possible human remains." Although it wasn't unusual for citizens to call in reports of human skeletons, most turned out to be only the remains of animals. A few were Native American graves, where tribe members had been buried a hundred years earlier, unearthed now by bulldozers, as the cities of the Northwest were more and more enlarged by suburbs.

Orvig's perusal of the scene told him that this was no coyote or elk. The skull was clearly of human origin. He was joined at the scene by Sergeant Sam Hicks and Detectives Bob La Moria, Frank Tennison, and Dave Reichert and King County Deputy Medical Examiner, Gordon Anderson.

The young investigators, most of them not long out of the Patrol Division, surveyed the scene, where someone had either wandered into the brush and died or, more likely, where a killer had attempted to hide a body. They could see fragments of bone and torn weathered clothing, but the time wasn't right for an intensive crime scene search. Already the chill of the early fall evening made them shiver, and the setting sun made the woods murky. If they attempted to work the body site now, they might overlook something vital. The body had lain here for at least three months; twelve more hours wouldn't matter. The detectives left patrol deputies to guard the area until they could return in the morning light to process the scene.

Shortly after eight the next day, Detective Sergeant

Roy Weaver and Detectives Lockheed Reader and Frank Atchley arrived at the body site. First, they took many rolls of photographs, then they drove stakes into the ground so that they could always re-create the location of the body parts and any other pieces of physical evidence by using triangulation measurements. At a later date, this precise technique might prove to be vitally important.

Decomposition, animals, and the elements had removed all the body's soft tissue. The skull was still attached to several cervical (neck) and thoracic (chest) vertebrae, but the rest of the skeleton had been scattered, presumably by animals. A single tennis shoe with a sock and a desiccated leg bone still inside it was on top of two deadfall logs.

Who was the person who had once lain here? The clothing, rotted and sun-bleached, appeared to be that of a young girl. The detectives picked up and bagged each piece: a mint green short-sleeved velour shirt with white trim and the label Cuckoo's Nest, a hooded sweatshirt with dark blue appliquéd stripes, a pair of flared blue denim jeans, and a white bra.

Next, Reader and Atchley sifted the dirt and leaves in the wooded glen. They turned up more bones, and more pieces of cloth, one being a blue-and-white knotted strip of cloth found close to the dirt road. Twenty-one Explorer Search and Rescue Scouts, under the direction of Lee Hahn and Officer McDowell, fanned out through the woods. They too found more bits of evidence: the other blue tennis shoe, a fingernail with silver polish, some nylon material that proved to be torn panties, a clavicle bone, a rib, and various pieces of material either cut or torn from the victim's clothing.

But there was nothing that would help identify the

body quickly. No purse, no identification. Nor was there anything that might be deemed a weapon.

Dr. Donald Reay, the King County Medical Examiner, arrived to remove the fragments of bone that had once been part of a living human body. The first tentative presumption of just who the victim might have been would have to come from Dr. Reay's examination.

Forensic pathology is a remarkable science and can give detectives a handle on a case that otherwise seems to be a loser from the start. On this one the King County detectives were at a definite disadvantage going in. They were called to the body site many months after the victim died, they didn't know who she was or how she had died, and they had no witnesses. The trail was not only cold; it was icy.

Dr. Reay was able to determine many things from his initial examination. A rotting brassiere, its hooks fastened in the back, still clung to the thoracic portion of the skeleton. The front midline of the bra had been cleanly sliced through by some sharp object. Reay also found a linear one-inch cut in the right cup that appeared to have been made by a knife blade or a razor. This slice in the fabric had not been roughened by the rotting material. The right sleeve of the velour shirt was gone, apparently cut off. There was a tear in the green cloth over the right breast portion, and it fit exactly over the cut in the bra beneath.

The logical assumption was that someone had stabbed or cut the victim with considerable force and that the knife or sharp instrument had probably continued through the cloth into her flesh, maybe even into her heart or lungs. But there was no body tissue left to confirm that.

Oddly, the lower part of the velour shirt had been sliced off horizontally, again by a sharp instrument.

One leg of her blue jeans was turned inside out, and the denim material next to the zipper had been cut. It appeared that the killer had literally cut the clothing from his victim then killed the nameless girl with a stab wound to the right breast. Dr. Reay examined the skull and found no blunt-force injuries, nor did he find any marks on the bones retrieved that might be from a bullet or a knife. Granted, many bones were still missing, but, given those parts he had to work with, the medical examiner could only conclude that the woman had been stabbed to death.

Reay could make certain judgments about the victim's size and age by measuring the femur bone and studying the growth ends of other bones. He estimated that she had been between 14 and 20 and approximately five feet four inches tall and slender. When the medical examiner unraveled a few tangled hanks of the blondish-brown hair, it measured from six to ten inches in length. The girl's teeth were in excellent repair. She had polished her toenails with the same silver polish as the lone fingernail.

Somewhere, someone must surely be worried about her. She had to be someone's wife, daughter, sister. But whose?

The King County Sheriff's Office immediately issued a nationwide bulletin with the description of the girl as she had been in life, along with photos and a detailed description of the clothing found in the woods. Not surprisingly, they were deluged almost immediately with calls from other agencies. In an era when so many young women hitchhiked and sought out rock concerts and commune lifestyles, there were dozens, scores, hundreds of girls classified as runaways or missing persons at any given time.

Ted Bundy had just been convicted of numerous murders in a Florida courtroom. No one had yet heard of Randy Woodfield—The I-5 Killer—or Gary Ridgway—the Green River Killer. But the world seemed to be growing more dangerous all the time.

One by one, missing women in other areas were eliminated. Some were found alive and well. Some were accounted for with the discovery of their bodies in Oregon or California or Iowa or Texas. Dental charts sent from other agencies didn't match. Or either the hair color, height, and weight were wrong or the dates of disappearance did not mesh with the estimated time of death of the victim. This nameless girl in the woods had probably been killed and left there sometime in late May or in June. Somehow, she had gone undiscovered for three to five months.

In the end, the detective team found they hadn't needed to look farther than the Kent-Renton area in the south part of King County to discover the name of the murdered girl. When the detailed description of the victim appeared in Seattle and suburban papers, they received calls from teenagers who had wondered about the sudden disappearance of Jacqueline Annette Plante, 17. Jacqueline, whose family had lived in the Timberlane area until the previous February, attended the Thomas Continuation School in the Kent School District. When her family moved to Utah, Jackie went with them. Then, according to friends, she flew into Seattle for a visit in late May.

"She was here just a day or so, staying with her

boyfriend, Buck Lewis, and then she just disappeared," was the story detectives heard over and over. The general description of Jackie Plante matched the description of the homicide victim, but it was only that: "general."

Detective Lockheed Reader contacted the Thomas Continuation School and learned that Jackie Plante had transferred earlier in the year to Dugway High School in Dugway, Utah. When Reader contacted the principal of the Utah school, he learned that Jackie had attended school there until the end of the spring term. "Her sister's here, though," the principal offered to Reader's surprise. "Do you want to talk to her?"

Reader most certainly did. Talking with her sister, he learned that Jackie had flown to the Seattle area in late May and that the family had not heard from her since the day of her arrival. She said it would be difficult to reach the girls' parents. They could be contacted only by leaving a message at a toll station near an isolated ranch in Skull Valley, Utah.

On September 28, Jackie Plante's parents called the King County detectives. Worriedly, they listened as Detective Sergeant Sam Hicks read them the description of the clothes found with the unidentified body. Yes, Jackie had clothes like that, they told him.

Jackie Plante's parents knew the teenager had arrived safely in Seattle and that she had been staying at the Lewis residence. They had grown increasingly concerned about their missing daughter but had tried to believe she had simply chosen to live in the Seattle area. Her mother explained that she had never reported her daughter as a missing person, even after her calls to Buck Lewis's home in the early part of the summer elicited only vague answers on Jackie's whereabouts. The Lewises said only that Jackie had moved out of their house, leaving most of her belongings behind.

Her family tried to convince themselves that Jackie was staying with other friends in the Seattle area and that she would return to Utah to start school in the fall, as she had promised.

"We knew that she got there all right, on May 28," her mother said, "but they said she'd left and they didn't know where she was."

The Plantes gave Hicks the names of dentists their family members had gone to in the Kent-Renton area. Reader and Hicks checked with several dentists who treated the Plante children over the years and finally located a Kent dentist who remembered treating Jackie. He turned over her dental X-rays, which were rushed to the King County Medical Examiner's office. Reader talked to Dr. Bruce Rothwell, a forensic odontologist, who found that the dental X-rays and charts from the Kent dentist matched up exactly with those taken from the skull and mandible found in the woods near Timberlane.

There was no longer any question. The homicide victim was Jackie Plante. Detective Reader called the sheriff's office closest to the isolated ranch in Utah where the dead girl's parents lived. He asked that a deputy go to Jackie's mother and father and give them the tragic news of their daughter's death.

An hour later, Jackie's mother called to talk to Detective Reader, hoping against hope that the message about her daughter's death wasn't true. He had to tell her that it was indeed true.

•   •   •

The King County detectives knew now who their victim was. They were on the first rung of a tall ladder, but they had a long way to go. Now they attempted to trace Jackie Plante's movements from the time she left Utah, happy and excited about a visit to see her boyfriend and her old school friends, to the moment she had vanished. Perhaps somewhere in so many witnesses' remembrances of her they could find a lead to her killer.

Several of Jackie's girlfriends in the Kent area told the detectives unsettling stories about young men who had hit on Jackie during the first few days she was back in Washington. Several of them were extremely insistent that she date them. The most frequent rumor was that Jackie had attended a "kegger," a beer party held near a quarry in the deep woods near Timberlane, on the night of May 30. Although she went to the party with Buck, her longtime steady boyfriend, others at the kegger recalled that a strange young man hassled Jackie, making suggestive remarks.

"We told Buck about it," one girl said, "but he said she could take care of herself."

The obvious place to start unraveling the sequence of events in late May was at the Lewis home. Detective Reader and Sergeant Weaver contacted Buck Lewis's father.

"I wasn't here when Jackie flew up from Utah," the father recalled. "I was over in eastern Washington, but my family said Jackie only stayed a few days. I thought maybe she'd gone over to Coeur d'Alene, Idaho, where she had friends. My boy, Buck, said she left his car parked way up at the entrance to Timberlane. And then, she just took off."

Buck's older brother remembered that Buck sent

Jackie a plane ticket to come to Seattle because it was her birthday. "He bought her a watch, too. She only stayed a couple of days, and I heard she took off for eastern Washington. I can show you the stuff she left behind."

He led the detectives to a basement bedroom and showed them a box full of Jackie's clothes and shoes. Even her purse was there. Her wallet was missing, and there was no money in her purse, but her address book was there.

Buck Lewis's stepmother also corroborated that Jackie Plante had flown into Sea-Tac Airport shortly before her birthday; Jackie was going to turn 17 on May 30.

Weaver and Reader had a feeling that Jackie Plante had probably lived for exactly seventeen years. The investigators hadn't found anyone who actually saw her after she was at the beer bash in the woods. May 30 might well prove to be both the date she was born and the date she died.

While "Lockie" Reader was taking a statement from Buck Lewis's stepmother, Buck himself arrived home. He talked to Sergeant Weaver about his last recollection of the girl he had hoped to marry. "I picked her up at Sea-Tac on Monday, May 28, about 9:30 PM, and we drove straight to my folks' place near Timberlane," he said.

Buck said they slept late the next morning then spent the next day visiting friends in Kent. That evening, Jackie called her mother to let her know she had arrived safely in Washington. Then the couple had made a round of parties in Kent. Early in the evening, they went to a birthday party for a mutual friend. Lewis admitted that Jackie was critical about his drinking at the party. "She said I'd changed for the worse, but she said she still wanted to marry me when she finished school in Utah in the fall."

On May 30, Buck and Jackie had spent most of her birthday lying out in the sun. Then they went to visit friends again. That evening, they attended the kegger at a gravel pit near Black Diamond. Buck admitted that he'd been drinking a lot that day and was quite drunk when they arrived at the party.

"Jackie had only one or two drinks," he remembered. "We got separated about ten PM. I was standing next to the bonfire talking to two friends, and Jackie wandered off into the dark someplace. She was talking to some people I didn't know. We sat down by the fire drinking, and some guy came up to me and said, 'Your girlfriend is being hustled,' and I said she could handle herself okay. I figured if she was in any trouble, she would come over and get me. So we drank the keg down to the bottom. When it was time to leave, I went looking for her, but everybody said she'd left."

Buck said he drove his car home and his two friends followed in their car. They had all had a lot to drink. He intended to go right to bed, but his friends wanted to go out to eat.

"I left with them in their car," he said. "I left my car parked in front of our house."

"What time was that?" Weaver asked.

"Maybe one or two AM. We headed for the Jack in the Box in Kent. But I was too wiped out to eat, and I fell asleep in the backseat of my buddy's car.

"So it's about two hours later when my friends woke me up. We were at the entrance to Timberlane, and my car was parked out there. I don't know why it was parked so far from my house. The guys dropped me off, and I drove my own car home and went to bed."

Buck told Weaver that the next morning he found a piece of cardboard torn from a beer carton on the windshield of his car. It was a note from Jackie. It said, "Buck, I drove your car down here. Jackie."

His first reaction was anger. Jackie had obviously come home, changed clothes (he found the blouse she wore to the kegger in her room), and driven his car as far as the entrance to Timberlane. She hadn't needed a key; it could be started by turning the ignition slot. But Jackie didn't know how to drive a standard transmission, and he figured she must have decided to dump his car blocks from his house. Then he found another note she left on the coffee table in the house, saying she was going out to look for him.

It sounded as though she had been worried about him. But he couldn't understand why she ran out on him at the party in the first place and why she hadn't come home all night. She was upset about his drinking but not *that* upset. After all, he paid for her plane fare and bought her a watch for her birthday. Buck said he talked to his brother, who spoke with Jackie when she came back from the kegger. "He said that she only left because she was going to go looking for me."

All he could figure was that she had gotten a ride with someone after she'd left his car several blocks from his house. It had been in the wee hours of the morning, so it would have to have been someone she trusted, someone who would drive her around to look for him.

Buck waited for a call from her. None came. He spent five days driving around Kent looking for Jackie. No one had seen her. It wasn't a big city. How could she have disappeared so completely? He said he came to blame himself for being so drunk that he didn't check on whoever was trying to pick her up at the kegger. There were scores of young people there, many of them complete strangers to one another.

As things stood, Buck Lewis appeared to be a likely suspect in Jackie's murder. He was with her the last night she was seen alive, and they'd argued about his drinking. It was possible that he wasn't telling the truth. Maybe he *had* found Jackie after his friends dropped him off in the wee hours of May 31. They might have argued because she took his car without permission and then ditched it.

That was all within the realm of possibility, but Buck Lewis truly didn't know what had happened to his fiancée. He cleanly passed a lie-detector test administered on October 1. No, Buck hadn't killed Jackie. He came to believe that she left him of her own volition. As the summer months passed, he stopped looking for her, figuring that their lifestyles were too different and that she no longer wanted to marry him. He was only 18; she only 17. A more mature man might have worried more, but Buck soon found a new girlfriend, believing that Jackie would write to him from Utah someday and explain why she left so suddenly.

According to their friends, Buck still thought getting drunk was fun, but Jackie had been trying to change. She was no longer interested in smoking pot, and she drank very little. If tragedy had not intervened, Jackie Plante seemed to have been on her way to becoming a responsible adult. She looked forward to high school graduation and a job.

The King County detectives interviewed as many young people as they could find who had attended that kegger near the quarry in Black Diamond on the night of Jackie's seventeenth birthday. Many recalled the man who tried to pick her up but said Jackie had turned down his advances. "The last time we saw her, she was hitchhiking home to Kent," said one girl.

Jackie made it safely back to the Lewis home. The investigators knew that. The only conclusion they could draw was that she had thumbed still another ride, this time with a killer. Or perhaps he had forced Buck's car to the curb and forced her into his vehicle. No one in the family neighborhood saw or heard anything long after midnight. There were no witnesses. No one saw Jackie at all, not for four months, not until her skeletonized body had been found in the wooded copse in late September.

On the chance that there might still be some bit of evidence in the car owned by Buck Lewis, Lockie Reader tracked down the new owner who had purchased it from Lewis. Although they processed the car carefully, they didn't find anything helpful to the investigation.

Reader did find a young man, Ben Prosser,* who bragged about having dated Jackie Plante. When Reader confronted him, he seemed terribly nervous. He quickly said that he hadn't even seen Jackie Plante during the summer she vanished.

"I took her to a drive-in movie once," he said. "That's all—and that was *last* summer. I didn't even know she moved to Utah."

At the same time that Sergeant Roy Weaver's team of detectives were investigating the Plante homicide,

Sergeant Sam Hicks's squad was working on two rape-assaults, and several kidnapping cases that were so vicious that they had come close to being homicide cases. Hicks felt a lot of pressure to catch the rapist. He would kill a woman soon if he weren't stopped; his rage at women was scary.

One rape had occurred on August 18, the other on September 26, only one day after Jackie Plante's body was discovered.

The two detective squads met with Lieutenant Frank Chase, commander of the Major Crimes Unit, to discuss both the sexual assaults and the murder case. There were enough similarities to make sheriff's investigators wonder if there might be a connection. All of the crimes against women had occurred in the South King County area.

Sometime between 7:30 and eight on the evening of August 18, April Collins,* 15, set off with her pet dog to walk to a girlfriend's home south of Renton. The petite dark-haired girl noticed a maroon car as it drove slowly by her. The driver seemed to be looking for an address. But then he turned his car around and came back. He called to April, asking for directions to the Aqua Barn in Renton. April walked over to the car so that she could look in the window and see whom she was talking to. The moment she got close enough, the driver grabbed her by the arm and held her fast.

"I'll cut you with this knife if you scream," he threatened. He was very strong and pulled her into the car. Her dog jumped in beside her. April was forced to lie with her head down on the front seat, and the man pinioned her body with one leg as he drove away.

She was too shocked and frightened to cry out for help. And then he took the utility knife with a single-edged razor blade in it, and held it to her back, threatening again to cut her if she made a move. Terrified, April obeyed.

The man drove to an isolated area off the Kent-Kangley Road east of Kent. There he dragged the teenager roughly out of his car.

Then, surprisingly, he reached into the car and handed her a can of Budweiser beer.

"Drink it," he ordered.

"No," she refused. "I don't drink."

He told her to lie on the ground on her stomach. Then he straddled her. Using the utility knife, he sliced a band of cloth from the bottom of her sweatshirt. He used that strip of cloth to tie her hands behind her back.

Next, the man pushed April into the trunk of his car. He began to cut the leg of her jeans, apparently enjoying himself as he cut off her clothing with the razor blade that fit into the slot of the utility tool. Without thinking, she told him to stop, "These are my best pair of jeans!"

This annoyed her captor, and he ran the blade along her leg until blood welled up all along the cut. Then he slammed down the lid of the trunk.

April was trapped in the pitch-dark trunk, and she was bounced and jostled cruelly as the car plunged over rough roads. She could think of no way to get out or even to signal to other drivers. Even if she could have, she sensed they were in a lonely place where there were no other drivers.

At length, the car slowed and then stopped. She waited, terrified, to see what he would do next. She heard the driver's door open and slam shut and then approaching footsteps.

The stranger opened the trunk, pulled her out, untied her, and barked, "Take off your clothes!"

April Collins was an exceptionally bright and brave young woman. She knew it was futile to fight the man who held her captive, so she did as she was told, knowing that she was about to be raped and knowing that there wasn't a thing in the world she could do about it. She hoped now only to survive with her life. He led her to the front seat and pushed her down.

Even as she endured the sexual assault, she studied the rapist, determined to memorize everything she could about him. He was slender but fairly muscular and quite tan. She thought he probably worked out of doors. He had wild, wavy light-brown hair, light blue eyes, and a mustache and hadn't shaved for at least a week. She thought he might be as old as 35 to 39, but it was hard for her to judge age. He was old enough to be her father.

When the man was done with her, he told April to put her clothes back on, all but her blouse. She thought that he was going to let her go now.

She was mistaken.

"Stand in front of the car," he commanded. "Now lie down right there, on your back."

The man sat on top of her chest, while he took her blouse and held it against her throat.

"What are you doing?" she gasped.

"I don't want to get blood on me if it spurts out when I cut your throat," he replied in a strangely flat voice.

April hadn't fought him until then. It had seemed utterly useless to try, but she realized in horror that he did mean to cut her throat as he actually drew the blade deeply into the right side of her neck, moving it down toward her shoulder . . . one inch . . . two inches. Suddenly, she was galvanized into action by a tremendous will to live. With every bit of strength she could muster, she knocked the knife from his hand.

Then she began to talk, asking him, "Why? Why are you doing this to me?"

"I have to," he said simply. "If I let you live, you'll be able to identify me. I'll get caught."

April had an advantage over the man. Not in strength but in IQ points. When he asked her what her name was, she told him. "I'm telling you the truth," she said. "If you don't believe me, look in my wallet. It's right over there. You can look in and get my address and everything. If I told anyone, you could come back and kill me. See, you'd have that power over me, so I wouldn't dare tell."

He seemed to be mulling that over. April kept talking; she could see the man was getting confused. "I'm going to be sixteen next week," she said. "I don't want to die before I have my sixteenth birthday. I want to see what my presents are. I deserve to live that long. Can't you see it's not fair to kill someone who hasn't even had a chance to live yet?"

"Well, I don't know . . ."

April's neck throbbed with pain, and she could feel the blood coursing down her breasts from the deep cut in her neck, but she couldn't think about that now. She had to keep talking, keep the man off balance. She could see that he wasn't able to think as fast as she could.

"I swear I won't tell," she repeated. "I just want to be sixteen. I've been looking forward to it for so long."

He seemed to have taken the bait. "If you tell, if you even tell anyone, I'll have this," he said, holding up her learner's permit from the Department of Motor Vehicles. "I know who you are and where you live. I'll come back and finish the job. I'll kill you."

"Yes, I know you will. Yes, yes, yes. See, you could do that," she repeated. "You *know* I wouldn't dare tell anyone."

Incredibly, the brave little teenager had outfoxed her attacker. He put her back into his car and drove her to a street near a junior high school. There he told her to get out. As soon as the car disappeared, April ran to a nearby home and called her parents. They called an ambulance and told them where April was. Then they headed there themselves.

April Collins was rushed to Valley General Hospital south of Renton, where surgeons stitched up her deep neck wound and the long vertical cut on her leg. They agreed that the weapon had been razorlike, and that it could well have been the utility knife April described. It was the kind of knife that workers who install linoleum or wallboard use. A blade is replaced by a fresh one whenever it becomes dull. The blade used on April's neck had not been dull; the wound actually extended into the muscle tendons. Just a bit more pressure and she would have died quickly from hemorrhaging. As it was, she had suffered profound loss of blood.

Lieutenant Frank Chase rushed to the hospital and talked to the brave young victim. She was a remarkably good witness. She was able to describe the car as a late sixties white-over-maroon Ford Fairlane or Falcon or a Chevy Nova. She was able to describe the site where she had been taken first but was not as sure about the isolated place where her captor had taken her while she was in his trunk. "I could recognize it if I saw it again," she said, "but I couldn't see the roads he took to get there."

April was more worried about her dog than she was about herself. The stranger had put her pet out of the car after the first stop. She was heartbroken that it was probably so lost that it would never find its way home.

Part of the MO used by the rapist—the way he cut away the strip of April's clothing—was very similar to the way Jackie Plante's clothing was cut. Her jacket was also sliced at the bottom, presumably to get strips of cloth to be used as bonds for her hands.

The second unsolved rape followed the same MO. On September 26, Jodi Lukens,* 16, was hitchhiking on Highway 99 in front of the Rain Tree Restaurant-Disco at 8:30 PM. At the time, the news of the discovery of the skeletal remains in nearby Kent was featured in newspapers and on television, but Jodi—like so many teenagers—didn't think anything could happen to her. She laughed at friends who warned her not to hitchhike.

A yellow Dodge "Charger-type" car passed Jodi, turned around, and came back. Jodi hopped in. The driver, a slender man with bushy light-brown hair, drove south along the highway for about five miles and turned into the parking lot of the sprawling Sea-Tac Mall in Federal Way. Then he changed his mind and drove back to the spot where he'd picked Jodi up. He told her that he needed some change, gave her a five-dollar bill, and sent her into a small convenience store to get five ones. She returned with the change and then agreed to go with the stranger to "a friend's house in Kent" so he could pick up some marijuana.

Jodi hoped to get a ride all the way to Tacoma, about fifteen miles south of where they were. She told the driver that she didn't mind the detour as long as it wouldn't take too long.

She didn't know that April Collins had been driven to Kent and up the Kent-Kangley Road six weeks earlier and had barely escaped with her life. Still Jodi became nervous as the driver turned onto narrow roads that seemed to be further and further away from a populated area. They finally ended up on a lonely gravel road that led into a deep woods.

She knew she was in trouble when the driver grabbed her by the hair and forced her down on the front seat. He quickly reached into the backseat and produced a utility knife with a razor edge. He pushed Jodi out of the car and demanded that she perform oral sex on him.

When he was finished with her, he began to methodically slice away her clothing with the knife. To get better leverage, he forced her to the ground and sat on her while he cut the bottom edge of her blue jacket away in strips. Then he used the cloth to tie her hands behind her, all the time threatening to slice her throat if she resisted.

The rapist had his vicious MO down to a well-thought-out plan by now. He pushed Jodi back into his car and told her to keep her head down as he drove to another location. Each time she tried to lift her head up to see where they were going, he grabbed her by the hair and knocked her back to the seat.

"I'll bash your head in," he snarled. She didn't doubt that he would.

Jodi managed to get just a glimpse of where they were at one point; they were east of the Timberlane area off of

199th and SE 259th. She had no way of knowing it, but they were extremely close to the area where Jackie Plante's body was discovered. Jodi had never heard of Jackie nor of April, either.

Convinced that this man was going to kill her as soon as the car stopped, Jodi managed to free one of her hands from its bonds. She might have a slight chance to live if she could just get out of the car. Surreptitiously, she managed to unlock the door on the passenger side. As they pulled into the rutted road to the woods, her abductor became agitated at the sight of a car parked there. His attention drifted away from Jodi for a moment as he slowed down, preparing to turn around.

Jodi grabbed her last chance. As she pushed the door open, the rapist tried to slash her leg with his knife, but she grabbed the knife by its handle. They struggled until Jodi was able to knock the knife to the floor. She tumbled backward out of the passenger door of the slow-moving car, not knowing what she would hit or if the driver would turn and run over her. But the yellow car sped away, and she ran toward the lights of a house in the distance. There she asked the residents to call the police.

Just as April Collins was, Jodi Lukens was an excellent witness, her ordeal having left her memory crystalline. As she lay on the front seat of what she believed was a Dodge Charger, she had observed everything within range of her hearing and vision.

"The car was jacked up in the rear," she told Detective Bob La Moria, mentally ticking off all the details she had memorized while she wondered if she was going to live to tell someone. "And it had a loud exhaust," she continued. "There was a CB radio under the dashboard, bench seats, light-colored interior. Automatic transmission. The glove box opened up instead of down, and the car had a column shift lever."

She had remembered *everything*. "The man drank Budweiser beer with tomato juice while we drove around," Jodi said, "and he smoked Marlboros. He wore brown trousers and a dark, reddish shirt."

One other thing that Jodi recalled was that the man who kidnapped her told her that his younger brother had recently been killed in an automobile accident.

"He said his brother had either been drinking or doing drugs and he was in a car crash," Jodi said. "This guy kept telling me about it."

There were just too many factors that linked Jackie's murder and the two sexual assaults to be mere coincidence. Both the rape victims and the homicide victim had had their clothing sliced with a sharp knife. Although the bonds had been removed from Jackie Plante's wrists by animals as her body decomposed during the long hot summer months, knotted bits of fabric found at the site were almost identical to those sliced from the jackets of the two rape victims.

All of the crimes occurred in the same general area, and Jodi Lukens was driven to the site where Jackie had been left. If she hadn't managed to escape, her corpse, too, would probably have ended up there.

It was possible that Jackie was hitchhiking when she met her killer. More likely, her killer might have been the man she met at the kegger. He could have followed her to Buck's house, then grabbed her as she walked away from Buck's car when she couldn't figure out how to work a manual transmission.

Jodi had definitely been hitchhiking, sure that she could tell the good guys from the bad before she accepted a ride. The cars were different, but the descriptions of the rapist given by the two surviving victims matched right down the line.

The clinching connection came when Sam Hicks and Bob La Moria checked through the dozens of envelopes of evidence picked up at the site of Jackie Plante's body. Among those bits of cloth, those pieces of clothing sliced by the sharp knife, was one knotted strip of cloth that matched none of Jackie's clothes. But it did match April Collins's jacket.

The blue-and-white strip with the zipper attached matched up perfectly with the bottom of April's jacket. It seemed unbelievable, but April had to have been taken to the spot where Jackie's body lay undiscovered for almost three months. Luckily, April had not seen Jackie's remains or her attacker would almost certainly have killed her. Indeed, Jackie's skeleton wasn't even found until six weeks after the attack on April.

In a grisly ritual that presumably only he understood, the killer had taken both April and Jodi to the very location where he'd left Jackie, apparently planning to create his own macabre private graveyard.

After the spunky teenager talked the man who raped her out of slitting her throat, he drove April away from the spot, but he failed to notice that the strip of cloth from her jacket had been left behind. When Lockie Reader picked it up, he assumed it was connected to the Plante case. Instead, it was evidence from the Collins case, and it was likely that it would eventually nail the killer to the wall.

With help from Jodi and April, a police artist made a

sketch that the rape victims agreed was a good likeness of the man who kidnapped and attacked them. The King County investigators wanted him, and they wanted him fast. His sadistic teasing with the sharp knife blade, teasing that rapidly escalated to his actually cutting his victims, his preference for teenage girls, and his being the prime suspect in three cases occurring within a four-month period all indicated that he would surely continue his prowling and terrorizing.

But how could they find one man who looked much like thousands of other men in an area with a population of one million? How do you locate a suspect vehicle when the abductor apparently often changed vehicles? They knew his MO, they knew his basic physical description, but that was all.

They began what Lieutenant Frank Chase terms "good, old-fashioned detective work." He figured that any man capable of such violence had a record of similar sex offenses and had probably come to the attention of law enforcement agencies before. "We've been lucky enough to have two excellent witnesses," Chase said. "We've got two teenagers who gave us some of the most precise descriptions we've ever had. Let's go with that. I don't care how long it takes. Let's go back four years and pull every file we've got on sex crimes. We'll winnow them out each time we get a match on either physical description or the way he operates."

Computers were not yet valuable tools in police work; they could have searched through the files with lightning speed. This search was by detectives, who took on the tedious job of reading each file. The sex cases over the previous four years were stacked in as many huge piles, and most of them took hours to look through. Investigators from the Intelligence Unit were called in to help the Major Crimes detectives check through the files for similarities. Each file was compared with a list of similarities furnished by Bob La Moria and Sam Hicks.

It seemed a thankless and fruitless task at first. What if the killer had moved into the King County area just before the attacks? What if his criminal record lay in dusty files halfway across the country, not in the King County Sheriff's Records Bureau?

And yet, steadily, slowly, the stack of files with matches began to grow. Those files were given to La Moria and Hicks to check out further. They then went through the mug shot files and pulled photographs of the men convicted in earlier cases.

One morning in the first week of October, Sam Hicks came to work to find five cases that had been pulled as "possibles" sitting on his desk. His lieutenant had set them aside because they had interesting similarities to the modus operandi of the nameless man they were all looking for.

Hicks looked up the booking numbers and went to the mug shot file to check the photographs of these known sex offenders. As he thumbed through the mugs, he was unable to see the booking numbers until he actually removed a mug from the file because they were on the lower edge of each photo. When he came to one picture, he paused. He was looking at a mug shot that was almost a perfect likeness of the artist's drawing. As he lifted it from the file, he saw that the booking number was the one he was looking for.

Bob La Moria was sitting at his desk working when Sam Hicks walked up behind him. Hicks didn't say a word. He simply flipped the mug shot onto La Moria's desk and waited.

"The hair on the back of my neck just stood up," La Moria recalls. "It was him. We grabbed that mug and ran into Lieutenant Chase's office and said, 'We got him!' It was intuition. I knew we'd found the man we were looking for."

The man in the picture was William Gene Scribner, 28. He was no stranger to local law enforcement agencies. He had a police record going back to his early teens. Even back then, he'd had a serious alcohol problem. He had been sent to several correctional institutions for juveniles after he was involved in car thefts and runaways. After he was released from reform school, he joined the army.

Scribner's adult rap sheet began with petty crimes after he was dishonorably discharged from the army for being AWOL. He spent time in jail in Yakima, Washington, for drunk driving and failure to answer a traffic summons. Then his crimes escalated to petty larceny and larceny by check. But he escaped doing hard time. The disposition of his cases stipulated that he would make restitution and remain on probation. He was required to hold a job and submit to periodic lie-detector tests and urinalysis to verify that he was avoiding alcohol.

None of this would have brought him to the attention of King County investigators working on sex crimes cases. However, events in the two and a half years before Jackie Plante's murder marked William Scribner as a man of perverse sexual impulses, almost always when he'd been drinking.

Two years before, on March 22, a Renton woman who was acquainted with Bill Scribner agreed to go with him to rural Maple Valley "to cop a lid of pot." She took her small daughter along. To her shock, Scribner stopped the car in a wooded area and pointed a gun at her head. He wanted her "to perform." She assumed that he meant he wanted to have intercourse with her. If she didn't oblige, he would shoot her. But oddly he first insisted she chug-a-lug four bottles of Budweiser beer at gunpoint.

When she finished, he demanded oral sex, roughly grabbing her by the hair and forcing her to fellate him as her tiny daughter screamed in terror.

The woman told Renton detectives that she finally talked Scribner into unloading the pistol and putting it on the dashboard of his car. He did that, and she breathed a sigh of relief. Then he pointed into the dark woods and told her to "take off."

She didn't know where they were, and it was dark and stormy. If she had been alone, she would have run, but she had her child with her. "Couldn't you just drive us to the main road," she pleaded. "My daughter's sick and it's raining. I have to get her a ride home."

She should have taken her chances, because her request had enraged Scribner. He growled, "You blew it, bitch! You had your chance and you blew it." Then he dragged her out of the car by her hair and punched her several times in the face.

Apparently satiated, he pulled her back into the car and drove her and her little girl back to her apartment. She held her breath the whole way, hoping she would be able to grab her daughter and leap from the car if he became angry again.

The victim said that Scribner was very drunk, but his intoxicated state hardly accounted for his violent sexual attack and the beating that followed.

When Bill Scribner was arrested, he admitted only to having had an argument with the woman. He acknowledged that he had given her a black eye, but he blamed his behavior on his drinking problem. He begged for help to conquer his addiction to alcohol. He completely denied that he had used a gun to threaten her or that he'd forced her to perform a sexual act.

There was another attack on a woman later that year. A young Kent woman was stranded in a stalled car late one evening. She looked around for help and noticed a man, Bill Scribner, working on his car near an apartment complex. She asked him if he could take a look at her car.

"He told me that he didn't have the tools to fix my car," she told the police later, "but he offered me a ride to the lounge [the Sundowner] where I was supposed to meet my friend."

He seemed like a nice enough guy, but as he drove into the parking lot of the cocktail lounge, he suddenly grabbed the woman and threw her down on the front seat of his car.

"I'll bash your head in," he said between clenched teeth as he ripped her blouse from her neck to her waist.

Fighting for time and hoping someone would notice what was going on, the frightened woman grabbed the stranger's keys from the ignition and threw them out the window to the ground. They continued to struggle, and both of them tumbled out of the car onto the asphalt parking lot. At this point, the disheveled woman managed to break free and run to the lounge for help. She spotted a man she knew, and he hurried out to the parking lot with her.

"There," she said, pointing. "That's his car." The man who had attacked her wasn't in it, and he didn't seem to be anyplace close by. The assault victim's friend removed a wire coil from under the hood of the car so it could not be driven. Then he drove the woman around the neighborhood looking for her assailant. It had happened only five minutes before, and she soon spotted the man who attempted to rape her.

Her protector, a husky man, stopped Scribner and detained him until the police arrived. They smelled beer on him, but he didn't appear to be really intoxicated.

The woman had obvious finger marks on her neck from the attempted strangulation, a bruised face, and contusions all over her body. Even so, the man, whose identification said he was William Scribner, once again had an explanation for everything. According to his version of the story, he had only been trying to help a lady in distress. When he couldn't start her car without jumper cables, he had offered to give her a ride to the Sundowner. Yes, he admitted that he had put his arm around her and asked her for a date. "She told me, 'Maybe Friday night.'"

Scribner became vague when the police asked him why she became angry at him and ran into the tavern. He had no idea why she suddenly flipped out. He hadn't hurt her, he insisted, and hadn't said anything disrespectful to her.

He couldn't get his car started, so he got out and started walking home. At that point, the woman came back with "a big guy" who grabbed hold of him and made him wait until the police drove up.

Scribner was charged with one count of assault and one count of simple assault and was again back in the criminal justice system. He was ordered to talk to counselors and psychiatrists. They tried to find out why he felt so much anger toward women when his impulses were released by imbibing alcohol. He repeated his version of his life history as he had often done before. He constantly blamed his troubles on alcohol, never on himself.

Bill Scribner was the eldest of five children and had been married twice. He married first when he was twenty-two; that lasted fifteen months. His second marriage was three years later; after three years that wife left him, too.

The psychiatrist who examined William after the two violent attacks on the women who managed to get away from him found personality traits which are all too common in recidivist criminals. His diagnosis was that Scribner suffered from "severe antisocial personality disorder and chronic alcoholism." The report continued, "In my experience with antisocial individuals, good intentions reflect more the anxieties and concerns of the immediate moment than any basic change in personality. The defendant suffers not from lack of good intentions, but from the gross inability to conform his behavior to the norm in the face of conflict, and [from] severe social disorganization."

In layman's terms, the psychiatrist was saying that William Scribner was sorry only because he had been caught and that he was likely to repeat his violent behavior in the future. When Scribner pleaded guilty to the two assault charges, he was sentenced to ten years on one count and one year on the second count (to run concurrently). It sounded as though he would go to prison for ten years, but in the convoluted machinations of sentencing, he ended up serving only ten *months* in the King County Jail and several months more in the Cedar Hills Rehabilitation Center.

He hadn't been rehabilitated long before Jackie Plante was murdered.

Detectives showed mug laydowns of several men—

including one of Bill Scribner—to April Collins. She picked Scribner's photo immediately. "That's him! That's the man!"

Sam Hicks and Bob La Moria learned that Scribner was working as a roofer and living in a home some four miles away on the West Valley Highway south of the city of Kent. On October 10, Hicks and La Moria sat on a stakeout at Scribner's residence while Deputies Leo Hursh and Dave Reichert parked near the roofing firm.

At ten minutes to five that afternoon, Hursh and Reichert notified La Moria and Hicks that a Dodge—jacked up in the rear as described by victim Jodi Lukens—had just left the roofing company. The car was not yellow; it had been painted over with a black primer coat.

"He's headed for Highway 18 and probably in your direction," Reichert advised.

Four minutes later, the newly painted Dodge pulled into the driveway of Scribner's residence. Hicks and La Moria contacted the radio operator and asked that a call be placed to Scribner so that he would be on the phone and therefore less likely to grab a weapon when the two detectives knocked on his door. Minutes later, Hicks, La Moria, Hursh, and Reichert went to the door and arrested William Scribner without incident.

He was advised of his rights and informed that he was under arrest for suspicion of murder and rape. When the detectives looked at the black car, it was obvious that it had recently been yellow. A relative of the suspect appeared to ask what the county sheriff's cars were doing there. When he was told about the charges, he was cooperative, revealing that Scribner had painted his car black only a week before. This put the sloppy paint job within a week of the rape and abduction of Jodi Lukens.

Scribner was booked into the King County Jail. He declined to give any statements without the presence of his attorney.

On October 12, Detective Sergeant Harlan Bollinger contacted William Scribner's estranged wife. She told him that her husband had changed cars frequently over the summer. In late May, when Jackie Plante vanished, he drove a red Pontiac Le Mans. He sold that car, and the investigators tracked the new owner through the Department of Motor Vehicles. The new owner gave them permission to process the Le Mans but he said he had cleaned it thoroughly when he took possession. If there had been any evidence of Jackie La Plante's murder there, it had long since disappeared.

Scribner's second car that summer was a white-over-maroon Dodge Dart; he traded the Le Mans for it. La Moria and Hicks processed the Dart, vacuuming up several hairs from the trunk area. These proved to be microscopically alike in class and characteristics to April Collins's hair. They were probably left there when she was held captive on August 18. But this wasn't absolute physical evidence; it was only "highly probable." If it had been ten years later and if the hairs had been yanked from April's scalp, they would have had "tags"—roots—on them, sufficient for DNA comparison. But it was still a decade too early for that kind of DNA analysis.

The yellow Dodge used in the abduction of Jodi Lukens also gave up hair samples. These matched Jodi's. Moreover, Jodi's description of the Dodge's interior was as accurate as if she had had a camera to photograph it. Scribner's hurried paint job on the exterior had accomplished virtually nothing to throw the detectives off track.

Deputy Leo Hursh drove April Collins and her brother to the Timberlane area to see if she could pinpoint the spot where her attacker raped her and held her down as he attempted to cut her throat. Hursh was careful not to give her any body language signals that might let her know where Jackie Plante's body or the strip of cloth from April's jacket were found. In truth, he was chosen for this trip because he didn't know the exact spot, either; he knew only the general region. Still, as they drove north on 199th then turned onto a gravel road at SE 259th and up a steep hill, April tensed. She was sure they were now very close to where she had been assaulted.

April cried out, "That's the hill! I know it is."

Hursh crept along in low gear, turning at her direction onto a road to the left. There were two large mud puddles ahead.

April was pale as she said softly, "That's the exact place. I remember it perfectly."

She had to be right on target. The Explorer Search and Rescue Scouts who had searched the area had left small colored flags to mark where Jackie had lain. But April wasn't looking at those. She seemed to be reliving the attack she had suffered.

"After he took me out of the car," April remembered, "he cut that strip off my shirt. When he freed my hands, I saw him throw the piece of cloth on the road. I wonder if they found it."

Of course, they had found it. And that single strip of cloth was one of the most vital pieces of physical evidence the prosecutors planned to use in William Scribner's trial.

The sun was setting as Hursh drove April and her brother away from the isolated region. April sighed and looked back. Her voice conveyed tremendous stress as she said quietly, "It's really weird looking at my own grave."

It most assuredly *would* have been April's grave. She came so close, and yet somehow she managed to confuse her abductor enough to convince him to let her go.

Sergeant Sam Hicks obtained a search warrant for Scribner's house. Hicks and Bob La Moria found several utility knives with slots for razor blades and two newspaper clippings describing the automobile accident in which Scribner's brother was fatally injured, just as he described it to Jodi Lukens. They also found a pair of brown pants and a wine-colored shirt—the clothing that Jodi said her attacker wore—a CB radio, a door panel from the maroon Dodge Dart, and, most important of all, the two pieces of denim cloth that were cut from April Collins's jeans.

On November 1, two King County deputy prosecutors, Rebecca Roe and Mary Kay Barbieri, a duo known for their determination to convict men who committed violent sexual assaults on vulnerable women, brought formal charges of first-degree murder, attempted murder, and two counts of rape against William Gene Scribner. His bail was set at $100,000.

It seemed right that this man charged with crimes against women face female prosecutors, who would now speak for the dead girl who could no longer speak for herself. Gently, they would elicit testimony from the brave teenagers who had been able to think quickly enough to escape the same fate. Barbieri and Roe had a strong case. They were armed with both physical and circumstantial evidence, brought to them by detectives who spent countless overtime hours to snare William Scribner. They had April and Jodi's testimony, and both the prosecutors and the detectives deemed them "fantastic witnesses."

William Scribner's lawyers based his defense on his alibis. He always had an alibi, no matter how far-fetched it was. Whenever he was accused of beating and sexually assaulting women, he concocted reasons why he was either far away from the scenes of the crimes or why the women could not be telling the truth.

This time, however, his alibis collapsed of their own weight, even though his most recent wife testified that he had been with her a half hour after midnight on the night of May 30–31 when Jackie Plante vanished. She told the jury that Scribner went to bed at her house and was there all night. Testimony by women romantically involved with defendants is rarely convincing, and the ex-Mrs. Scribner had no way to delineate that particular night from any other during the summer.

Scribner had no shortage of intimate female friends, a frequent circumstance with rapists. He was not sexually starved, but he apparently enjoyed the thrill of the hunt and the sense of power he felt when he attacked helpless women. Now, the women who had enjoyed consensual sex with him spoke up on his behalf.

One of his girlfriends testified that he had been with her at her home since six on August 18, when April Collins was attacked at 7:45 PM. She recalled that he had a headache and had fallen asleep on her couch. She said she was positive that he had remained there until four AM.

In rebuttal, the prosecutors produced their own witness, a friend of the girlfriend's son. He testified that Bill Scribner hadn't been at the woman's house at all on August 18. He had been there a day later, on August 19.

The final attack, Jodi Lukens's case, occured at 8 PM on September 28. Again, Scribner's former wife gave him an alibi. She said she had received a collect phone call from him around midnight on that date. The call had originated in Ellensburg, Washington. The defense put forth that Scribner could not have driven across Snoqualmie Pass to Ellensburg in four hours. But that was ridiculous. If it had been winter, the pass might well have been blocked for hours by avalanches, but on September 28, the I-90 freeway was clear, and he certainly could have reached Ellensburg in less than two hours. Ellensburg was only ninety-five miles from the place where Jodi was assaulted. That would have taken about an hour and a half, even driving at the speed limit. Detectives checked traffic records just to be sure. There were no accidents on the pass that night. This alibi had negligible impact.

Dismissing all the arrows that pointed again and again to William Scribner in the three cases, the defense attorneys maintained that it was all a case of mistaken identity. Scribner was a good-looking man, who dressed for court in conservative clothes. In this venue, he looked harmless, even sympathetic.

But the jurors didn't buy it. On March 8, 1980, they returned verdicts of guilty of first-degree murder, attempted murder, and two counts of rape.

Lieutenant Frank Chase commended his detectives and gave credit to the prosecutors, Mary Kay Barbieri and

Rebecca Roe. He particularly singled out the survivors.

"I can't say enough about those two teenage girls. They were smart and were two of the best witnesses our detectives had ever encountered. They were a major part of solving this case. They remembered everything—*everything*—and they helped us to find the guy and bring him in."

And yet, some twenty-five years after the terror, so much damage remains. As so often happens, victims of long-ago crimes contact me, still needing something to free them from their nightmares. The teenage girls that William Scribner attacked are now women in their early forties. Even though he is still locked behind prison walls, the horror of what he did to them hasn't gone away. It clings like silky cobwebs to an old brick wall.

Jodi Lukens never hitchhiked again after the night that Bill Scribner picked her up. Although her memory was perfect shortly after she was attacked and during his trial six months later, her recall gradually clouded over, the mind's own defense.

Some twenty-five years later, Jodi is still fearful of Bill Scribner, but she remembers only scattered bits and pieces of the actual attack. She recalls that he forced her onto the floor of his vehicle and that somehow she managed to get the passenger door open, fall out, and run for help.

She can no longer remember where the woods are where she got away from him. However, she was recently driving with friends when a terrible feeling of dread washed over her. Although she could never have retraced the route to the place where she almost died, she *knew* that they must inadvertently have stumbled upon that awful site where he had taken his victims. It brought the nightmares back again.

Jodi remembers Bob La Moria, the King County detective, now retired, who along with Sam Hicks was responsible for catching Bill Scribner. "He was the only one who told me that none of it was my fault," she says today. "His caring about my feelings meant so much to me."

One of Jodi's close friends has signed on to Washington's Victims Watch Program so that she can be aware of where Bill Scribner is at all times. It is important to Jodi to know that he is not out on the streets, trolling for more victims.

Scribner is now fifty-three years old and still in prison, currently at the Washington State Penitentiary in Walla Walla. His earliest parole date is June 14, 2047. If he is still alive by then, he will be in his nineties and presumably no longer much of a danger as a sexual predator.

Most of the King County detectives who tracked William Scribner have retired. Tragically, on June 17, 1982, Sam Hicks and Leo Hursh walked into a fusillade of bullets as they approached a farmhouse in Black Diamond to question the resident there about the murder of a Seattle rock musician. The man inside had sworn he would never go to prison. Caught in the open, Hicks was killed instantly and Hursh was wounded.

Dave Reichert, one of Hicks's closest friends and a frequent partner on investigations—as on the night they staked out William Scribner just before they arrested him—was grief-stricken. Many years later, Reichert went on to become the sheriff of King County, and he was also one of the prime investigators into the Green River murders for which Gary Ridgway was eventually arrested.

Today, Reichert is a Republican Representative from Washington State.

Ironically, Scribner's crimes were very like those that Ridgway began to carry out two years after Scribner was convicted. They operated in the same general area, took their helpless victims to lonely spots, and trolled the Pacific Highway south of Seattle. Fortunately, William Scribner was caught before he could run up a toll as high as Ridgway's.

Old Man's Darling

This case *came to me almost accidentally. I happened to be signing books in a Sam's Club in Denver, Colorado, when Captain Joseph Padilla of the Denver Police Department stopped to introduce himself and have his copy of* Green River, Running Red *signed. Like all cops and former cops, we started telling "war stories," and Padilla told me of a strange shooting he and his officers were involved in the year before. They didn't have to go out on the streets of Denver to investigate; the situation came to them on their own turf, literally in their parking lot.*

Because the principals had acted out an age-old dramatic end to a once-passionate affair, it sounded routine at first. Then I realized that the story Padilla was telling me was not at all the usual scenario of love gone sour.

When I got home to Seattle at the end of my book tour, I decided to research the case. The more documentation I read, the more interesting the case became. And

261

so I returned to Denver, one of my favorite cities, to learn more about the story of a sensually beautiful young woman who was dumped by a withered old man.

Her name was Teresa, and she probably could have crooked her finger and had any man she wanted. But she didn't want just any man; she wanted Justyn, who was nearly 80 while she was barely 40.

And Teresa was not prepared to just let him walk away from her. As many males have said about the women who try to leave them, "If I can't have her, nobody can," Teresa felt the same way.

If she couldn't have Justyn, then nobody would.

1

Denver, the mile-high city, has air so thin that it causes some sea-level tourists arriving at its Bedouin-tent–shaped airport to run out of breath, at least until they acclimate. Although the Denver International Airport's unique design seems more a mirage than an actual structure, its tough, translucent cloth roof is perfectly designed and withstands summer heat and winter blizzards, welcoming planes that often bounce in the turbulent air currents familiar to Denver. The trip into the city offers glimpses of prairie dogs. They seem like cuddly rodents to strangers, and they maintain a very complex and caring society beneath the ground, even burying their dead. The locals, though, aren't always as entranced by them.

Denver is full of history and the ghostly presence of early citizens. The Brown Palace Hotel is scarcely changed from its early days; piano music soars upward through the hotel's central atrium to the corridors ringing it several stories up. LoDo (Lower Downtown) has been restored to a trendy district, and the Cherry Creek neighborhood is a most desirable place to live. The Tattered Cover Book Store is a must destination for authors on tour.

Indeed, there are few spots in Denver or in all of Colorado that don't offer history and beauty to the natives and the increasing number of people who move there.

Teresa Perez was one of the thousands who came to Denver hoping, more than most, to find a new start. Although her final surname was Hispanic, Teresa's biological parents were not, and she looked more Irish than anything. Looking at her, one would think she had everything in the world. Sadly, her early years had been chaotic, marked by neglect and abandonment. Her parents, Sonya and Jerry, divorced when she was just 3 years old. They lived in California then. For some reason her mother either didn't want to raise Teresa and her older sister, Monica, or was found unsuitable in custody disputes.

Their father took the little girls with him when he moved back to Zanesville, Ohio. He soon remarried, but his new wife had no interest in being a stepmother. Their father turned the little girls over to foster home care, and they moved into a house with no running water, a house where ten children lived. Teresa and Monica entered the world of foster care children, a world where they never knew for sure how long they would stay with each new family. If the foster care families had children of their own, youngsters placed with them by public agencies were sometimes made to feel second class. Often, they had to change schools in the middle of the year. Occasionally, Teresa and Monica were placed with families they grew attached to, and that made it worse when circumstances made them move on yet again.

Teresa particularly longed for a stable father figure she could count on. Of the two sisters, she was the tomboy who loved sports. If someone teased Monica, it was Teresa who stepped up to defend her, even though Monica was older. They were "welfare children," and there were always cruel kids and bullies to remind them of that.

Teresa cut her hair short, wore baggy overalls, and loved to ride horses and shoot baskets. Before she reached puberty, sometimes it took a close look to tell whether she was a girl or a boy. The more vulnerable she felt inside, the tougher her facade grew. She didn't want anyone to know when she was hurt or disappointed. She was a fighter, something she continued to be for the rest of her life. If she felt cornered, she didn't cower; she lashed out.

"She had a very tough childhood," a woman who knew Teresa for a long time said. "She was never parented. She didn't grow up surrounded by love and encouragement as other children are. That was the root of her problems."

By the time she was 14 and blossoming into young womanhood, Teresa was no longer mistaken for a boy. She was too pretty and had a lovely figure. Fortunately, at that point she found someone who truly cared for her.

Teresa was taken into Patricia Wietzel's Ohio home. For the first time she found a foster mother who was almost like a real mother. "She was a good kid," Wietzel remembered. "She really was."

For two years, Teresa had a home, but then her father decided to have a reunion, and he moved her to Denver. Too much time had passed, however. Teresa couldn't get over the sense of abandonment she felt when she was a little girl and her father picked his bride over his daughters. If he expected a perfect daughter, he too was disappointed. Their reunion didn't take, and soon Teresa was on her own in Denver.

She kept in touch with Patricia Wietzel, but she couldn't go home again to Ohio. She wanted to have the kind of life she had never known, and she wanted a nice house, expensive clothes and a car. She soon realized that her looks attracted men, men with money and the means to give her what she wanted so badly. Almost all of her life, people had looked down upon the "welfare kid." Teresa wanted to show them all.

Inside her, a ferocious anger burned. She could have crumpled under the weight of her lonely, neglectful childhood. Instead, she directed her resentment and the feeling that she deserved much better to achieving her goals. And she did well—except when someone rejected her. She could not bear that; it infuriated her, probably because it brought back her bleak response to being deserted and reinforced it.

Teresa was attracted to older men. It wasn't something she faked. All of her life, she'd looked for a "good daddy" to replace the "bad daddy" who disappointed her. It was natural that older men appealed more to her than callow youths who didn't have anything to offer her. They weren't mature enough to care about her feelings, and they didn't have the financial means to buy her much more than a hamburger and a movie. Still, ultimately, she took out her anger on the last "good daddy" she found.

When she was 17, Teresa moved in with Bob Costello. He was fourteen years older than she was but at 31 still a young man. According to his statements to police many years later, they were married in 1981 and divorced in 1983. On October 2, 1983, Teresa bore Costello's child, a daughter they named Lori.* Even after they divorced, the couple were together sporadically for a long time. Costello became someone Teresa could always turn to when she was troubled.

But Teresa moved on. She was 25 in the fall of 1988 when she married Vincent Rieger, who was 66 and a successful real estate developer. He was a navy pilot in a war that ended long before Teresa was born. Rieger shot down a half-dozen enemy planes in World War II and had the medals and the documentation that proved he was a hero when he was only in his early twenties.

At the time they married, Teresa was three months pregnant with Rieger's child. That may have been why he went through the ceremony with her or he may have hoped that her temper—which he had seen flare before— would calm down once they were married. At any rate, he paid for the lavish wedding she wanted.

Not even three weeks had gone by before the newlyweds separated and filed for divorce. Shortly before Teresa gave birth to a son, she and Rieger decided to give their marriage another try, but it didn't work. Their son, Brent,* was born in June 1989; by October, they were again seeking a divorce.

Along with Denver Police detectives, reporters from the *Rocky Mountain News* and the *Denver Post* carried out an exhaustive research of Teresa Garrett Costello Rieger Mansfield Perez's background. There was a lot of information to be gleaned from the Arapaho County divorce court files about the end of the Riegers' short-lived marriage.

As loving and seductive as she sometimes was, Teresa made a manipulative enemy. While living with Rieger in their high-end neighborhood—just south of the Denver city line—the couple had several drinks one evening. Teresa decided she didn't want to cook, so she demanded that they go to a restaurant. While Rieger was getting ready to go, she sneaked away to a phone out of his hearing and called the police. Pretending to be a neighbor, she reported that a drunk was about to drive. As a good citizen she felt she had to report it. She gave her husband's license number and described his car. As they headed out to eat with the children in the car, an officer pulled them over. Rieger refused to take a Breathalyzer test, which meant an automatic arrest. This led to his losing his driver's license.

In an affidavit filed during their divorce proceedings, Rieger also claimed that Teresa broke into his office to read his diary and steal documents, and that she had beaten him with one of his golf clubs. She sought ownership of their home but didn't get it. She reportedly took her revenge by taking Rieger's war mementos, medals, and log books, all that he cared most about from his glory days.

Sometime later, Vincent and Teresa fought over Brent's custody. Although no one who knew them—including Rieger's grown daughter—ever said that Teresa didn't love the boy, the Court felt she was not stable enough to be the custodial parent.

Judge Lynne Hufnagel found Teresa to be self-absorbed, emotionally needy, lacking in empathy, and slow to forgive. "Her profile," the Court wrote, "reflects a person who has difficulty in maintaining close relationships, who is reluctant to trust others, and a person who is vulnerable to feeling victimized."

Rieger's daughter commented that the boy touched Teresa's tender side. "She totally loved Brent, and she was as good a mother as she could be. She wanted only the best for him."

But Teresa had never had parenting models, and she herself was as hungry for nurturing as a child. It was too late for her to ever catch up. Try as she might, her emotional outbursts made her a less-than-perfect mother.

In the end, Vincent Rieger was given custody of their son, although Teresa was allowed visitation.

In 1993, Teresa took another husband: Mike Mansfield, a realtor, twenty years older than she. That union survived for three and a half years. A year later, she married her fourth husband, Mario Perez, 42.

Teresa was 32 now, but her weaknesses had only been exacerbated; her temper was more likely to erupt than ever. Perez made a good living as an expert in finance who worked for an oil and gas corporation.

Teresa drank a little too much and may have started using drugs at that point. She also had another, much stronger addiction that took over her life and signaled trouble for her marriage. She had discovered the rush that came to her when she gambled. She owed almost $10,000 to more than a dozen casinos before she married Perez. Armed with his credit cards, she became an even more frequent sight at the casino tables and machines. She was out of control, and before Perez realized it, she had maxed out his cards and put him in debt to the tune of $42,000. She also forged his name on checks and was looking around for a way to embezzle even more money.

Within two hours one day, she withdrew $1,000 in each of five ATM transactions. Always an addictive personality, Teresa was obsessed with making a fortune at the casinos, enough that she would not need to depend on a man to survive. But at every casino, the House always has the advantage, and her chances of becoming independently wealthy through her gambling were almost nil. The judge warned her that she was in way too deep and that she had a serious problem, advising her to enter rehab to deal with it.

She didn't listen. Although her marriage to Perez had come to the end of the road, she had a backup plan. Her husband may not have known that Teresa had been unfaithful to him for two years before they ended up in divorce court. She was seeing an older man—a much older man.

This time, her lover was *forty* years older than she was. And he was rich. He couldn't marry her; he was already married and had been for decades. Still, Teresa believed that becoming his mistress would give her the status and the kind of life that would make up for everything she had missed out on. When she began with him, she didn't know that she wasn't his only lover. Would it have mattered to her? It's impossible to say now. Their affairs were like a French movie, lovers in a circle with each one betraying the next.

Justyn Rosen, also known as J.R., was in his early seventies when Teresa was hired as a salesperson at one of his car dealerships. He was extremely wealthy.

As a young man, Rosen started with a used-car lot, one of thousands around Denver. He was a natural salesman, and his business thrived. He had been married to Marian Novak since they were just 18. She was beside him as he worked his way up from nothing, and they raised their two daughters together.

His father-in-law taught Justyn the automobile sales business, and Rosen honored him by using Novak's name in his businesses long after the old man was gone.

When he was 35, Justyn bought Phil Reno Ford and soon turned it into Rosen-Novak Motors. He worked for three decades to build up Rosen-Novak Motors into the thriving Cadillac-Ford dealership it became in the nineties. He and his businesses were well known in the Denver area, and he had a staff of a hundred people, many of whom had been in his employ for three decades. He was known for his contributions to good causes and memberships in both Jewish organizations and businessmen's clubs. A number of people saw him as a businessman with a heart.

Although he was past retirement age when Teresa met him in 1996, Rosen was still a vibrant, youthful-acting man. He wasn't particularly tall, and his hairline had long since receded. He looked a little like the actor Ben Gazzara. And he had what Teresa needed: money to spend on her and the maturity to be yet another surrogate father.

When Teresa went to work for Rosen-Novak, she caught her boss's eye, even though he was already involved with another woman besides his wife, a woman he called "Angel." With Teresa in his life, Angel was soon unceremoniously dumped.

Rosen had juggled his loyalties for a long time and had seemingly come to a place where he didn't feel guilty about his extramarital activities as long as he was always there for his wife and his family. "Angel," however, recalls him with bitterness, still hurt and resentful that he was cheating not only on his wife but on her while he grew increasingly attracted to Teresa Perez.

"There should be a whole book written about him,"

Angel wrote in an email. "The way he treated me—and others. I was with him for a long time before he started up with Teresa."

In the beginning, Rosen and Teresa Perez confined their friendship to an occasional coffee break and then to having lunch together. There was such a discrepancy in their ages that no one took their relationship seriously. But Teresa apparently fell in love with J.R. and demanded more and more of his time. She told her foster mother that he had taken her to Arizona with him for a convention and to one of his vacation homes for her birthday. His grown daughters disputed that later, saying that their father hadn't left the state without taking his wife along for at least seventeen years. They said he was home for dinner every night.

Perhaps. More likely, no one can keep track of adults without hiring a private detective to trail them, and Rosen's family had no reason to do that. He had always been discreet, and he gave the women in his life cash so there would be no paper trail to follow.

Teresa's emotions and maturity seemed to be frozen as she experienced them in her teenage years, like insects trapped in amber. She had no education and no life experience beyond scrambling for money to live. She had never really grown up and was both histrionic and full of impossible dreams. She ignored the reality of Justyn's marriage, refusing to even ponder the warning sign when he stayed with his wife for their golden wedding anniversary and well beyond.

"She was sure he was *the* one for her," her foster mother said sadly. "They were going to walk the beaches and into the sunset."

Teresa was more convinced of that when Rosen offered to get her a really nice apartment, pay her rent, and give her money for groceries and other necessities. Although he wouldn't be able to move in with her, he would visit her. He did have one proviso. Her daughter, Lori, who was 14, would have to move out. He told Teresa he wouldn't feel comfortable having the teenager around when he called on her mother.

Most mothers would have balked at this request, but keeping Justyn Rosen in her life was of the ultimate importance to Teresa. She had continued to stay in touch with Bob Costello. He knew about Teresa's life since they'd parted and was devoted to his daughter. Now Teresa called him to tell him that Lori would have to live with him and his wife. He agreed.

And so Teresa had moved into a lovely apartment on Louisiana Street. Her stay there may have been the longest she had ever lived in a home of her own. Despite her hardscrabble life, she had good taste, and she wanted expensive furniture and paintings.

It was ironic that for the moment having a home meant more than having her daughter. Teresa herself had been abandoned; now, as much as she loved Lori, she abandoned her, choosing to be with Justyn no matter what the cost. She may have reasoned that once she married her wealthy benefactor she would be in a financial position to take better care of Lori.

Or maybe Teresa didn't reason at all. Her mind flitted from one thing to another. She was no longer working as a car saleswoman. In some IQ tests she took over the years of child custody suits, she hadn't scored very high, but there was too much cleverness in her to downplay her native intelligence.

Now she no longer had to work if she agreed to Justyn Rosen's terms for his support. She told herself that this was just an interim thing. Teresa wanted to live in a big house the way he and his wife did. She wanted to be taken care of for the rest of her life.

At 14, Lori detested J.R. If it weren't for him, she would still be living with her mother, and it was natural that she resented him.

Being his mistress worked for a while, and Teresa was placated by the easy life she was living. It wasn't as if she were with Justyn just for the money, either. She really believed that she loved him with all her heart. As long as she had hope for their future, she could be sweet and accommodating. She still wanted to marry him. But as the century turned and nothing changed, and she saw Justyn grow older and older, she began to doubt him.

It was as if her daddy was leaving her again, abandoning her no matter how much she loved and needed him. The tighter Teresa clung to Justyn, the more uncomfortable he became. He had seen her temper now and how venomous she could be in an argument. Her beauty wasn't enough to make up for the ugliness she exhibited when she was angry.

As the seasons changed and coolness crept into Colorado in September 2003, there was a sense of finality in Teresa Perez and Justyn Rosen's relationship. He was 79 and quite probably suffering from cancer. No longer the virile, vigorous man he was seven years before when he was entranced with Teresa's beauty and facade of charm, he wanted only to be free of her. She would not let him go. She threatened to commit suicide or expose their relationship to his wife and family.

Teresa was just as frightened as Justyn was. What would she do without him? She was forty. She had a lot of *things;* her apartment was lavish and furnished impeccably. She had always kept it clean; she'd seen enough clutter and dirty houses when she was a foster child. And she wanted it to be perfect when her lover dropped by. But he didn't come over anymore, and she realized that she really had nothing. On her own she couldn't pay the $800 a month rent, and she had no particular skills.

She had already played one of her top cards: she sent a letter to Justyn's wife, thinking that would end his marriage. But it didn't. After sixty years, his wife was not going to let him go.

In the summer of 2003, Teresa warned him that she was prepared to do more. She had pictures and places and dates that she intended to send to his daughters and to other members of his family and his friends. If he tried to leave her, she would send them and reveal his secrets to the community where he was used to being revered and respected.

Her threats were those of a woman who lived in her own world, who was delusional and desperate. At his wits' end, Rosen contacted a lawyer to see if he could obtain a restraining order that would shut Teresa out of his life. He said that she was stalking him. She left terrible messages on his answering machine, and wherever he drove, he felt that she was following him.

Craig Silverman, the lawyer retained by Justyn Rosen, sent Teresa a registered letter on September 15. It contained a stern warning. He told her that she had to stop calling or writing Justyn or his family. Having checked her background, he included a reference to her arrest ten years before for having used a credit card not her own and piling up charges before the owner realized what she was doing. Silverman submitted that her stalking Rosen was a case of Abuse of the Elderly. The letter had a chastising tone that angered Teresa, and it carried a warning: "Mr. Rosen is nearly eighty years old and your days of bothering him are now over."

He was wrong.

The letter from Justyn's attorney was a slap in the face to a woman who was unable to understand that her own actions had caused it. Teresa was in so much pain and anxiety that she lost what little ability she had to empathize with anyone else. When she was cornered, she had always been able to ferret out her opponent's weakness and would play on it. She knew that the man who had forsaken her was extremely committed to his religion. Being Jewish was important to Rosen. She now made fun of his religion, denigrating it, telling him that he was supposed to suffer as all Jewish people were because they were "bad."

When she told Bob Costello that she didn't understand why that upset Justyn so much, he tried to explain to her that she had gone too far; that having been born after World War II, she obviously didn't understand what Hitler's regime had done to the Jews.

"She asked me if I would have left her over that," Costello recalled, "and I told her yes."

Teresa's world revolved around herself; it always had. She was narcissistic and antisocial, so stunted emotionally from her childhood of abandonment that she constantly saw herself as a victim.

As always, Teresa called the people who had been there for her, even when she was exasperating. She talked to her foster mother in Ohio, sobbing over the phone that Justyn didn't want her anymore. Patricia agreed to call him and ask him why he was leaving Teresa. When she did, he explained that Teresa had become too controlling. He told the Ohio woman not to call him again. It was over.

Still, Teresa followed Justyn. She was even more beautiful than when he first met her, and most men would have been pleased to have such a statuesque woman walking just behind them, *if* they were unaware of her obsessive tenacity. But she was unhinged. Costello had suggested that if she felt she must confront Rosen, she should hire an attorney and confront him that way. She said she might consider that; she could sue him for palimony.

On October 2, Justyn Rosen, through his lawyer, Craig Silverman, filed a sworn affidavit asking for a restraining order that would stipulate that Teresa Perez must keep at least a hundred yards away from Rosen at all times. It was not unlike the requests that thousands of females who are victims of domestic violence ask for. Even if they obtain these orders, they are basically only pieces of paper that have proven to have little impact on jealous or deranged stalkers. But it would at least provide a reason for the police to arrest Teresa if she violated the restraining order.

It was probably humiliating for the old man who had a good reputation in Denver to admit that he was being emotionally blackmailed, and he must have worried that it would cause gossip, but he had few options.

"While I initially welcomed Ms. Perez's company," the statement read, "I have many times recently sought to end my relationship with her. In response, Ms. Perez has consistently demanded money from me to support herself and she is unwilling to let me terminate our relationship."

Although he did not describe the details of his relationship with Teresa, he noted that she had sent a letter to his wife. "She has recently made clear to me her willingness to deliver similar packages of information to my children and other people I care about.

"I made the mistake of giving her money in the past, and now she feels she is entitled to more money. She is not."

He was an old man who was receiving treatment for cancer, still wealthy but not the powerhouse he had once been. His hands were gnarled, and he wore a classic Burberry cap to cover his bald pate. It was easy to feel sorry for him and for his wife, who was also 78 or 79. Even so, his chickens had come home to roost, and he had chosen the wrong woman for his last hurrah as a man with a beautiful young mistress.

His statement revealed that he was afraid. He had come to dread Teresa's messages on his voice mail and the constant glimpses of her in his rearview mirror or in the city so close to him. How did she always know where he was?

"Teresa Perez represents a threat to my mental and physical health," Justyn Rosen stressed, citing his age and his illness. "I feel as if Teresa Perez has long been manipulating and taking advantage of me. I need it to end now."

Judge Kathleen Bowers granted a temporary order prohibiting Teresa from getting within a hundred yards of the Rosen home in the Hilltop neighborhood or of his car dealerships. Another hearing was set for October 16.

Process servers attempted to reach Teresa at her apartment, but she hid behind her locked doors, crying. In hysterical tears, she called her former foster mother.

She was panicked and heartbroken. She was also angry and desperate.

2

Shortly before six PM on Friday, October 3, Captain Joseph Padilla was on duty as the head of the Denver Police Department's Gang Bureau at 2205 Colorado Boulevard in the center of Denver. The Gang Bureau was housed in an old firehouse located on the western edge of the city's sprawling City Park, just northeast of the Denver Museum of Natural History. The park was lush and green and boasted two lakes: Duck Lake and the much larger City Park Lake. The onetime firehouse was also close to Saint Joseph's Hospital, the Presbyterian Saint Luke's Medical Center and the National Jewish Medical and Research Center.

Padilla, a big man with a thick mustache, had twenty-five years of experience as a cop, nineteen of them with the Denver Police Department. He'd been in some tough scrapes before, two where he had to fire his gun. He hoped never to have to do that again. This Friday evening was quiet. It was shift change at six, and red-haired Officer Randy Yoder left the gang unit to walk to his black Ford F-250 pickup truck, where he'd parked it hours earlier in one of the lots near the police building.

It was still light out, although the sun would set at about twenty minutes to seven. The forerunners of winter hadn't hit Denver yet, and it was dry and mild with temperatures in the low sixties. The weekend lay ahead, time off for most of the cops stationed at the Gang Unit substation.

Yoder stood at the passenger side of his rig as he took off his police equipment: his police radio from where it was clipped to his shoulder, his gun belt, the bulletproof vest that was a somewhat bulky—but necessary—part of his uniform, and his blue uniform shirt. Wearing just a black T-shirt and his uniform pants, he put the other items into his bright blue gym bag. He was the only cop in the lot at the moment as he scanned it idly.

He watched as a new white Ford Expedition SUV turned at relatively high speed into the driveway southwest of the Gang Unit building. The driver appeared to be a man, and there was a woman in the passenger seat. The driver didn't park in one of the slots set aside for the public but instead drifted into the spaces reserved for patrol units and cops' personal vehicles. It pulled up close to Randy Yoder, whose truck was headed south.

"I was in my driver's seat at that point, and I got out and walked up to the SUV," Yoder recalled. "It kind of struck me as odd. The window was cracked just a little bit, like a half-inch. I guess I was kind of expecting him to roll down the window and say, 'Where can I go?' But he says, 'Are you the police?'"

Yoder saw an elderly man at the wheel. "I told him, 'Yeah, I'm the police. What can I help you with?' And before I could finish [saying that], he flings open the door, kind of bumps into me, and takes off running. And he runs around, and as he's running, he says, 'She's got a gun! She's got a gun!'"

Startled, Yoder looked into the SUV and saw that the woman in the passenger seat did indeed have a gun. She was pointing it at him. He wasn't going to stick around and ask her why.

Yoder backed up to his pickup truck and frantically started to search for his police-issue weapon and radio. As he did that, he kept his eyes on the woman.

She got out of the Ford Expedition, and Yoder could now see that she was still holding a silver handgun. She began to walk toward him, asking, "Where is he? Where is he?"

Yoder could see the old man trying to hide behind Officer Joey Perez's vehicle. At the time, Joey Perez (no relation to Teresa Perez) was inside the Gang Unit's offices.

Yoder found his radio first, but he couldn't turn it on by just feeling the buttons while his attention was distracted by the woman. Finally he felt a thrill of relief as his hand closed around his service weapon, a .45 caliber Sig Sauer, Model P220. The woman had walked to a point between the white SUV she was riding in and Yoder's pickup truck.

"I am a police officer," Yoder shouted at her. "Drop your weapon. *Now!*"

He yelled it three times, but the woman only stared at him. Then she placed the gun, which appeared to be a 9mm Smith and Wesson, to her head, as their eyes locked.

"Shoot me," she said. "Shoot me. Well, just go ahead and kill me."

Never taking the gun from her head, the woman began to move toward Yoder, and he edged away, trying to keep his truck between them. His eyes still fixed on the woman with the gun to her head, Randy Yoder managed to get his police radio turned on. He tried to break into radio traffic. When the air was finally clear, he spoke into it, calling out an emergency warning: "TAC thirty-six. I've got a party holding a gun to her head."

"While I'm talking," Yoder remembered, "she's still moving about."

He was warning his fellow officers inside the building and asking for help at the same time.

"And then," he said later, "she goes and gets back into her car, into the passenger side, and she's sitting in there, and she's yelling and ranting and raving, but I don't know what she's saying. Because now I'm focused on this guy. I'm trying to get him; I'm hollering at him. I'm watching her, and I'm hollering at him to come over to me, because I was going to throw him in my truck."

Randy Yoder figured that if he could get the old man into the open door of the passenger side of his pickup truck, he'd be safe from the woman, who seemed intent on shooting him.

"He doesn't respond, and I tell him several times. . . . Well, finally, he does. He comes running as fast as . . . Well, as fast as an old man can run. There, my door is open."

The old man was almost safe, but as he ran, the woman spotted him, and jumped out of the white Ford. Yoder shouted to the man to get into his truck, but he couldn't move fast enough. "She made a beeline toward him," Yoder said. "I saw her coming around the truck, and I began to back away from her."

Yoder was at the tailgate of his pickup truck when he

heard the woman's pistol go off. "And I hear two pops! I
see him go down, and I see her pointing the gun at me. I
didn't know that I had been hit or what had happened. At
that point, adrenaline's kind of running. She doesn't even
skip a beat, though. She's not lollygagging through here;
she's on the move. She goes right to him, I hear the pops,
and she's standing over him, and she's just continually
[firing]. One. Two. Three."

Randy Yoder retreated toward a nearby tree to get
some cover. As he ran, he felt two shots hit him in the
side. At that point, he turned and shot at the woman. He
didn't want her to hurt anyone more than she already had.

Inside the station, Captain Joe Padilla heard the radio
call for help and realized that, unbelievably, Randy Yoder
was right outside in the parking lot.

Padilla headed for the door. As he did so, he caught a
glimpse of another officer's gun belt lying on a table in
the roll-call room and knew that Officer Daniel Perez
(Joey's brother) was still in the office, someplace. Padilla
called out a warning to Perez, "Danny! She's got a gun!"
hoping he would hear it, and then Padilla plunged out into
the parking lot.

"I saw a woman first, tall, slender, good-looking, in a
shooting stance," Padilla recalled. "And my first thought
was that she was a police officer and that she was holding
a suspect at gunpoint."

Padilla was armed with a .45 caliber Glock Model 21
semiautomatic pistol. Its magazine had a capacity of thirteen rounds, and it could have one additional round in the
chamber.

It was important later on to know the type of weapon
everyone involved in this strange tableau was carrying.

Danny Perez, alerted by his captain, rushed out of the bathroom, where he was changing out of his uniform. He grabbed his fanny pack, which held his handgun, a 9mm Glock Model 17 semiautomatic pistol. This model held seventeen rounds in its magazine and one in the chamber. As Perez exited the police station, he saw Padilla running west toward the parking lot. He also saw a white SUV and caught a glimpse of Randy Yoder standing near the back of his own pickup.

Police officers are trained to size up a situation in as short a time as possible. Before they ever hit the streets for the first time, they are placed in staged situations where they have to decide whether to fire their weapons, bearing in mind that things are not always what they seem to be and that they must avoid hurting innocent bystanders or hostages.

One of the best police training films is titled "Shoot—*Don't* Shoot!" Trainees must decide in an instant or so whether to push a button in response to figures popping up in front of them. Often, they shoot, only to realize that they have just fired at an innocent victim or someone with a child in his arms. What might seem so easy to a layman is in reality a maze full of deadly pitfalls.

Pierce Brooks's book, *Officer Down: Code Three,* is another invaluable training resource. But in the end each cop must make his own decision of what to do. And in real life, there may be even less time to decide. In Denver, on this soft October evening, the Gang Unit team walked or rather *ran* into a shooting gallery in their own parking lot. They had no idea what motivated the beautiful hysterical woman with the gun. They were afraid that Randy Yoder might be fatally shot. From Padilla's viewpoint, it appeared that the woman—who he now realized was not a police officer—was about to shoot Yoder.

He didn't know that Yoder was already wounded. Having taken off his body armor just before he encountered the couple in the white SUV, he wore only a thin black cotton T-shirt over his chest and abdomen, the most vulnerable areas of his body. Shock kept Yoder from realizing that he was bleeding heavily, and he felt little pain . . . yet.

The woman was still pointing the gun at Yoder. She switched her aim between him and the old man on the ground, whom she continued to shoot. Yoder fired at her in a vain attempt to stop her from shooting the wounded man.

As he tried to dodge the woman's bullets, Yoder caught a glimpse of a blue uniform and saw it was his captain, Joe Padilla. He was also aware of another officer in the lot, whom he couldn't see well. It was Danny Perez, who had gotten down on one knee near Randy Yoder's truck so he could see the figure lying beneath it.

"I saw movement first," Padilla says, "and I started running that way, and I see a woman come out behind the SUV, and she raises the gun up."

Padilla ran to the southwest of the Gang Bureau office until he was "roughly parallel" with the woman with the gun. He saw her raise her gun again and begin shooting. At the same time, he saw Randy Yoder ducking and bobbing near his truck. Then the red-haired officer disappeared.

With a sinking heart, Padilla feared that Yoder had been fatally shot. He sighed as he recalled his split-second decision to fire at the woman.

"And because her hands went like this [he gestured at a diagram showing where all the personnel and vehicles were] . . . I fired at her. I thought Randy was hit because I never saw him [pop up] again. And she ran around by this black truck, which was Randy's truck. And I ran up to the front of the car. I think it was a little further back, but I had a view of his door—open—on the black truck. I'm hearing gunshots, and I'm crouched down like that. I don't know where Randy's at. I'm thinking she's shooting at Randy over here [pointing to chart], so I fired again at her underneath the door as she's down. And I believe I hit her because after I fired [that shot] her body just slumped."

Any cop will tell you that the officer who has to shoot a human being is injured just as badly as the target, injured in the heart and soul and conscience, even though he had no choice. Joe Padilla was no different. He was heartsick at having to shoot the woman and dreaded moving around the black truck and probably finding that one of his men was dead, too.

As Padilla moved around Yoder's truck, he saw the woman, who seemed to be unconscious or dead, and for the first time realized that there was another person lying on the ground. It was an elderly man, who lay on his back and appeared to be mortally wounded. Padilla had had no idea that a second civilian was involved in the parking lot shoot-out.

The gun was no longer in the woman's hand, and Captain Padilla called out, "Cease fire!"

Brothers Joey and Daniel Perez were both there during the barrage of gunfire.

Daniel watched the action from his viewpoint of the

underside of Yoder's truck, a large diesel jacked up high off the road. He described seeing the woman's legs "from the midthigh down" and assumed she was shooting straight down into the elderly man's body. He then fired three or four shots at the part of the woman he could see from his kneeling position.

Joey Perez, who was working plainclothes inside the Gang Unit, had rushed to the parking lot to provide Randy Yoder with backup. He heard Yoder shouting at someone but in his line of sight, he couldn't see who it was. He then heard a number of gunshots. He crouched and moved around to the back of Yoder's truck.

It was dead quiet now. The acrid smell of gunpowder still drifted in the air. The Perez brothers and Captain Joe Padilla stood near Randy Yoder's truck. Padilla leaned over the still figure of the woman and now saw a handgun underneath the old man's leg. If the bleeding woman should suddenly regain consciousness, she could reach it, so he kicked it away, then carefully picked it up and put it on the floorboard of Yoder's truck.

Randy Yoder had been hit twice in the abdomen a few inches beneath his heart and lungs, but he wasn't dead. Padilla already had fire department paramedics on the way.

The most dreaded call police can hear went out over the radios of patrol units in the area. "Officer down . . . officer down."

The first uniformed officers to reach the scene on Colorado Boulevard expected the worst; they saw a motionless man and woman and an officer on the ground.

Randy Yoder had been incredibly lucky as he stood in the middle of what was a virtual shooting gallery trying to save the life of the old man, who scuttled for safety in vain. Yoder was bleeding profusely from what proved to be two grazing rather than penetrating wounds.

Paramedics from the Denver Fire Department inserted breathing tubes into the unconscious man and woman and attempted to force oxygen into their lungs, knowing as they did so that it was probably no use.

Then the female shooter, the elderly man, and Randy Yoder were rushed to the Denver Health Medical Center's emergency room. Yoder was admitted in fair condition. Dr. Katie Bates wiped away the blood on his belly and found that his wounds were painful but not critical, though a few centimeters either way and it would have been a different story. He was treated and observed for several hours then was released.

Dr. Andy Knaut checked the shooter and her victim. At eighteen minutes after six he pronounced the elderly man dead. A minute later, he pronounced the woman dead.

The case was assigned to homicide detectives Dave Neil and Dale Wallis. Along with many officers and crime scene experts from the Denver Police Department, they arrived at the Gang Unit.

People were leaving the nearby IMAX theater, kids were playing football in the park, and nearby residents were standing in their yards, wondering what had happened as they listened to sirens, watched whirling blue lights atop cruisers, and saw a score of police vehicles pulled up close to the parking lot where the shooting had taken place.

Detectives swarmed over the lot, whose surface was sprinkled with dull brown oak leaves and fresh blood, some of it in pools, some of it a path of dots, as if someone actively bleeding had run between the SUV and Randy Yoder's truck. Its doors open, the SUV was parked headed north. Yoder's truck, also with its doors open, was headed in the opposite direction. They were four to five feet apart.

The investigators marked the myriad spots where evidence lay: bullet casings, fragments and expended rounds, a cell phone, a man's Burberry wool cap, and sunglasses. Every bullet or casing was noted with a yellow billboard-shaped marker with a number. There were almost two dozen on the ground near Yoder's truck, and five under the tree between Justyn Rosen's SUV and a green metal picnic table.

One of the most interesting items lying on the asphalt driveway was a small tape recorder with the tape inside intact.

The detectives took scores of photographs and diagrammed and measured the area. Practically in City Park, it was also close to homes. The crowd on the other side of the yellow crime-scene tape grew, their voices hushed and curious.

Identification of the two deceased people came as a shock to many Denverites. Justyn Rosen, 79, long familiar because of his automobile dealerships and as a benefactor of numerous charities, seemed to be the last person who would die in a shoot-out.

The woman, whose lovely face later appeared in *The Denver Post* and *The Rocky Mountain News* and on the eleven o'clock television news was familiar to only a few. She was Teresa Perez.

The members of the Gang Unit had no idea what led

up to the bloodbath in their parking lot, but they soon learned about the end of the affair between Rosen and Perez and then what detectives found when they traced their lives back to their childhoods.

The tape in the recorder unveiled much of the story of the relationship between the old man and the beautiful younger woman. It was a soundtrack for the last reel of a true-life *Fatal Attraction*. Of course Justyn Rosen in no way resembled Michael Douglas, but Teresa was as attractive and obsessed as Glenn Close was in that memorable—and frightening—movie.

Teresa apparently felt the need to let the world know why she was choosing what she believed was her only way out of a tangled and tragic life. That tape, combined with interviews detectives and reporters had with people in Rosen's and Perez's lives, explained many of the whys of the carnage outside the Gang Unit.

After brooding and sobbing all day on October 2—her daughter Lori's twentieth birthday—Teresa grew more upset. She hid from process servers who knocked on her door to deliver the restraining order to keep her away from Justyn. She called Bob Costello and asked him if God would forgive her if she committed suicide. She had threatened to kill herself before, so alarm bells didn't sound as loudly as they would have for the average woman. Costello assured her that God would forgive her, and he asked Teresa to call him back later so they could discuss the matter. That approach usually worked to calm her down, and it would give her time to think.

But she had thought about her life for a long time, and she had apparently found only hopeless dead ends. One warning sign that indicated her desperation was that she gave her precious dog, a little Yorkie named Shelby, to her daughter, Lori, for her twentieth birthday.

Teresa Perez had made up her mind. She was not going to be ignored. The next day, she also called her foster mother in a hysterical rage. "He scammed me all along, didn't he?" Teresa demanded to know. "I could've gone on with my life and done other things. But I sat here and waited for six years!"

She seemed to be out of control, heartbroken and angry that the man she truly appeared to love—despite his age and infirmity—was using legal means to get rid of her.

Perhaps both Teresa Perez and Justyn Rosen were thinking about their religious beliefs during the final few days. She wanted to be sure she would go to heaven if she killed herself, and Justyn, a devout Jew, might have been adhering to his religion. Yom Kippur, the highest Holy Day of the Jewish religion, would be on Sunday, October 5. It is the Day of Atonement, on which Jews make amends for their sins of the year just past with fasting and prayer. By Sunday, Justyn would need to demonstrate his repentance and try to make up for his sins. If he wanted to change the judgment written in the book in which God inscribes all names, he needed to accomplish it the next twenty-four hours. The fasting would begin before sunset on Saturday night and continue for twenty-five hours until after dark on Yom Kippur with many of Denver's devout Jews praying for hours in their synagogues.

Now it was approaching sunset on October 3. Justyn Rosen and his family would, in all likelihood, pray on Yom Kippur at Temple Emanuel. Arguably, the old man had much to atone for.

Hours earlier on that Friday evening, Teresa had decided to be in charge of her last act. She rented a dark-colored SUV so that Justyn wouldn't recognize her own white car. Once she was in the posh Hilltop neighborhood, she parked near the bottom of his driveway, partially blocking an exit. She left the engine running as she knocked on the Rosens' door, forcing her way in at gunpoint when it opened.

Justyn's wife and daughter later found Teresa's rented car. Curious, they looked inside and saw a backpack, an empty gun case, and some envelopes with notes in them. They felt they knew who they belonged to, and they told a friend that the messages were from a woman who "wanted money from their family." He glanced at one of the notes and sensed that it was really a suicide note. He called police and waited for them to arrive. The date on the suicide note was January 24, 2002, almost two years earlier. Nevertheless, it was ominous. Several paragraphs began, "In the event of my death . . ." and ended with instructions for Teresa Perez's funeral arrangements and what bequests she wanted her children to have. But she hadn't killed herself then; hopefully, Bob Costello was right. Teresa was just off on another of her wild tears. His family didn't know it yet, but Teresa had, quite literally, kidnapped Justyn. He was gone from home. She had already mailed new suicide letters to those who were on her mind, people she loved and those she resented.

And then Teresa had forced Justyn into his new white Expedition and told him to begin driving. It was rush hour on a Friday afternoon and traffic was heavy.

The voices on tape indicated that they drove aimlessly

around Denver as she railed at him, telling him that neither of them was going to live.

Histrionic as always, Teresa wanted the world to know her story. She memorialized their conversation on the small tape recorder, perhaps thinking—as some dramatic would-be suicides do—that she would be able to listen to it one day, not comprehending that she would not be around to relive what she was doing. She thought she would feel the shock waves that would wash across Denver. She believed that she would be able to watch television news and see her name—and Justyn's—on the front page of area newspapers.

For the moment, the knowledge that she was terrifying the man she considered a faithless lover seemed to be enough. *She* was in charge of their lives at last.

Her voice on the tape rambled on, out of touch with reality. She was clearly distraught and emotional. Her vocabulary was profane as she repeatedly threatened Justyn Rosen.

Teresa addressed her taped remarks alternately to Justyn and his lawyer, a man she intensely resented. "Craig Silverman," she said scornfully. "I already got all the letters out in the mail, to newspapers, everything. It's all out. All the money's going to one of my relatives that I have. You have pushed me [over the edge]."

Her voice broke as she talked to Rosen. "You're a dead man tonight, and I'm a dead woman 'cause of you. You went too far. You do one wrong thing, and I'm gonna shoot you.

"I saw [*sic*] your lawyer calling me, and here's your lawyer with an [unintelligible]. You're setting me up."

"Bullshit," Rosen muttered.

"You're setting me up," she warned, as she criticized Rosen's driving, apparently wary that he might deliberately cause an accident to thwart her. "If you hit that car, you're—as soon as you fuck up on the road, I'm shooting you and then me. So be ready. And I don't want to kill you, but I'm gonna embarrass the fuck out of you. *I'm* gonna die 'cause I want to go to heaven. If I kill me, I can go to heaven, but if I kill you, I won't. But I'm gonna shoot you. You're gonna be shot tonight. Give me your cell phone now. *Give me your cell phone!*"

"I'm not gonna do it," he said firmly.

It was clear what she intended to do if he tried to call for help. "Okay. When you pick it up," she said, "then you're shot. Why have you lied to me for six years?"

In crude terms, she recalled her view of their sex life together, reminding him of all she had done for him, sexual favors that only she could provide. She repeated her recollection of what she claimed had been their most intimate moments.

It sounded, too, as though she were giving him driving directions. "Turn here . . . turn there . . . Pull over . . ."

Sometimes Teresa insisted that he stop the car, always with a threatening tone in her voice, which sounds implausible as she was clearly on the fine edge of total hysteria.

They were apparently on Colorado Avenue, close to the Gang Bureau offices, at this point on the tape. It dovetailed precisely with Randy Yoder's recall of the first glimpse he had of Rosen's SUV.

"If you get out of the car, you're shot," she warned him. "Drive the fucking car up there now. If you . . . Drive the fucking car! Geez, what are you trying to do?"

She sounded surprised and frightened. "Go straight! What are you trying to do to me?"

"Nothing," Rosen's voice said, trying to placate Teresa as he turned into the parking lot. "I just want to . . ."

It was obvious that she realized Justyn was headed toward the police substation. "Keep driving," she ordered, "or . . . [unintelligible]. Go up there."

She capitulated by allowing him to drive toward Randy Yoder's truck. "Go up there," she said. "Oh, you want to be with the police when you die? Okay. If you tell this guy anything, you're shot now. [unintelligible] *I mean it.*"

Teresa's voice suddenly sounded weary, accepting that it was all over. "Okay," she said flatly. "You're done, and I'm done."

There was an unidentifiable sound on the tape, then Rosen's voice could be heard asking someone, "Are you the police?"

"Yeah, I'm the police." It was Randy Yoder's voice, getting louder as he approached the driver's window.

There were more sounds, hard to pinpoint, staticky noises, and voices in the background.

"Let me see your hands," Yoder said. "Let me see your hands! Drop the gun. *Drop the gun!*"

Now there was chaos on the tape.

". . . the gun . . ." was the last word before four distinct "pops" sounded.

Then there was nothing at all. The tape fell out of Teresa's hands and clattered on the asphalt pavement.

Police officers who have been involved in a shooting are always placed on administrative leave while the event is investigated. While Randy Yoder was being treated in the ER, Captain Joe Padilla and Officer Danny Perez were transported to police headquarters to be questioned and debriefed.

Under Colorado Revised Statutes, the circumstances under which a peace officer can use deadly force are precisely spelled out: "(1) To defend himself or a third person from what he reasonably believes to be the imminent use of deadly force; or (2) To effect the arrest or to prevent the escape from custody of a person he reasonably believes has committed or attempted to commit a felony *or* is attempting to escape by the use of a deadly weapon."

There are many more subparagraphs, but that is the essence. The State of Colorado doesn't require a police officer to retreat from an attack rather than use deadly force. It asks only that he take appropriate action to handle a situation.

The shooting in the parking lot seemed to have lasted an hour, but it was really over in a matter of minutes. Now detectives would try to match the bullets, casings, and fragments to the four people who had apparently fired weapons: Teresa Perez, Captain Joe Padilla, Officer Randy Yoder, and Officer Danny Perez. Joey Perez had not fired his weapon because he did not have a clear view from his position and was afraid he would hit his fellow officers.

The morning after the shooting, October 4, Dr. Thomas Henry, the chief medical examiner for the Denver coroner, did the postmortem exam of Teresa Perez. She had been shot six times. Quite probably, she was struck by rounds from Randy Yoder and Danny Perez, who were trying to stop her from shooting Justyn Rosen, and by Joe Padilla, who was trying to keep her from killing Yoder. One bullet entered her right chest, passed between her ribs and perforated her right lung. It then passed through her diaphragm and liver and fractured her twelfth thoracic vertebra before it came to rest in the soft tissue of her back; this bullet came from Randy Yoder's gun. Another bullet entered her right lung and also fractured a rib. The third bullet entered the left side of her thorax then passed through her stomach. The fourth entered her left hip, fracturing bones in her lower back, the fifth only grazed her, and the sixth fractured the humerus in her upper right arm.

Tests for the presence of metabolites from alcohol and cocaine were positive. Teresa's blood alcohol level was .224, more than twice Colorado's standard for drunk driving. The cocaine level was not high—704 mg/ml—suggesting that she had ingested a small amount of the drug some time before the shootings and metabolized most of it at the time of her death. There were traces of nicotine and the Benadryl she took in a futile attempt to sleep. None of these results were surprising; Teresa Perez had been a walking emotional time bomb, fueled by drugs and alcohol.

Oddly, in death Teresa looked more peaceful than she had in the adult years of her life. She had no injuries at all to her face or head. She was still quite beautiful.

Dr. Henry also did the autopsy on Justyn Rosen's body. He had been shot *fifteen* times, so many times that it was impossible to tell if some of the wounds might not have resulted from the same bullets' entry and exit, and even re-entry, of his body. The fatal bullets had been to his chest, abdomen, and groin, but he had a number of "defense wounds" in his forearms and hands indicating that he had tried to hold off the bullets as Teresa stood over him, continuing to fire. And lastly, the old man had suffered a few leg wounds. These were attributed to Danny Perez's attempts to shoot Teresa's legs, visible to him beneath the undercarriage of Randy Yoder's truck. Danny Perez had been trying to stop her from shooting Rosen, but she was virtually standing over him and it had been hard for Perez to differentiate between her body and Rosen's.

It had been a desperate situation.

Toxicology reports on Rosen's blood and urine showed no signs of alcohol or drug metabolites.

On Tuesday, October 7, 2003, funeral services for Justyn Rosen were held at Temple Emanuel. Three hundred mourners gathered to remember him for his philanthropy. His daughters and grandchildren and lifelong friends spoke of the benevolent side of the well-known Denver businessman, the husband of sixty years, the loving father.

Rosen had lived a long life; one couldn't say he was cut down in the salad days of youth. But in the end Teresa ended it, and she also embarrassed him and his family, just as she meant to do. And she did more than that; she left them with deep grief, shock, and the knowledge that all the good Rosen had done in his life was blemished and sullied.

There were no public services for Teresa. Her life was much shortened, and she died at the height of her beauty, leaving her children to mourn and wonder why it had to be that way. They knew about her relationship with J.R., although many who thought they knew Teresa well were stunned to hear about the six to seven years they were together. When she needed to, she was quite capable of keeping secrets.

"She wasn't evil," Bob Costello, her first husband, said. "She was sick. I'm not condoning what she did. I am horrified by it . . . her daughter is horrified . . . but [she was] made into a monster. She's not a monster."

Teresa's sister, her foster mother, her ex-husbands—even their current wives—agreed that she truly loved Justyn Rosen. She had talked of him with such affection. "It wasn't about the money; she wanted the man."

On Thursday, Teresa's children, 20 and 14, visited the apartment on Louisiana Street. It was neat and clean as it always was, decorated with simplicity and taste. They looked at the many pictures around the rooms, most of them of their mother, posing with them at different stages in their lives. She had liked glass-topped tables and crystal that channeled rainbows when the sun hit them. She'd collected elephant statuettes.

The suicide letter that Teresa mailed to Lori before her last desperate drive arrived on Monday, October 6.

I'm so sorry, sorry, sorry. I'm out of options, confused but so hurt by Justyn Rosen. He lied so much about being with me. Can't take the pain. I'm sorry, sorry.

Please forgive me.

I hope I can still go to heaven.

Love always, Mom.

Please stay real close to Brent. It would have been nice to have a brother like him and sister like you while I was growing up. Love to you again, Mom.

I'm sick inside and feel like I've already died. This man killed me.

Didn't pay rent for Oct. It's $800.00—make sure you got everything out for you and Brent.

Love Love Mom

Find nice people to share your life

There were echos of Marilyn Monroe in Teresa Perez. All the physical beauty in the world and a terrible hunger for money and security coupled with a complete lack of self-esteem and a loneliness so profound that it could never be cured.

Justyn Rosen didn't kill Teresa. Something that happened a long, long time before probably accomplished that: A little girl watching her father walk away from the crowded foster home where he'd left her, so he could be with his new wife.

Teresa Perez didn't kill Justyn. His inability to understand the desperation behind her glamorous facade and his decision to make promises he could not keep did. He, too, walked away from her, preferring to be with his wife.

And in the end, it was all ashes.

• • •

On February 18, 2004, Bill Ritter, Denver's district attorney of the Second Judicial District, announced the conclusion of his investigation of the October 3 shoot-out between Teresa and the Denver police officers. It had been a long and painful four months for Captain Joe Padilla and Officers Randy Yoder and Danny and Joey Perez. Each of them lived the shootings over and over in the waking hours and in their dreams, regretting that they had had no choice but to do what they did that night.

"When Justyn Rosen turned his vehicle into the Denver Police Gang Bureau's driveway in search of help," Ritter wrote, "Teresa Perez's actions set in motion a chain of events that led to their deaths and to her shooting and wounding Officer Randy Yoder in the process.

"The three Denver officers who fired their service pistols in this deadly confrontation were clearly justified in doing so in an effort to stop Teresa Perez from continuing to fire. This conclusion is not altered by the fact that two of the bullets that hit Justyn Rosen were apparently fired by Officer Daniel Perez. . . . Seeing Teresa Perez standing over Justyn Rosen and repeatedly shooting him from point-blank range, the three officers, from varying positions, were attempting to shoot Teresa Perez to end her murderous attack. The actions of these officers were reasonable, appropriate and necessary. . . . Officer Joey Perez's decision not to fire . . . demonstrated sound judgment and weapon control on his part.

"Without an instant of hesitation, these four officers responded to this life-threatening confrontation. . . . Their willingness to put their lives at great risk to help another is deeply appreciated and is in the highest tradition of protecting and serving our community."

Randy Yoder, Joey Perez, Danny Perez, and Captain Joe Padilla received Denver's Medal of Honor for their bravery on October 3, 2003.

They are all grateful to be alive, but they wish that it had never happened. Randy Yoder carries two deep scars from Teresa's bullet. They all bear the emotional scars that come from being involved in the violent deaths of others.

All for Nothing

The following case is one of the strangest, saddest, and most brutal multiple murders I have ever encountered. The human beings involved are the last people that anyone—including me—could picture being caught in such a violent situation. They were all winners, intelligent, attractive, successful, high-functioning, admired. They were relatively young, with the whole world in front of them.

This was not a case where one could trace their lives back to their childhoods and predict what lay ahead. Their deaths shocked not only their families and their friends but an entire city.

In the end, what happened can be blamed on jealousy, mindless, raging, uncontrolled jealousy. When the green-eyed monster grips someone, the most mild-mannered and organized individual becomes unrecognizable.

In a way, that simple truth explains the end of the story; in another way, nothing can ever explain it. I suspect that not even the killer can say why he did what he did.

I don't think I can, either.

Sometimes true-crime cases hit much too close to home. This one involves someone whose life touched mine a few times, if only tangentially. Early in my career, I did some work for him, but we never actually met in person. Like most television viewers in Seattle, I often watched Larry Sturholm's segment on KIRO-TV's nightly news. He and his older brother, Phil, both worked for the CBS affiliate. Phil, a gentle, quiet, and very intelligent man, was a cameraman and later the executive editor of the news at KIRO.

In his part of the news, "Larry at Large," Sturholm was both hilarious and sensitive. He did the lighter side of the news and always managed to come up with intriguing offbeat subjects. One of his funniest shows was about a Canada goose that decided a certain suburban driveway and garage door would be his territory, and he literally flew in the face of anyone who dared come close, including Larry Sturholm.

Anyone who was innovative or adventurous or any well-known eccentric living in the Greater Seattle area eventually found himself spotlighted on "Larry at Large": A family that was building an igloo; an elderly mother and her grown son who regularly crashed high-society parties, filling purse and pockets with buffet items and souvenirs; bizarre would-be politicians who jousted with city fathers; attention-seekers who dyed their hair purple or pink; they were all ideal subjects who could count on getting a call from Larry Sturholm. He never seemed to run out of feature stories, and no matter how grim the hard news was, you could count on Sturholm to end the broadcasts with something that made you smile.

Larry had a good, solid Scandinavian-American face and a head of thick brown hair. He was very nearsighted and usually wore horn-rimmed glasses. He was a friendly guy, and most Seattleites spoke about him as a favorite acquaintance, even if they didn't know him personally.

Back in the late fifties and early sixties, Larry Sturholm went to high school in Sweet Home, Oregon, an idyllic American town with a population of about 8,000. My brother, Luke Fiorante, taught at Sweet Home High School and was the football coach, too. It was a small school in a small town, and most of the citizens were enthusiastic supporters of the games and track meets.

During the summers of 1961 and 1962, Luke worked as director of parks and recreation and ran Sweet Home's recreation program in the fields in back of the high school. His assistant was Larry Sturholm, who was then 17 or 18. It was a good summer job for both of them. Far from any large cities, kids in Sweet Home depend on the town's park department to provide sports and activities during the long, sleepy summer months.

Together, Luke and Larry invented a device that was really an early version of what is used today for T-ball, fashioning the apparatus from a brake drum, a metal pole, and a thick rope to hold the ball while the little boys swung at it. Larry was in charge of midget league baseball. Never much of an athlete in high school, he was always patient and cheerful with the kids in his charge.

"IT'S REALLY WEIRD LOOKING AT MY OWN GRAVE"

Sex killer William Scribner planned to add to the graveyard where he'd left his first victim. Luckily, he wasn't clever enough to overcome the next victim he chose.

Denver detectives looking for the motivation behind a deadly shoot-out with most unlikely participants had to look no further than this tape recorder that lay on the ground next to the bodies. It was all there.

Randy Yoder's pickup truck. CSI placed placards to mark bullets and casings. As Yoder tried to save Justyn Rosen and himself, they were caught in a "shooting gallery."

Justyn Rosen's new Ford Expedition SUV after the shoot-out outside a Denver police station. Rosen flung open his door and scrambled for safety behind Officer Yoder's truck as Yoder desperately tried to save him.

Denver police officer Randy Yoder had just gone off duty, removed his body armor, and stashed his radio and service revolver when he encountered the most dangerous felon of his career.

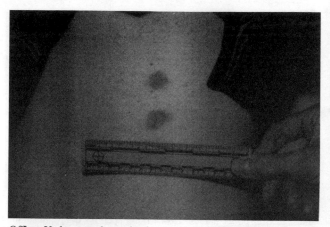

Officer Yoder was shot twice by a woman with a gun as he tried to save her real target's life. These wounds are scant inches from his heart and lungs, and he had just taken off his body armor. He was very, very lucky.

Justyn Rosen, 80, chose his final mistress for her beauty, never realizing how dangerous she could be when her heart was broken.

Teresa Perez had many loves in her short life, but Justyn Rosen, a married man old enough to be her grandfather, was the only one she seemed to love with all her heart. She simply could not let him desert her.

These four Denver police officers were plunged into a deadly shoot-out in their own station's parking lot. Here they receive the department's Medal of Honor for their actions on the night of October 3, 2003. Left to Right: Officers Randy Yoder, Joey Perez, Danny Perez, Captain Joseph Padilla.

ALL FOR NOTHING

Radio Station Staff, Turkey, 1968

Larry Sturholm, one of two victims in "All for Nothing," is shown here (third from left) with the staff of the armed forces radio station at the base he was assigned to in 1968 in Samsun, Turkey. His hilarious scripts for soap opera style "dramas" brightened up the bleak days at the "superspy" base.

Debra Sweiger, 35, was a tall lovely blonde. She had a new business that was taking off, a new Jaguar, a new house, and the world belonged to her. Sadly, there was one man to whom she was worth more dead if he couldn't have her for himself.

Larry Sturholm, nearing 50, seemed like a friend to everyone in the Seattle area who watched his television news segments, "Larry at Large." He had great talent as a writer, a commentator on the funny side of life, and as a performer/producer. In the summer of 1989, he made another kind of news, saddening thousands of people.

This is the house Debra Sweiger owned in the suburbs of Seattle, the scene of the double murders and an attempted suicide. Homicide investigators were shocked at the violence they found inside.

High-ranking Naval Reserve officer William Pawlyk, 48, had graduate degrees, the respect of the leaders in his city, and a successful career. But jealousy overrode everything else, and his rage destroyed three families.

Lee Yates, senior deputy King County prosecuting attorney, who, along with senior deputy Jeff Baird, prosecuted William Pawlyk in the shocking "overkill" murders of Debra Sweiger and Larry Sturholm. Yates had represented the State in dozens of major homicide trials, but this was one that vividly stood out in his memory.

The D'Autremont brothers made headlines all across America in the 1920s. Larry Sturholm wrote a memorable book about the train holdup that failed, and the tragedies that ensued. From top to bottom: Roy, Hugh, and Ray D'Autremont. (*From* All for Nothing)

Larry Sturholm's book, *All for Nothing,* recalled the daring and tragic robbery of a gold train. In 1923, Ray, shown here in the Washington State Reformatory at Monroe in his first prison sentence, lured his twin, Roy, and younger brother, Hugh, into the ill-fated plot. (*From* All for Nothing)

While Ray had the mind for criminal plots, Roy went along with his identical twin brother. Their story fascinated Larry Sturholm, who wrote a very successful book about them. (*From* All For Nothing)

A DESPERATE HOUSEWIFE

The staff at Morgan Stanley, Dean Witter of Bellevue were friends as well as coworkers. They all liked Carolyn Durall and spoke of how considerate she was, the woman who was always smiling. In happier days, they posed together. Carolyn is on the far right, and Denise Jannusche is in the middle in the back row.

The Jannusches, Denise and Gary, and the Duralls, Carolyn and Bob, were friends for years, but the young wives became best friends. Denise was at the forefront of the massive search for Carolyn after she simply disappeared one morning.

John Henry Browne, one of Seattle's most accomplished—and flamboyant—defense attorneys, represented Bob Durall initially. Early in
his career, when he was a public defender, he also represented Ted
Bundy.

Carolyn Durall loved to ice skate and to ride her horses. Here she's on a skating outing with her children.

Carolyn at a party for her at Morgan Stanley, Dean Witter. She is pregnant in this picture taken not too long before her daughter was born.

MISSING PERSON

Carolyn Durall

Last seen the morning of August 7, 1998 leaving her home in Renton Highlands area. Driving a 1990 maroon colored, Ford Aerostar Van. License Plate #166 CWI

Female, Caucasian, approximately 5' 7", 120 lbs.
35 years of age. Short, blond hair. Blue eyes.

If you have any information or have seen Carolyn, please call (425) 455-8026.

Carolyn Durall is pictured on the "missing" flyer that her friends distributed within forty-eight hours of her mysterious disappearance.

Several of Carolyn's friends planted this flowering cherry tree in a park in the Renton Highlands neighborhood where she once lived. Linda Gunderson and Denise Jannusche are on the right.

All for Nothing

Soon, his adventures took him far away from Sweet Home. In the late sixties, Larry Sturholm was in the United States Air Force, and his duty assignment with a TUSLOG unit sent him to one of the most isolated bases of all, near Samsun, Turkey, on the Black Sea. Although the troops' accommodations were spartan, the weather was relentlessly challenging, and the food was often iffy at best, the men there were grateful that they hadn't been sent to Vietnam. TUSLOG was a surveillance post, a spy base, and the duties and assignments of the army and air force servicemen stationed there were kept secret from most of the world. The personnel stationed at Samsun weren't particularly popular with most Turkish citizens, but they did form solid friendships with one another. Their entertainment consisted mainly of watching yet another replay of movies they had seen a dozen times before or wrestling with one of their camp's two pet bears. (The whole base mourned when an overeager MP fatally shot the smaller bear, unaware that the bears were so tame they were allowed out of their cages at will.)

Larry Sturholm's wild sense of humor saved his buddies from depression and sheer boredom from the tedium that marked TUSLOG. He joined several other servicemen to run AFRTS, the camp's radio station. Larry wrote scripts for two hilarious satires of radio dramas. "As the Stomach Turns" and "Down Our Street and UP Your Alley" kept the camp laughing. "Most of the writing for these was done by Larry," an old buddy recalls, "with some totally crazy brainstorming sessions including the whole team. Larry's unique sense of humor simply fed the insanity of the other men."

The radio staff airmen had "a conspiratorial mind set," the long-ago buddy says, "that may have been because we were stationed on a spy base. We even questioned the 'reality' of the moon landing, wondering if it had been staged in a studio somewhere. A favorite pastime was starting insane rumors and then sitting back as they spread like wildfire around the base."

It was there on a lonely base in Turkey where Sturholm first experimented with combining humor and news, and it became his forte.

When he was finally back in the United States, Larry married his girlfriend, Judy, and moved into professional radio and television jobs.

Sturholm was an entrepreneur and a visionary; he always had some creative project going, usually having to do with writing or producing in television or radio.

In 1979, a former college friend of mine was preparing to publish a book written by Larry Sturholm, and he asked me if I would edit it. It was titled *All for Nothing,* and it was a remarkably well-researched true story of Ray and Roy D'Autremont, twin brothers born in Oregon as the twentieth century dawned. On October 11, 1923, they made headline news all across America, although not in the way they envisioned.

The twins, 23, enlisted their younger brother, Hugh, in their meticulously choreographed plan to carry out what newspapers of that era termed "the last great train robbery in America."

Ray D'Autremont had already served time in a Washington state prison for his union activity. He said later, "Thousands of women and children were starving and dying. Thousands more—honest working men—were receiving less than half of what they should."

Though the charismatic twin brothers bragged about their goal of outwitting the boss barons who were living high on the hog, they didn't actually want to help the poor. For them, charity began at home. Seeking adventure and wealth, they went to Chicago, where they figured they could become gangsters and enjoy the perks of the Roaring Twenties.

But the brothers from Southern Oregon weren't exactly welcomed into the gangsters' world. They were viewed as country hicks who didn't fit into the big city. They came back west, and it was then that Ray came up with his idea to rob a Southern Pacific train.

He believed he had the perfect plan to make them all rich: one of the trains that roared south through the Rogue River Valley in Oregon to cross the Siskiyou Mountains into California was called the Gold Special because it was said to carry huge cargoes of both gold and cash.

Ray heard that there would be half a million dollars in gold on the train on October 11. He assured Roy and Hugh that money could be theirs.

With stolen dynamite, Ray waited at the south end of Tunnel Number 13 while Roy and Hugh jumped on the train. That was easy to do because the train slowed to a crawl as it entered the three-thousand-foot-long tunnel and chugged up to the summit of the mountain. Roy and Hugh leapt down into the engine and ordered the engineer to stop the train. Then the brothers packed the dynamite against one end of the mail car. Their plan was to set it off, grab as much gold and cash as they could, and escape into the forest.

But as Sturholm described it in his book, they used far too much dynamite. It ripped up the steel mail car like a can opener, killed the mail clerk, and set fire to the train. The D'Autremonts could see nothing at all through the black smoke and flames that filled the tunnel, much less steal anything. Much of the cash in the mail car had literally been shredded, and the gold was buried in the wreckage. The train itself was jammed in the tunnel by the mangled mail car, and could move neither forward nor backward. When the brakeman came back to see what had happened, he spooked Ray and Roy, and they shot him dead. Then they shot the engineer and the fireman. They were now not only train robbers but also cold-blooded murderers.

Without so much as a bar of gold, the three D'Autremonts scrambled into the woods, which they knew well. Somehow, despite a huge manhunt, they managed to stay free—if virtually penniless—for four years. Hugh was caught first, turned in by an army buddy who recognized his photo from a wanted poster. Roy and Ray were caught shortly after that in Ohio.

The story of the D'Autremonts had enthralled Larry Sturholm from the first time he heard about them. They had become media celebrities on a par with Bonnie and Clyde, John Dillinger, Al Capone, Bruno Hauptman or—today's counterparts—O. J. Simpson and Michael Jackson. The public wanted to believe that they were basically good men who were striking back for the underdogs and working stiffs in America. And the D'Autremont twins were as good-looking as movie stars, happy to pose for newspaper cameramen.

Sturholm set out to re-create the story that had been

lost in time. He discovered that Roy had gone insane in prison and been forced to undergo an experimental frontal lobotomy, which didn't work. He died in the Oregon State Mental Hospital. Hugh was paroled in 1958 and died soon after of cancer. Ray, the instigator of the botched train robbery fifty years earlier, had his sentence commuted in 1972. Once he sued the railroad that ran trains past the Oregon Penitentiary in Salem, claiming that the sound of the whistles disturbed his sleep and gave him nightmares. His suits were thrown out as frivolous.

The onetime glamour boy of train robberies lived to be eighty-four and was a formidable resource for Larry Sturholm's book. Sturholm interviewed the surviving D'Autremont in his old age, and he also obtained amazing photographs taken at the time of the disaster. *All for Nothing,* his book, told the true story to readers who had never heard of the D'Autremont brothers and to the elderly who recalled the headlines.

In 1979, I had yet to publish a book myself, and I was grateful to be hired to edit the rough draft of *All for Nothing.* Working on Larry Sturholm's book bought my family a lot of groceries. I was impressed with his ability as a writer and the way he could create suspense and bring back the scenes and personalities after more than fifty years. He didn't need any editing in storytelling, so I confined myself to checking his grammar and spelling. His words caught the futility and the tragedy of the desperate men whose foolish crime ended their hopes and dreams and also the lives of their innocent victims. His title, *All for Nothing,* was right on target.

One day, that title proved to be grimly ironic.

Sturholm wrote another book, this time on the bravery of law-enforcement officers: *In the Line of Duty: The Story of Two Brave Men.* It detailed the struggle of a Portland, Oregon, police officer who fought brain damage and paralysis after a devastating car crash. Once more, it was a gripping read, and Sturholm told it with sensitivity.

Neither of Larry Sturholm's books were national best sellers, although they did sell very well in the Northwest, and are still available by order through bookstores. His fans looked forward to more books.

His television viewers hoped to be able to enjoy his sense of humor and genius with new ideas for years to come. He was a natural; he had already won a number of Emmy Awards, and he was only 46.

Larry and Judy Sturholm stayed together in a marriage that other people envied. They were happy, although they never had children. As they both turned 40, they realized that they probably never would. But their lives were full; Larry always had his hand in new projects, producing short subjects, documentaries, and even commercials. And of course he had his KIRO features.

In midsummer, 1989, Larry Sturholm's fans were disappointed when he announced that he was taking a sabbatical from "Larry at Large" and Seattle and was going to head "into the sunset" on a new adventure, a project in the Cayman Islands. Disappointed, but not surprised. He was a man who constantly tested his limits, looking for new ways to create and entertain and educate.

On the night of July 31, 1989, the end of the five o'clock news ran pretaped footage that Sturholm had prepared for his good-bye to viewers. It showed him on water skis, close up at first, waving good-bye, then his image growing smaller and smaller as he disappeared into a beautiful sunset.

Sturholm and his crew were scheduled to fly that evening to the Cayman Islands. Judy drove her husband to Sea-Tac airport and kissed him good-bye. She didn't expect to hear from him until his flight and connecting flights touched down. They had been married for twenty-two years. She had never had any reason to doubt his faithfulness.

A few hours later the King County Police got their first disjointed call for help from paramedics dispatched from a hospital in Bellevue on the east side of Lake Washington. At the same time, a citizen was reporting a stabbing, with wounded people and possibly even a murder at a house near Issaquah. Issaquah was once a very small town near the foothills of Snoqualmie Pass that burgeoned in the eighties.

A female victim, who had suffered a massive loss of blood, had apparently been declared dead on arrival at Overlake Hospital in Bellevue. Other reporting callers said that there had been some kind of fight or assault at the home in an upscale neighborhood outside of Issaquah.

Deputies were dispatched to meet with the paramedics, and other units were sent to the address given in Issaquah. As they began to sort things out, they realized that the woman, who had died of exsanguination (blood loss incompatible with life), had apparently called her friend and business partner for help, gasping that there was trouble at her house. Unaware that anything more than one of her partner's increasingly common verbal confrontations with an ex-boyfriend was taking place, the friend sent her husband to the victim's house, the same house in Issaquah, where deputies were sent.

The woman, a nurse, was alive when her friend's husband reached her home. But she had been savagely stabbed, and her throat was sliced open deeply from one side to the other. As they headed for the hospital, she somehow managed to grip the edges of her slashed neck, trying to stop the flow of blood from her severed arteries. As a registered nurse, she would have known full well that she had to stop the bleeding and that she needed emergency care immediately. She had indicated to the man who'd come to help her that he must keep driving.

He drove as fast as he could, but even if the paramedics or the emergency room doctors had been right there fighting to save her, she was so terribly wounded that it would have taken a miracle.

The word was that she died in her friend's husband's arms before they could get medical help.

Deputies back at her house opened the front door and began a search of the downstairs rooms. From the saturation of blood, they knew that something disastrous had occurred there. During a sweep of the downstairs, they discovered a man wedged between the tub and toilet of the bathroom. There were indications of an immense struggle in the bathroom, and there was no question that he, too, was dead. He had probably attempted to lock himself in the bathroom, then barricaded the door against his attacker. He had been stabbed an estimated 180 times, too many times for a pathologist to get an accurate count. Even for trained and experienced police officers, the interior of this lovely home, the sight of the dead man, and the pools and sprays of blood throughout the house were almost too much to take in. This was shocking, senseless overkill.

They immediately called for backup and also requested that detectives from the Major Crimes Unit respond. Then they set about stringing yellow "Crime Scene: Do Not Cross" tape to guard the scene from contamination.

At the same time, other deputies walked cautiously through the strangely silent house. They had located the deceased man there. A few miles away, paramedics confirmed that they had declared a woman dead. According to the male friend who tried futilely to save her, she had lived in that house and her name was Debra Sweiger. The officers had no idea what her relationship to the dead man was. First word was that this house belonged to her. They didn't know yet who had done what to whom—or, more ominously—who might still be inside the house.

They searched the downstairs area and determined that there was no one hiding there. They headed up the stairs, their guns in their hands, expecting some madman to leap out at them at any moment. Then, as they opened the bathroom door, they found another man. He was in the tub, submerged in bloodied water. Dead.

This appeared to be a triple homicide or perhaps a double homicide and a suicide. The deputies and their supervisors knew that radio and television reporters monitored police calls, but it was difficult to call in over their police radios without giving details. Inevitably, by the early morning hours of Tuesday, August 1, the rumor that there had been three violent deaths in Issaquah had leaked to the media.

Media cars, their station's call letters visible on the sides, crept up as close as they could to the crime scene, only to be prevented from getting near enough to find out much before they were turned back by deputies stationed to guard the perimeter of the scene.

The Seattle stations KOMO-TV, KING-TV, and KIRO-TV (ABC, NBC, and CBS, respectively) all had their newsrooms on alert, standing by to get the first news of the rumored murders in Issaquah. Phil Sturholm was the news editor for KIRO, and he waited at the television station near the Space Needle in the Queen Anne neighborhood of Seattle. From the rumors, the Issaquah situation sounded as though it would be a top-of-the-hour story for the noon news. Bombarded by bad news and tragedies, radio and television newsmen and women learn quickly to grow a thick hide so that they won't take it all home at the end of a shift, but most of them do feel the pain. Field reporters have to knock on the doors of people still in shock from hearing that they have lost someone they love to violence. Reporters come to learn that life is ephemeral. They also lose some of their own to helicopter crashes and vehicular accidents as they race to where news is happening.

More than those in most occupations, media personnel are well aware that it can happen to them or to someone they love, too. But there was nothing about the first reports emanating from police radio transmissions to make anyone think that this incident was anything more than a huge crime story.

At the perfectly appointed home on the east side of Lake Washington, there was no longer any need to hurry. Although an aura of violence and terror still hung in the air, the King County detectives, led by Joe Purcell—who became the lead detective on this horrific case—worked slowly and methodically inside the murder house. They photographed the quiet rooms and drew sketches and measured so they could re-create the placement of the bodies and possible physical evidence later. They also tried to identify the three people who died the night before.

Joe Purcell looked for evidence in the upstairs bathroom where the corpse of the second man still lay in the tub full of bloody water, water that was quite cool now. As Purcell knelt to examine something, he thought he heard the sound of water splashing behind him. Of course, that could not be. A prickling ran up his spine, and he turned slowly around to see what had to be impossible.

The body in the tub had just sat up.

There is such a thing as bodies reflexively moving as dead muscles contract during rigor mortis, but this couldn't be caused by that. The guy was sitting straight up.

The dead man wasn't dead at all. He had bled quite a bit from where he'd slashed his neck and wrists in a suicide attempt, more than enough to turn the water in the tub crimson, and, as blood chemistry tests later showed, he had also taken an overdose of sedatives, enough he evidently believed would kill him. But he had not cut himself deeply enough to bleed to death nor taken enough pills to suppress his lungs' ability to draw breath. As the hours passed after the murders were discovered, the temperature of the water in the tub cooled enough to wake him from his drugged sleep.

It would be a long time before Joe Purcell, having experienced the sight of a body that almost literally rose from the dead, would be able to turn his back on a corpse. Indeed, he was never again able to work a homicide crime scene without a sense of trepidation.

Who were the three people who had come together so violently?

Records showed that the house was owned by Debra Sweiger, 36, a registered nurse. She was also the head of a corporation. In the past few years, she had turned her knowledge of nursing into an extremely successful enterprise, enough to buy this house, the fabulous wardrobe in her closets, and the sports car in her garage.

In the mid-eighties, there was a severe shortage of highly skilled nurses in America, partially brought about by their low salaries, long hours, and the lack of respect accorded them. Despite the lack of financial rewards, nurses were also expected to take on huge responsibilities for the welfare of their patients. For a decade or more, registered nurses had complained about the inequities in their careers. It came to a head in the eighties. Many of them simply quit their profession and found something that paid them a living wage.

The lack of top nurses that affected patient care the most were those RNs who were particulary skilled in the ER, ICUs (intensive care units) and in CCUs (coronary care units). No one could blame them for giving up on nursing when their requests for salary raises were ignored. The nurses who remained were in high demand.

Debra Sweiger was one of those highly trained nurses. So was her friend Joyce Breakey.* Debra and Joyce put their heads together, and came up with the idea for a referral service where they would link the top echelon of nurses to medical facilities willing to pay them what they were worth. Cascade Nursing Services was an idea whose time had come, and the women incorporated in 1987.

Joyce and Debra each had her own skills: Joyce was the hands-on person in the actual business; Debra gravitated more to public relations. In the early days of their business, they had only ten to twelve nurses to place in jobs, and the demand was great for "super nurses." Debra and Joyce took shift assignments themselves. They worked really hard, but they had faith that the day would come when all they had to do was run Cascade.

And it did. Debra brought in business and was the one who lobbied to state senators in Olympia to establish that Cascade's policies on taxes and unemployment compensation met existing statutes. A friend recalled, "Debra really enjoyed the schmoozing and dealing with things in the political arena. The whole 'who's who' was really important to her. She was a socializing machine, and she was very good at it."

Debra was married twice at a young age and she had two children, who didn't live with her full time. At 35, she was a divorcée making up for the years when she had too much responsibility and missed out on having fun. A man who was married to one of Debra's clients recalled his impression of her. "Debra was like a young college student who went off to school and had never experienced drinking and went to every sorority and frat party around. She was definitely a fun-loving person and enjoyed herself."

Debra was a slender blonde, very attractive. Originally

from the South, she still spoke with a charming honeyed accent. She was about five feet ten inches tall and would have been hard to ignore, even if her looks hadn't been so dramatic. She was usually the center of attention wherever she was. She dressed impeccably and a friend recalled that she had "big hair" and "great clothes: party dresses." No one ever saw her looking less than perfect.

"Debra was professional, self-confident, a flirtatious woman with a lot of nerve and energy," one platonic male acquaintance said. "She was boisterous and not afraid of embarrassment; she spoke loudly at a restaurant telling an inappropriate joke. Others might look on in disbelief, but it was all in good fun. Lots of fun, in fact."

Not surprisingly, Debra Sweiger attracted men. It wasn't unusual for her to have at least "three serious dates" with three different men in a week's time.

As their corporation thrived, the State maintained that nurses could not be classified as *professionals* while Cascade paid them as *independent contractors*. That was the whole point of Cascade's existence: highly capable nurses who were tired of being treated as nonprofessionals and being paid low wages had found their niche with Debra and Joyce and were loath to give it up. Washington State wanted to reclassify Cascade's nurses as Cascade employees. A lawsuit was filed, and, after a long struggle, Cascade won. They wouldn't have to pay business taxes, social security withholding taxes, and other fees the IRS and the state charged employers. The nurses, working as independent professional contractors, would be their own bosses, a big step upward for their bargaining powers in wage demands.

Joyce and Debra enjoyed a newfound sense of power,

power for women and power for nurses. To celebrate, they bought matching Jaguars. They hosted lavish black-tie parties for their contractor-nurses, and they lived far more carefree lifestyles than they had known in the days when they were simply nurses with tired feet and never enough money.

The two women upgraded their computer system, and their office procedures became even better organized. They prepared to start branches of their business in other cities. A Kansas City franchise was their first goal.

They deserved their success; they had worked tirelessly. Joyce and her husband, Mark,* were like a sister and brother-in-law to Debra. Debra was the one who gloried in being the hostess of their upscale parties and in the social life at the state capital with the movers and the shakers. She did most of the traveling, but she found time to have fun. This was probably the best part of her life.

Those who knew her well believed that Debra dated only casually, but they were concerned because many of the men she met wanted more serious commitments than she did. She had had that. Now she was enjoying a carefree life. While many women in their mid-thirties want to settle down, Debra Sweiger didn't. That only made her more attractive and more of a challenge to men.

One man fell totally under her spell, becoming besotted with her to the point that he was willing to give up everything he had going for him just to be with her in a committed relationship and, hopefully, in a marriage. His name was Bill Pawlyk, he was 48, and he had a great deal going for him. He had a master's degree in business, and he was a highly respected business leader in the Tri-Cities area of Washington (Kennewick, Pasco, and Richland on the east side of the mountain passes that divide Washington). He was the chairman of the Richland Economic Development Board, a highly placed executive with the Boeing Company's Computer Services Division, and a high-ranking naval reserve officer who was cleared to command submarines.

Pawlyk had been married a couple of times, unions he described to an acquaintance as "disasters," and he had a son and a daughter. He didn't have a single black mark on his professional record or any skirmishes with the law. Originally from New York, he was tall and good-looking, urbane, and classy in every way. He had money and prestige, and Debra was attracted to him. It was mutual. In one friend's words, "For him, along comes Debra with her charismatic, fashionable style and her southern accent, and Pawlyk found her very attractive."

Debra Sweiger took Bill Pawlyk by storm. She enjoyed dating him and the attention he lavished on her. A woman who was jealous of Debra said, "Debra tended to play games with men's emotions. I think she liked the drama of it all."

If Debra was behaving like a high school or college girl who enjoyed being the belle of the ball, sought after by many male suitors at the same time, she was also playing a dangerous game. And it began to backfire on her. Almost before Debra realized it, she was in way too deep with Pawlyk. Some said he had proposed marriage to her; at the very least, everyone who knew them agreed that he was madly in love with her.

Debra drew back; she was definitely not looking for marriage, and his possessiveness had become suffocating. Even though they lived almost two hundred miles apart, he made the trip to Issaquah to see her every weekend, far more often than she wanted. He didn't want her to date anyone but him, and he questioned her constantly about who she saw and what she did when they were apart. The more he clung to her, the more she fought to slow their romance down until, finally, she attempted to break up with him. He could not believe she was serious.

Bill Pawlyk was distraught. Although Debra had not asked him to do it, he had placed her ahead of everything else in his life, and he'd left himself no escape parachute at all. Without her, nothing mattered to him. He was alternately brokenhearted and enraged. His jealousy was almost pathological. He could not bear the thought that she might be with some other man.

It was more than that. Pawlyk's pride was shattered; he had spent a lifetime building up his reputation as a confident man, a man in charge in his business world, his navy service, and a man used to being treated with respect. Now he felt deceived and cuckolded, an object of derision, if not actually, at least in his own mind.

Love, passion, and overwhelming jealousy know no age, and Bill Pawlyk, nearing 50, was a runaway train, consumed with jealousy.

By this time, Debra Sweiger had met Larry Sturholm. No one is exactly sure how they met, although it was probably when he contacted Debra for a feature story. He was certainly a celebrity in Seattle, a garrulous, clever man who was a lot of fun to be with. Compared to Bill Pawlyk's gloomy presence, Sturholm was a breath of fresh air for Debra. They shared an interest in exploring new businesses, they talked about intriguing and innovative ideas, and they shared a lot of laughter.

"In my opinion," one man who knew them both said, "they were emphatically *not* having an affair, even though it might all have looked terribly bad. They liked to have lunch and talk or party together. He was probably poised for a midlife crisis, and their relationship was definitely headed in the wrong direction, but I don't think it had progressed to that point."

But Bill Pawlyk thought it had. He was convinced that Debra was having an affair with Larry Sturholm, and he couldn't stand the thought of that.

Pawlyk's breaking point came on July 31, 1989. He didn't know that Debra Sweiger was going on a trip to the Cayman Islands with Larry Sturholm and his film crew that night, but he was suspicious of everything she did. He wanted to talk out their relationship and somehow convince her to come back to him. But he had slipped over the edge; if she didn't take him back, he was fully prepared to kill her, a terrible choice that seemed better to him than to let her go to another man.

What happened next was a stunning example of how a whole lifetime—even life itself—can be shattered into minute fragments when someone reacts with rage as violent as a volcanic eruption or a tsunami, unexpected, unheralded, and totally devastating.

When Larry Sturholm arrived at the Sea-Tac airport that Monday night, he didn't go to the departure gate to await his flight. He carried out one of the few major deceptions of his life. His reason may have been as simple as not wishing to worry his wife. Most wives wouldn't be thrilled to learn that their husbands were flying off to a romantic spot with a woman as glamorous as Debra Sweiger was. And it's quite possible that Sturholm had envisioned the trip that lay ahead as more than just a business trip for him and Debra.

At any rate, Larry had not told Judith about his friendship with Debra Sweiger nor that she was going along on the trip to the Cayman Islands. After he said good-bye to his wife, Sturholm rented a car and drove away from the airport, headed for the Issaquah area. He planned to pick Debra up when she got home and take her back to the airport with him.

He didn't know that the house wasn't empty. Debra had given him a key to her house so he could come in and wait for her, but he didn't need it: he found the door unlocked. As he stepped in, he was confronted by Bill Pawlyk. But it wasn't the same Pawlyk that his family and friends had known for decades; instead, he was a man on a deadly mission.

On Sunday, the day before, Pawlyk had purchased two razor-sharp hunting knives. He'd taped them to his socks where they would be hidden by his trousers. He knew exactly what he was going to do as he made the long drive west from the Tri-Cities area.

He didn't know that Debra was almost home free or that Larry Sturholm was planning to wait for her in her house. Had Pawlyk delayed only one more day or even a few more hours, they would have been on a plane headed toward an island paradise and their lives would have played out in entirely different ways.

According to Pawlyk, Sturholm was as surprised to see him standing there in the foyer of Debra's house as he was to see Sturholm.

There is no way to validate what happened next because only one eyewitness remains, and he had reason to fabricate. Bill Pawlyk said later that the two of them had a friendly enough conversation at first. But Sturholm had soon realized to his horror why Pawlyk was there. He tried to reason with a man possessed who had no intention of letting Debra go.

It was like reasoning with a mad dog. The thin veneer of civility and polite conversation fell away, and it all went sour. Larry Sturholm was a great talker, a man whose decades of interviewing people had taught him to understand the frailties and bitter disappointments of other men, but he was not a fighter. He had no reason to be armed, and he must have been totally shocked when Bill Pawlyk reached to his ankles and produced the knives he'd bought to kill Debra.

In a blind rage, Pawlyk struck out at Sturholm. Victims who have survived stabbings say that they never felt the cuts; instead, they recall only the sensation of someone hitting them with what felt like a closed fist. Hopefully, that is true. Trapped and unprepared, Larry Sturholm died rapidly from more than a hundred fatal thrusts and the exsanguination that followed.

Pawlyk left Sturholm's body where it could not easily be seen by someone entering through the front door. Then he took time to shower and shave while he waited for Debra.

When she arrived home, she found to her surprise that Bill Pawlyk was there to meet her. He was committed now and perhaps angrier than he had been before. He had proof that Sturholm had a key to Debra's house. In his mind, that was also proof of her infidelity.

According to Pawlyk, Debra also tried to reason with him. Since he had cleaned himself up, his clothing wasn't blood-stained. She probably didn't know that Larry Sturholm had been attacked and was dead and that her ex-lover had waited for hours in her quiet house for her return.

Again, no one can know for sure what happened next. Pawlyk said he allowed Debra to make a phone call to her partner, knowing that no one could possibly arrive in time to stop him from what he planned to do. Joyce quickly picked up on Debra's coded words, realized that she was in trouble, and sent her husband, Mark, racing to Debra's nearby house.

Already wounded but still conscious, Debra asked Pawlyk if she could write a good-bye note to her daughter. He permitted her to do that. It was a short note, stained with her blood: "Jenny, I love you. Mom."

And then Bill Pawlyk carried out his original plan. No matter how many years have passed since that terrible night, writing about it is very difficult. It always will be. Pawlyk cut Debra Sweiger's throat in a final cruel act of revenge and jealousy after he had already stabbed her dozens of times. Believing that she was dead or fatally wounded, he left her in a welter of her blood. He planned that they would die together soon enough. He recalled later that he went upstairs to the bathroom. His lack of sleep and the overdose of sedatives he'd taken had made him "tired." He described how he tried to cut his throat on the right side as he gazed into the mirror over the sink, but he couldn't bring himself to use as much pressure as he had on his victims. Instead, he sliced his wrists until blood welled up.

As his life fluid seeped out, Pawlyk ran a bath and stepped into the tub. There he finally passed out.

When Mark Breakey arrived, probably thinking he had come to calm down only an argument, he found Debra in a room drenched and sprayed with her blood. It was a scene that would never leave him for the rest of his days. She was still alive, fighting desperately to survive. She held her throat, putting pressure on the severed arteries just as she had done to save other lives when she worked in the emergency room. She managed to gasp, "That son of a bitch, Pawlyk, did this to me . . ."

Mark picked her up, carried her to his car, and headed toward Overlake Hospital. But he knew in his heart they wouldn't get there in time, and he couldn't drive and help Debra at the same time. He pulled into the driveway of a home along the way and pounded frantically on their door. The family who lived there opened their front door, and Breakey begged them to call paramedics. They did so immediately.

But it was too late. Debra died in his arms.

When the King County detectives saw that the "dead man" in the tub was still alive, they called an ambulance to rush him to the closest hospital. The first ER physicians who examined him determined that he wasn't in critical condition. (Pawlyk later complained bitterly that they made him stay in the hospital corridor on a gurney while they took care of patients who needed more urgent care.)

No one knew for sure yet who the other victim in Debra Sweiger's house was. Detectives learned from

Mark Breakey that Debra had made a dying statement that someone named Pawlyk had stabbed her. There were three vehicles at the Sweiger house. One was registered to Debra and one to William Pawlyk; the third was a rental car. There was a rental agreement in the glove box that had Larry Sturholm's name on it. The investigators had Breakey's identification of Debra, and they thought they knew who the two men were, but the official determination would have to be made by the King County Medical Examiner's Office.

News crews continued to stand by, waiting for more information. It was just before ten when Channel 7's Bryan Thielke took the M.E.'s call on Tuesday morning and listened with horror. The dead man was KIRO's own Larry Sturholm. Larry's brother, Phil, Thielke's editor, sat a few feet away from him. It was Thielke who had to break the news to Phil that his brother had been murdered.

"We'd had no idea one victim was a friend, colleague, and relative," Thielke wrote later in an article on journalistic ethics. "It's something every reporter wonders about and even fears, being on the other side of the mic [microphone] or notebook. What's it like that we were about to be a principal source in a news story at the same time you're covering it?"

Some of the KIRO staff wondered about the relationships among Pawlyk, Sturholm, and Debra Sweiger. A few of Larry's closest friends knew about his possible romantic involvement with a woman who lived in Issaquah and were even aware that she had been dealing with a jealous ex-lover. This was in a way the most difficult aspect of the tragedy for the news staff. They knew

Judith Sturholm, and they didn't want to cause her any more pain than she already faced. "We were torn between doing the best job possible and protecting our friends."

In the end, KIRO didn't have to make the decision; another network affiliate came out with the love triangle rumor as a possible motive. Phil Sturholm, a truly decent man who had lost his younger brother, didn't flinch. "Phil urged us to vigorously pursue the story of his brother's death, not to hold back," Thielke wrote. "Phil's urging helped all of us do what we knew, as journalists, had to be done."

All of the KIRO reporters were impacted emotionally by the loss of Larry Sturholm, and they would never again approach a crime or accident story with as thick a wall between the news and their own feelings. They decided to release some of the *Larry at Large* film, and his last time on the screen, heading into the sunset, was ubiquitous on the news over the next week. They would not, however, give permission to use it on the tabloid television shows whose producers seemed likely to pounce on the most salacious versions of the double murders.

I wasn't eager to write the story, either. Judy Sturholm came to my house a few months after she became a widow, and we talked for hours. She told me that she had had no idea that Debra Sweiger had a place in her husband's life until they were killed. When the couple's credit card bill came in the month after Larry was murdered, there was a charge from a florist for flowers that were delivered to an address Judy didn't recognize. Still trying to understand what had happened, Judith called the florist and asked who the recipient had been. It was Debra Sweiger.

Judy was far more sad than angry, and she was frustrated because she could no longer discuss what had happened with her husband. I suspect that in the long run the aborted trip to the Cayman Islands would have been only a blip in an otherwise solid marriage.

Judy decided that it wasn't time yet to write a book, and I promised to set it aside. As it happened, I waited sixteen years. Like Larry Sturholm's coworkers and friends, I struggled with my own ethics. Should I tell this remarkable story or let it go? Abiding by Judy Sturholm's wishes, I let it go—until I learned that William Pawlyk was trying to have his sentence commuted and until I met a woman to whom he confessed.

Cindy Versdahl, who was in her early thirties, had never been to a trial before, but she had been one of Larry Sturholm's devoted viewers, and she was saddened to learn that he had been murdered. "I was stunned," she said. "And then I was curious about why anyone would do that." When she learned that William Pawlyk was going to trial on two charges of aggravated murder, she decided to watch the legal system at work.

"I took the bus down to the courthouse in Seattle. It was standing room only, and they wouldn't let me in, but finally someone left and I found a seat."

Cindy went to Pawlyk's trial twice, fascinated by the testimony she heard. But she was disappointed when a defense attorney objected to a witness, and the judge cancelled the afternoon sessions on the second day so they could debate the problem. After taking a day off work, the long bus ride, and waiting to get into the trial, she had the whole long afternoon free.

"I was mad," she admits, "and so I decided to go over to the jail and talk to Pawlyk."

She wasn't intimidated by the fact that she knew nothing about procedures for jail visitors. She handed a note to the bailiff in the courtroom, asking what to do. She was told she could go over to the King County Jail and ask to see Pawlyk. It would be up to him and his jailers whether to grant her a visit. And that was what she did, taking the elevator to the floor indicated. Cindy waited for several hours then was led into a visitor's area. Bill Pawlyk came out to take a seat on the prisoner's side. He wasn't wearing the business suit he wore in court; he wore a bright orange jumpsuit, the kind reserved for "high-risk" prisoners locked up for major crimes. He was curious, too, about this stranger who had come to visit him.

"Who *are* you?" he asked her.

She explained that she wasn't a reporter or anyone special, just someone who wanted to understand him.

He didn't have many visitors, he told her, and he'd decided to see what she wanted. He spoke with what seemed to her to be a "New York accent."

"I understand who the victims were," she began, "but I wanted to know why did you kill Larry Sturholm? How could you do that?"

"I wasn't expecting to see him," Pawlyk said, as if that were a clear enough answer.

Pawlyk told Cindy Versdahl that he had traveled every weekend to see Debra. And she had betrayed him.

His marriages had failed, and his children didn't communicate with him. He had known what he had to do. He said that even though his lawyers were basing his defense on insanity, that wasn't true.

"I'm not insane," he said firmly. "It was premeditated. I planned the whole thing. I did it consciously."

She stared at him, temporarily speechless.

"It's over and done with now," he said easily. "No use talking about it."

He wanted to talk instead about his own life. He was born in New York City and had been raised in the "projects." He had one brother and a daughter and a son. He graduated from the Naval Academy and had expected to eventually become an admiral in the Naval Reserve. He had the distinction of having had two meetings with Admiral Hyman Rickover.

Pawlyk dominated the conversation and jumped from one subject to another, although he didn't seem crazy to Cindy. He liked to talk about books and advised her "Go up to Tower Records in Belltown [a district on the north end of Seattle's downtown area] and you can get cheap books there."

Bill Pawlyk asked Cynthia for her phone number, explaining that he could only call out of jail with collect calls. She was reluctant to give it to him but finally relented. He didn't seem at all interested in her as a woman, and he wasn't going anywhere. He wouldn't be showing up on her doorstep.

"He only called me once," she remembers. "And he talked steadily for half an hour—all about books. I could barely get a word in. He was very intelligent, and you could tell he knew it."

Lee Yates and Jeff Baird, senior deputy prosecuting attorneys for King County, represented the State in the case against William Pawlyk. Yates had been with the prosecutor's office for many years, and he had successfully prosecuted a number of high-profile cases. Baird had been there fewer years, and he went on to be the lead prosecutor many years later in the Green River Murder case. They made a very strong team for the State.

This courtroom was full of tension. Debra Sweiger's siblings were there, as was Larry's brother, Phil Sturholm, a constant presence as he took voluminous notes. Phil and Larry had been extremely close, and it was tremendously difficult for the older brother to hear details of Larry's murder.

The gallery was packed day after day with court watchers who could not imagine why anyone would kill the genial television star who had seemed like a friend to them.

Pawlyk had been examined by two eminent forensic psychiatrists, paid for by the State because he claimed that he was indigent. One, Dr. Emanuel Tanay, who had examined any number of nationally known high-profile offenders, including Ted Bundy, flew to Seattle to interview Pawlyk. He was the second psychiatrist the Defense hired. Tanay diagnosed Pawlyk as having suffered a psychotic break during which he killed Debra Sweiger and Larry Sturholm. Tanay opined that Pawlyk was legally insane at the time of the double murder and his attempted suicide.

Dr. Christian Harris, who was also hired by the Defense, found just the opposite. Harris, too, had many,

many years of experience in evaluating murder defendants. It was his opinion that Pawlyk had been fully aware of the difference between right and wrong when he carried out the savage stabbings and was cognizant of the nature and quality of his acts. The Defense had been aghast when they read Harris's report. So they hired Tanay. Satisfied with his report, they attempted to scratch Harris from the witness list. His diagnosis would be far more beneficial to Baird and Yates's prosecution than it was to Pawlyk's case. They wanted the jurors to hear only Dr. Tanay's analysis. Yates and Baird argued that both psychiatric evaluations should be heard.

The Court refused the Defense motion.

Just how bizarrely had Bill Pawlyk behaved on the fatal Monday of July 31? He purchased the hunting knives expressly for the occasion. He brought a gun for backup. Apparently his 200-mile drive from Richland hadn't been erratic, or he would undoubtedly have been stopped by Washington State troopers.

King County detectives traced his movements back to the time he left Richland and headed for Debra's house for a final showdown. They learned to their amazement that he was in her home, twice on the day of the murders. Apparently, he got hungry while he waited for her to come home so he drove back to the Snoqualmie Falls Lodge, a luxurious resort known for its fine cuisine, particularly its huge farm breakfasts.

There, Pawlyk ordered and consumed the lodge's seven-course breakfast. Sixteen years ago, the thirty-dollar charge for breakfast was the priciest in the area, but diners agreed that it was well worth it. Reservations for Sunday breakfast had a waiting list that was several weeks long, but this was a Monday. Pawlyk dined on fresh fruit, oatmeal with clotted cream, bacon, ham, eggs, waffles, and pancakes, the latter items part of a ritual at the lodge where waiters pour syrup from several feet in the air until it curls over the pancakes.

The investigators even located the waiter who had served Bill Pawlyk and learned that he ate his meal with gusto. The server had detected no overt signs of disorientation or despair in the man he waited on. Rather, he found him quite cheerful.

Then Pawlyk drove back to Issaquah to lie in wait for Debra's return home.

The defendant had an extensive lineup of impressive character witnesses, including the mayor of Richland, who extolled Pawlyk's service to the community in the Tri-Cities area. According to his friends and coworker, Pawlyk must surely have been out of his mind when he carried out the two murders. Yet the man sitting at the defense table looked eminently sane. Bill Pawlyk was relying on the not guilty by reason of insanity defense, but his actions before the stabbings seemed much too deliberate for a man who had lost touch with reality.

As it was, Bill Pawlyk had already escaped the most severe penalty for aggravated first-degree murder; the death penalty had been taken off the table. By mutual agreement between the State and the Defense, if he were found guilty, he would face life in prison with no early parole or commutation of the sentence. Once the death penalty was dropped, a life sentence would have no teeth if it could be softened and adjusted as the years went by.

But first, the jurors had to decide whether Bill Pawlyk

was guilty of the over-kill of two human beings who were taken completely by surprise after he carefully planned the details of the murder of Debra Sweiger.

Lee Yates and Jeff Baird summed up the shocking case in their final remarks and rebuttal. Of all the murder cases they had prosecuted, this was one where they expected a quick verdict, although they had long since learned that no one, not even experienced judges, prosecutors, and defense attorneys can truly read a jury by studying their faces and body language during a trial.

Juries who come back in a short time do, however, tend to vote for conviction. As their deliberation stretches into days, the likelihood of an acquittal grows.

There was no quick verdict. Indeed, the jurors in the Pawlyk trial deliberated for five days. But in the end, Yates and Baird and the evidence unearthed by the King County sheriff's detectives convinced them that Pawlyk was indeed guilty of a carefully choreographed plan to commit the murder of Debra Sweiger.

They believed that when he found Larry Sturholm in her house, Larry became expendable to Pawlyk. Did they actually have an initially friendly conversation? Pawlyk insists they did, but experts doubt that.

When William Pawlyk was found guilty of two counts of aggravated first-degree murder, he was sentenced to life in prison. No one—not even the prosecutors—knew of his frank confession to Cindy Versdahl. But the brutality of the murders could not be denied, nor could Dr. Christian Harris's opinion that Pawlyk was neither currently insane nor had he been insane under the law or medically on the night of July 31, 1989.

Pawlyk was sent first to the Washington State Prison

in Walla Walla. There he proved to be an ideal prisoner; there was no question that he was a brilliant man. He tutored prisoners who attended community college classes in basic math, calculus, science, and physics but worked mostly with those who were either trying to earn their GEDs or high school diplomas. He oversaw a small reference library and worked in preproduction for an in-prison television station.

He was president of the prison military service veterans' group; he had always been active in navy reserve activities. Pawlyk had many supporters, so many that he had to decide whom to trim from his visitors' list, as he was allowed to have only ten people cleared to visit him. He received many letters and cards. To keep up with his correspondence, he often had to write a single letter and make duplicate copies. He sent Christmas cards to scores of friends.

Several television stations requested interviews. He weighed the advisability of doing them. He was reluctant to grant those that emanated from Seattle. The third anniversary of the murders in Issaquah brought a number of requests in mid-1992. "I'm more reluctant to do those," he wrote to Cindy Versdahl, "because of the personal emotional drain and the stirring up of memories and emotions for people in Seattle."

He wanted people in Seattle to forget the double murder. He was working hard on an appeal of his sentence. The premise of his appeal was that he had not received a fair trial because the jurors heard Dr. Christian Harris say that he was not insane at the time he killed Larry Sturholm and Debra Sweiger.

Pawlyk and his court-appointed attorneys took that

tack for a decade, moving to higher and higher courts. The man who wrote to friends and supporters was perfectly sane, civilized, and even courtly in his correspondence. He said that his jurors were "good folks" and that three of them had even written to him.

It was almost as if he had been able to erase his responsibility for the murders of two people who had been much loved. When one of his jurors was quoted as saying (about Pawlyk) that "everyone can be driven to that edge [where they snap]" and that she would now "gladly invite him into her living room," it was very difficult for the victims' family members and for those of us who knew the details of what happened during that "snap."

Pawlyk remained in the Walla Walla prison for six years. Then his request to be transferred to the Washington State Reformatory in Monroe was granted. He was exhilarated; his appeal was headed for the Ninth Circuit Court of Appeals, just one step below the Supreme Court.

At the reformatory in Monroe, a medium-custody institution at the time, he shared a nine-by-six-foot cell with another prisoner. He had put on weight from the starchy diet served in prison and developed high blood pressure but otherwise was doing well.

Pawlyk continued to tutor other prisoners each morning, this time for Edmonds Community College extension courses, and to help men obtain their GEDs, and he worked eight hours a day for an outside industry. His tutoring, he said, "gives me a great deal of satisfaction in seeing changes in guys as they learn. Education is the best program to reduce recidivism."

He announced to friends in 1998 that he was vice president of the Lifers group, which sponsored positive programs in justice and corrections with Seattle University. He also belonged to a book club that brought authors into the prison for discussions. He took a sign-language class so he could communicate with deaf inmates, and he was in a group that helped two needy children.

Pawlyk had many visits from navy buddies who had graduated in his 1963 class at the Naval Academy. Photos of those visits were published in the newsletters that went out to scores of retired naval officers. His brother came to the Monroe Reformatory and the two men were allowed a trailer visit, where he enjoyed a semblance of freedom in one of the mobile homes kept on the prison grounds for family visits.

In 2001, the Ninth Circuit Court of Appeals turned down William Pawlyk's appeal. But he was determined to be free. He applied to the state Clemency and Pardons Board in 2004 after serving fifteen years in prison—only fifteen years of a life sentence. Governor Gary Locke was leaving office, and about eighty prisoners sought clemency and pardons. Pawlyk had built himself a superior prison résumé of good deeds and public service. His plea was set to be heard in late October 2004 in Olympia, the state capital.

Lee Yates, now assigned to the Appellate Department of the King County Prosecutor's Office, revisited the case he prosecuted some fifteen years earlier when he argued against clemency.

Pawlyk, who testified by phone, submitted a stack of letters from friends, prison officials, and even a few jurors who all felt he would never re-offend.

At long last, Pawlyk finally apologized for what he

had done. In his letter to the board, he wrote, "Having reflected much upon the horrible magnitude of what my actions wrought, I deeply regret the anguish and grief inflicted on the family and friends of Debbie and Larry. They didn't deserve to die."

Norm Maleng, the King County Prosecutor, said he had already considered William Pawlyk's crime-free life *before* the murders when he chose in 1991 not to ask for the death penalty. "The crime Mr. Pawlyk committed was among the most horrific in King County during my tenure. The life sentence he received was—and still is—commensurate with his brutal, premeditated, and prolonged act of violence against two unarmed people."

Debra Sweiger's brother was shocked that his sister's killer would even be considered for clemency. "I just think this process is so sick," he said. "I thought it was a joke. I said, 'It's impossible. He got life without parole.'"

Her brother remembered seeing Debra as she lay in her coffin with scarves carefully draped around her neck and her hair styled so that it clung to her cheeks. "It was to hide the knife marks on her beautiful face because she was literally sliced to pieces. . . ."

Phil Sturholm recalled that the Medical Examiner's Office had strongly advised him not to view his brother's body. He did not feel that seven and a half years per victim even approached justice. "Neither mercy nor clemency was uttered by Mr. Pawlyk [when he was stabbing his victims three hundred times]." Sturholm continued, "His crime was savage and cruel."

And indeed it was. Governor Locke, who was quite aware of the horror in Issaquah fifteen years earlier, chose not to override the recommendation of the clemency board. Pawlyk would remain in prison. He has said that he feels an obligation to do good. And, in prison, he has done that. He will almost certainly continue to teach and perform acts of kindness inside prison walls and fulfill his obligation there. But not even a forensic psychiatrist can predict how he would react if he were free and might once again be consumed with jealousy and a terrible blow to his pride.

The mass of men and women experience broken relationships, jealousy, wounded pride, and despair over lost love. It is never easy for any of us.

Only a tiny percentage of humans react with unbelievable violence.

In Larry Sturholm's own words, William Pawlyk did it "all for nothing."

Over the years, the stress of living through the murders of Debra Sweiger and Larry Sturholm took a toll on those who had cared deeply for them: Mark Breakey, who tried so hard to get Debra the emergency treatment she so desperately needed, died at a young age, still haunted by the images of that July night. King County Detective Joe Purcell, who headed the investigation team and was of immense help to the prosecution, retired early. He was never able to forget the shock of seeing a "dead man" rise up from a tub of bloody water like something in a horror movie. Judy Sturholm, Larry's wife, died at the age of 57 in 2001. Phil Sturholm, Larry's brother, stayed active in his television career, still believing that the news should be truthful, no matter whom it impacts. A faithful member of his church, he has tried to find forgiveness toward his brother's killer. It has not been easy.

Phil reportedly did finally have a conversation with Pawlyk about Larry's last moments, although what was said is an intensely private matter and will remain private.

I wish that I could find the answer to why Bill Pawlyk reacted to romantic rejection with such stunning violence, but I never have been able to. Men have been destroying women who try to leave them for centuries, and every day I hear from a few women who live in fear of reprisal from men who will not let them go free. Of course, some men do let go.

And some do not.

In prison, Bill Pawlyk helps many people. He plans to appeal his sentence in a few years. Freed from the restraints he lives under, would he ever again fall so passionately and possessively in love that he might once more be dangerous if he were thwarted?

I honestly don't know.

A Desperate Housewife

There is a bleak kind of irony in this case. The water-shed point in this remarkably unhappy marriage came about several years ago, and I began to write it long before the blockbuster ABC Sunday night show Desperate Housewives *took America by storm. To almost everyone's surprise, the new show captivated a major share of viewers almost from its debut. The lives of five gorgeous, totally fictional housewives living on Wisteria Lane in their perfect houses with their not-so-perfect husbands are full of romance, affairs, suicides, murders, drug addiction, nosy neighbors, money problems, and keeping up appearances. The plotlines are clearly designed to end each week's episode with a mysterious cliff-hanger and everyone has a secret—or two—or even three. Despite the constant threat of sudden violent death in the television series, the show is humorous. It's written in strokes that are much too broad to be taken seriously.*

In the true-crime genre I write, there are too many stories of real desperate housewives who find themselves trapped in relationships they never bargained for. They sought love and lifetime commitment only to find that they had married someone who, through the looking glass, was a man they did not know. There is nothing funny about the story of a real-life desperate housewife that follows. It is certainly rife with secrets and mystery, but the denouement is grim, and too many real hearts broke before it was over.

I will admit that I could not talk to the victims' friends or read the documents that accompanied this case without crying.

Every neighborhood seems to have one couple that appears to be enjoying an ideal life. It's easy to like them and at the same time to envy them. Their homes are too neat, their yards and gardens wonderfully manicured and alive with blooms. Their children always seem to be well behaved. While the rest of the block's residents have weeds in their yards, peeling paint, dogs that bark in the middle of the night, cars that need to be washed, and kids who break windows, miss the school bus, and rarely, if ever, get straight A's, the perfect couple avoids those problems. If they have arguments, they usually manage to do it behind closed doors. A marriage with no bumps at all is impossible; and who wants to be part of such a union, anyway? Still, it's a challenge to try to emulate people who seem to do it with so little effort.

To the casual observer, the couple in this case, Robert and Carolyn Durall, had a good marriage. Both held prestigious jobs with high incomes. After work, like most young couples, they shuttled their three children to and from soccer, baseball, church activities, Cub Scouts, and all the organized classes and clubs that are so important to youngsters growing up in an era when achievement and being the best have become more important than just playing. Kids don't play hide-and-go-seek or kick-the-can anymore. They don't climb trees or go fishing or read adventure books.

Robert and Carolyn Durall's children were no different: their parents wanted them to have a running start at success in life.

Even though the Duralls looked happy, at least to those neighbors who didn't know them very well, there was danger simmering there, little fires occasionally breaking out that might destroy their family if they took hold. Perhaps it was easier to hide their unhappiness because they had a nineties kind of life.

To a closer observer, there *was* an undercurrent that whispered trouble ahead. But even those who knew them well could not possibly have foreseen the terrible way the Duralls' marriage would implode.

Carolyn Durall was born on December 1, 1961. She was a truly nice little girl who grew up to be a woman who brightened any room she walked into. When she was eight, she made a birthday cake for the woman who lived next door. Nobody suggested it to her; she just wanted to be sure that her friend had a special birthday. She loved to bake even then, and her enthusiasm for cooking grew as she did.

Carolyn loved life, her family, her pets, and nature. She wrote poems when she was in grade school. Many of them were based on the changing seasons:

Autumn Leaves

When Autumn leaves whirl
In a neat little swirl
They fall from a pretty tree,
To meet the ground with glee

And birds fly south
To feed their mouths
   And when the wind is blowing
   It makes the snow snowing.

Carolyn always loved to cook, but ironically she married a man who ate only health food, organic vegetables, and no red meat at all. She went to extra effort to find sugar-free recipes and other ingredients acceptable to him. Since she couldn't very often bake treats for her husband, she baked things for her children, friends, neighbors, and coworkers. Every birthday of anyone remotely close to her was an occasion for a cake, and she often brought warm scones with raspberry jam to her office at Morgan Stanley Dean Witter and left them on her friends' desks. *Her* weakness was chocolate, anything chocolate.

As a child, Carolyn was captivated by horses, and she learned to ride at a young age; not just to ride but to show in competition, which included jumping and performing intricate movements around barricades. For most of her life, she had her own horse. When she was 36, her horse was named Drizzle, and she kept him in stables near her house and rode him whenever she could. She also loved ice-skating.

Whenever anyone describes Carolyn, they begin, "She was always smiling—always." And when you look through albums or watch videos, it's obviously true. Just as some people's facial muscles tend to fall into a frown even when they're not grumpy, Carolyn's face naturally lent itself to smiling.

She was a lovely blonde, and slender—when she wasn't

pregnant, as she often was after her marriage. She was five feet seven inches tall and usually weighed about 120 pounds. She dressed well, although she tended to spend more money on other people than on herself.

Carolyn grew up in a great family as one of two children, herself and a brother. She was especially close to her mother, Leni, and talked to her every day.

Carolyn met Bob Durall in the mid-eighties when they worked in a real-estate firm in Bellevue, Washington. She was very good at her job but had always looked forward to being married and having a family of her own. Bob seemed to have all the qualities she hoped for in a mate.

Bob Durall was intelligent, a high achiever, a National Merit Scholar in high school; and he had two college degrees: a Bachelor of Arts in accounting from the University of Puget Sound and a Bachelor of Science in computer science from the University of Washington. He was attractive, if slightly built, at five feet ten and only 148 pounds. Bob wasn't as outgoing as Carolyn was, and he had fewer close friends than she did, but that wasn't a problem for her, not at first; their personalities complemented each other. He came from a family background as solid as hers; his parents were ten to fifteen years older than Carolyn's, and he had a sister eight years older than he was, a warm and loving woman. His dad, Arnie, was fun and kind, and his mother, Bernice, very genteel and welcoming. She was a perfect lady, a little prim, but always friendly. Arnie was a salt-of-the-earth kind of man who didn't put on airs. They liked Carolyn right away.

The Duralls had lived in the south end of Seattle for

almost fifty years and raised their children in the Mount Baker Presbyterian Church. Bob's parents were in their forties when he came along on October 24, 1957, and they doted on him. He was a late baby much longed for. Everyone who knew them was happy for them.

As he grew up, he did them proud. They didn't really spoil Bob, but they certainly made him feel that he was a unique, extraordinary boy. Most of his parents' friends recalled him as being gentle and dependable, a nice kid.

When Carolyn met Bob, he was 25 and she was 21. He was confident and successful at his job, definitely a young man on his way up. Carolyn quickly fell in love with him, and she really liked his family. She was thrilled when Bob proposed. Together with their families, they planned their wedding. There was no question but that it would be in a church; they were both devout Christians. In 1986, they had a lovely formal ceremony in the Mount Baker church in Seattle, with a color scheme of white and beige. And then left for their honeymoon in Hawaii.

Carolyn gave Bob a Bible and wrote in its dedication that he was "one of the nicest men I've ever met."

Bob's mother took him aside during his wedding reception to give him advice that she didn't really think he needed. Nevertheless, she reminded him that his father "always treated me like a queen." She told him she hoped that he would cherish Carolyn in the same way and make her happiness his most important concern. Bob assured his mother that he would.

Bob's mother was delighted that he had chosen Carolyn; she was exactly the kind of young woman any woman would want for a daughter-in-law. Carolyn was nice to Bernice and Arnie, and it was obvious how much in love she was with Bob. Her parents approved of Bob, too. Bob and Carolyn were young, but they were responsible.

To Carolyn's shock, their honeymoon wasn't particularly happy. They argued a lot, and she realized that he was a man who was used to having things just the way he wanted. Even that far back, she had the feeling that she should not have married him. She tried to put their differences down to the natural difficulties any two people would have adjusting to living full time with each other. She was sure she could learn to do things the way Bob liked and that he would compromise about what mattered to her. But as they settled into marriage, it became clear that Bob was going to be the head of the household, and Carolyn deferred to him when it came to making decisions.

It was important to them to have a family. And, although Carolyn continued to work for a while, she stopped when she gave birth to the first of their children in 1989. It was a boy. A few months later, she felt once more that she and Bob should not be married, only to find that she was pregnant again. She had a second son in 1991. Carolyn adored her babies, but her marriage wasn't working. Bob insisted on counseling. He picked the therapist, and she agreed to go. Somehow, with all four of the counselors they eventually saw together, she always came away feeling that *she* was the partner in the wrong, and she felt guilty that she hadn't measured up to Bob's expectations. Or, apparently, to the counselors' either.

They attended religious services together in the same

church where Bob went most of his life. He taught Sunday school. In 1995, they joined the church and became even more active there. During the early years in their first house on Hoquiam Court in Renton, the Duralls outwardly seemed happy enough, although they had very different personalities. They participated in neighborhood get-togethers. Bob was a different kind of guy from most of the young husbands. One man described him as "a cocky guy, but I had the feeling: 'Is anybody in there?' when I talked to him. As if he wasn't really listening." Carolyn, on the other hand, was truly concerned about other people.

Bob was something of a job-hopper, although he usually moved up the financial ladder. But he was let go from a few jobs because he wasn't a man who went along with other people's programs. When he printed out his résumé, he simply didn't mention the jobs from which he was fired. He was a computer expert in a newly burgeoning area of business, so he never had trouble finding another job. Over the years, he worked for some time at IPC Pension Service and the Bon Marché department store.

In the early nineties, Bob accepted a job with Royal Seafoods. There he worked closely with a man named Gary Jannusch. Gary met Carolyn and knew at once she and his wife, Denise, would have a lot in common. He grabbed Denise at the company Christmas party and brought her over to meet Bob Durall's wife. Gary was right; Carolyn and Denise were soon best friends.

Certainly, they had their husbands' jobs in common, but it was far more than that. They got along, laughing at the same things. Since Carolyn wasn't working at the time, she was happy to babysit for the Jannusches' daughter, Tera, when Denise went back to work part time in a job-share arrangement at Morgan Stanley Dean Witter in Bellevue. Denise never worried about her little girl when she was with Carolyn.

The Jannusches found Bob a little strange, and his lifestyle was different from most people's. He was a health food nut, a compulsive jogger, and into meditation, strange ethereal music, and other fairly far-out mystical stuff. They felt a little sorry for Carolyn when they saw how she had to scurry to be sure Bob had his special natural foods before she could relax on any of their mutual vacations. But they didn't presume to judge anyone else's marriage. If Carolyn loved Bob, even though he seemed to control every aspect of her life, that was certainly her choice.

The Jannusches and the Duralls lived in the Highlands area of Renton, a Seattle suburb, and their homes were quite close. The neighborhoods there were made up of new houses occupied by couples in their twenties and thirties. The four of them socialized, and their children liked each other.

In 1992, Denise's job-share partner at Morgan Stanley Dean Witter left, and she asked Carolyn if she would like to work with her; that way each young mother would have an interesting job but would only have to work part time. Carolyn liked the idea, came in to be interviewed, and was hired. Now, they were not only best friends; they were also coworkers.

After having their two sons, Carolyn became pregnant again, an unplanned pregnancy. Bob wanted her to have an abortion, but she wouldn't even consider it.

Even though the marriage was limping along badly by 1994, Carolyn wanted the third baby. This time, she had a girl. Bob soon came to dote on his daughter. His neighbors said he absolutely adored her.

Carolyn stayed home with the new baby for a few months, then she went back to work. Bob still didn't help much at home, but she seemed able to handle both her job at the investment firm and her duties as a wife and mother with ease.

By January 1998, Carolyn was working full time for the investment firm. She and Denise were both assistants to executives in the Bellevue office. It worked out well because Carolyn's daughter was in a day care across the street from her office.

Morgan Stanley was a friendly place to work, and Carolyn fit right in. She was very artsy-crafty and made little gifts for more than a dozen of the women she worked with: crocheted and personalized little baskets for paper clips for their desks, or holiday cards that she designed and printed with stamps she carved. If she stopped to buy coffee for herself, she always brought in steaming cups for the women who worked near her.

At Morgan Stanley, there were Christmas parties and other get-togethers, but the big celebration of the year came right after the income tax deadlines had been met. After the staff had worked intensely for weeks to help their clients, the firm rewarded them by hiring limousines and taking them out for a gala evening they called "The Tax Party." Bob didn't approve of that, and it also meant that he had to look after the three children while Carolyn celebrated with her work friends.

The Jannusches and the Duralls spent more and more

time together; Gary and Bob worked for the same company, and now so did Denise and Carolyn. The men often carpooled, and while Gary liked Bob well enough, he noticed that Bob wanted things his way. When Gary drove, he couldn't turn on his car radio or play his CDs because Bob wanted the car quiet. And as always when they went camping, Bob Durall had to have special food—tofu hot dogs—when everyone else was roasting old-fashioned wieners on a stick.

While Bob enjoyed hiking or playing with his children, it was Carolyn who had to see to the details for every outing. He didn't want to be bothered. He rarely cooked for his children; that was a woman's job. If he fixed food for himself, he didn't clean up afterward. When he peeled an orange, he left the peels in the sink. It was a small thing, but one of Carolyn's friends thought it was inconsiderate, as if he were used to having a maid clean up after him.

Carolyn arranged all the dental appointments, haircuts, and doctors' appointments and was soon the parent who drove their sons to soccer or baseball practice. She was a Cub Scout leader. The Duralls' friends noticed that she never sat down; if the kids didn't need her for something, Bob did. She was sad that she had little time to just play Barbies with her daughter or board games with her sons, but there weren't enough hours in her days. Carolyn often took her youngsters to amusement centers like Chuck E. Cheese's Pizza for a quick meal. Most young mothers are busy, but she was parenting all alone, even though her children had a father who could have picked up the slack a little. *He* had time to play games with them, and if he was in the mood, he did.

Carolyn admitted to Denise Jannusch that she felt that Bob controlled her. Denise and the Duralls' neighbors noticed that Carolyn was jumpy and nervous around him, always glancing at him to be sure he approved of what she did and said. When she drank one beer at a company picnic, he chastised her as harshly as if she'd gotten sloppy drunk.

She told Denise that Bob's need to be in charge of everything began early in her marriage. "They were at a party and she told me that he wanted to go, but she wasn't ready to leave yet," Denise recalled. "He just picked her up and carried her out of the party and put her in the car and took her home. She was humiliated."

Bob often abruptly decided to leave functions where Carolyn was enjoying herself. One time the Duralls went with their children to see her parents, who were vacationing on an island in Puget Sound. They drove separate cars that day. Carolyn told Denise later that for some reason Bob announced he wanted to leave "right now." He told her to get everything packed into her car immediately so they could catch the early ferry. He took his car and left with the two boys while she scrambled to get all the children's gear, toys, diaper bag, and Bob's special food and supplies together and packed in her car. Then she raced with their baby girl to try to catch up with Bob and the boys.

"When she got to the end of the ferry dock," Denise recalled, "Bob had his car parked way up first in line. She waved frantically to him, but he just looked back at her and laughed. He drove on the ferry without her. He saw the gates close before her car got on, and he knew she would have to wait hours for the next one."

John and Linda Gunderson moved to Hoquiam

Court, into the house next door to the Duralls. "I remember the first time I met them very well," Linda said. "In all the stress of moving, I accidentally locked myself out, and our baby was inside. I was frantic, and then I saw Bob and Carolyn in their driveway. I introduced myself and told them what had happened. Bob said they couldn't stop to help me because they had to go someplace, but Carolyn said, 'Of course we'll help you.'"

The Gundersons realized that that was pretty much the way things would be. If Bob Durall had something he wanted to do or someplace to go, he couldn't be bothered with anyone else's problems. Carolyn always made an effort to help.

Linda noticed that it was Carolyn who mowed their lawn and took care of the children, while it had to be a special occasion for Bob to help. Once in a while, neighbors saw Bob in his yard while his children played outside, but if any other adult in their cul-de-sac came outside, he assumed that he no longer had to supervise and went in his house.

Carolyn had become very close to Bob's family, and she tried to keep her unhappiness from them. In a dozen years, she had become good friends with his sister, and she liked his mother, who was nearing 80. They shared traditions and celebrated holidays. Her mother-in-law always gave Carolyn scarlet geraniums for Mother's Day, planting them herself in a wine barrel near the front door. Sometimes the Jannusches came over while Bob's folks were visiting.

"Bob wasn't very nice to his parents," Gary Jannusch recalled. "They were great people—we really liked his dad—but he was just mean to them sometimes."

A Desperate Housewife

There came a time when Linda Gunderson wondered if her neighbors spent any time together. "When Carolyn came home from work," Linda said, "Bob left. And when he drove up, she would leave to go shopping or to ride her horse."

Denise Jannusch understood that. While Bob had never physically hurt Carolyn, he verbally abused her much of the time.

And he didn't make a secret of the possibility that he was seeing women outside the marriage. The Gundersons recalled a time when Bob was working at IPC. "He came driving up in a panic," John Gunderson said. "He said there was some crazy woman coming after him, and he had to get Carolyn and the kids out of the house."

While he did drive off with his family a few minutes later, the woman never showed up. A fellow worker at IPC verified that most people there were aware that Bob was seeing a woman he worked with. When he suddenly broke up with her, she suffered a nervous breakdown and ended up losing her job.

Bob left IPC. In the mid-nineties, he became the supervisor of the computer division of the King County Housing Authority, where he was responsible for all their information systems.

Thanks to a gift from his mother-in-law to both Carolyn and Bob, they belonged to a prestigious country club. It was Bob who took advantage of it. In photos, the couple still *looked* happy. But there was something in Carolyn's eyes that warred with her smile.

By the summer of 1998, they had been married for a dozen years. Their children were nine, seven, and four. They argued sometimes, but few residents on Hoquiam

Court realized the depth of the troubles in their marriage. All couples argue occasionally, and the Duralls weren't yelling and screaming at each other. Whatever their differences, they seemed quite civilized to one another, but they just didn't seem to be having much fun together.

The Duralls' marriage had long since fallen into a pattern that many wives are all too familiar with. Carolyn realized too late that to placate Bob she had given up little pieces of herself for years until she had virtually no power left. Their marriage was all about making Bob happy, a task that was daunting, if not impossible, to achieve.

Her close women friends, coworkers, and neighbors knew; they often talked about their relationships over coffee, and the women who went to neighborhood barbecues or office parties noticed that Carolyn was edgy when the time came for her to go home. Bob rarely validated her as a wife or as a person. He didn't trust her to handle money, even though they both contributed their salaries to the family income. Carolyn had to account for every penny, and Bob wanted to see all the receipts. His allowance was $200 a month; hers was $150 and out of it she had to pay the children's expenses. During her work hours, Carolyn was responsible for huge sums of money belonging to strangers, but her own husband didn't think she was capable of figuring out her grocery budget.

It was a relief for her when Bob went away on business trips. Only then could Carolyn feel comfortable in her own home. Bob wasn't there to dart looks of disapproval at her. She could laugh as loud as she wanted, wear casual clothes, and let the kids mess up the house a little.

"She told me that she dreaded going home after

work," Denise Jannusch recalled. "She didn't want to have to deal with Bob." Carolyn had dreams. She thought about being a writer; she had even written several short stories that were quite good, but somehow she couldn't write with Bob around.

Oddly, while it appeared that Bob was the one involved with other women, he was very jealous of Carolyn and constantly suspected her of cheating on him. For more than a decade of their rigidly controlled marriage, she had never looked at another man. Then in 1997, she met a man who was exceptionally kind to her and made her feel like an intelligent and valuable person. She'd spent time with him, a man who really liked her. Starved for love, she was an accident or, rather, an affair, waiting to happen. When she began having lunch with the other man, they could have become very deeply involved. Whether she physically consummated her friendship with him no one knows, but it made her realize that in her mid-thirties her life shouldn't be about bending to Bob's will. The other man had given her a glimpse of what life could be like without the suffocating black cloud that hovered over her constantly. She wanted that feeling again, but she didn't want to have to sneak around; that was against her conscience. She hoped to find love before it was too late, but Carolyn wasn't the sort of person who could commit to an extramarital affair, so she broke it off.

The timing was on schedule. Women who are unhappily married reach thirty-seven to thirty-nine and see forty looming. It's a milestone in aging that makes a lot of people feel as if the door to youth is shutting. All of the euphemisms about "forty is the new thirty" seem hollow when most models and movie stars are only twenty years old, and movies and ads are clearly aimed at the young.

None of the counseling Carolyn and Bob tried had helped their marriage. Instead, she realized, their counseling sessions just gave Bob a chance to point out what was wrong with her. Carolyn bought a book called *Too Good to Leave, Too Bad to Stay: A Step-by-Step Guide to Help You Decide Whether to Stay In or Get Out of Your Relationship* by a therapist, Mira Kirshenbaum. She read and reread it. When she showed it to Denise Jannusch, her friend noticed that Carolyn had underlined many sections of the book. She said it was helping her gain the courage to leave Bob. (She was not alone; one online bookseller had 143 positive reviews of Kirshenbaum's books from women who were apparently facing similar dilemmas.)

By 1998, Carolyn had finally made up her mind to divorce Bob, raise her children on her own, and hope to have a chance at happiness. She had thought of it for a very long time; now she was determined.

"She called herself a 'wimp,'" Denise Jannusch recalled. "She always used to say, 'I'm just so wimpy; I can't do it.' But then she built herself up and began to think that maybe she could."

Carolyn longed for freedom. And so did Bob. She sensed that and often wondered why he stayed. He resisted any conversation that might conceivably lead to a discussion of their problems. To her, the answer seemed plain. If he was as miserable as she was, why didn't he just face up to a mutual decision to split up? Money, probably. They had a nice house, and he didn't want to risk losing his share of the equity. Moreover, they had invested almost all their savings—$90,000—in some acreage near their home.

Most of all there were the children. Carolyn believed Bob loved their children, even if he no longer loved her. And one thing she was adamant about; she would ask for custody of their children.

They couldn't go on the way they had been. Carolyn cautiously began to hope that she could convince Bob that they should divorce. If they couldn't get it together after twelve years, they weren't likely to miraculously mend their marriage.

Bob was still handsome and trim, although he had gone bald before he was 40. His chestnut hair was now only a fringe. After being bald for a year or so, his vanity couldn't stand it, so he bought an expensive toupee that looked quite natural. Most of their new neighbors didn't even know he wore one.

It wasn't the way Bob looked, Carolyn explained to her friends. He was still an attractive man, but he was just too damned intractable. It was his way or the highway. Carolyn talked to her friends about her renewed hopes. She was only 36, she had a good job, and she longed for a world where she didn't have to tiptoe around her own home. Bob had taken over paying the bills six months earlier so he even had domain over their checkbook.

The marriage was dead. She just wanted to be herself again.

Carolyn's decision was reinforced one night after she went to a restaurant—Cucina Cucina—and a movie with her mother and Denise after work. Bob knew where she was, and he grudgingly agreed to stay with their children, but when she got home, she found he had locked her out. He didn't answer the door when she pounded on it and called out to him. Embarrassed, she had to go to the Gundersons next door to get the key they kept in case of emergency.

During the early summer of 1998, Carolyn Durall somehow found the confidence she'd lost so many years earlier. She bought some new clothes, had her hair cut and bleached a lighter blond, tried new makeup, and laughed more often. She opened a small bank account in her name only with a $400 gift certificate given to her by her bosses at Morgan Stanley. She added to it when she could; her goal was to have enough money to pay the first and last months' rent and the damage deposit on an apartment. There wasn't much in her account, only about a thousand dollars, but it was one of the very first independent things she had done in more than a decade.

Carolyn was on edge by the end of July 1998. Besides the bank record of her secret account, she kept anything remotely personal and private at her office. Bob was driving her crazy, virtually stalking her. If she went out for lunch or pizza with her women friends, he would suddenly show up unannounced. "He seemed to know her every move," one of her coworkers said. "How awful to have to live like that."

Bob tried to get home before Carolyn did so he could note the time of her arrival. If she got home first and he saw her van there, he would take off his shoes and socks and tiptoe barefoot into the house to see if he could catch her with a lover. When she talked to friends on the phone, both parties could hear a click that signified someone had picked up an extension. Bob made sure to pick up the mail before Carolyn did, and he went through it carefully. He listened to all their voice mail messages and monitored her Internet access. He was expert at that but found nothing.

Carolyn didn't have a lover or one in the wings. But she had made up her mind to be happy, which meant that one day she *would* find someone she could love. She hoped that she could keep in touch with Bob's family. His father had died shortly before, but she would miss his mother and her sister-in-law. They had been good to her, and she knew they would be shocked and saddened at the divorce. This year's red geraniums were flourishing near Carolyn's front porch.

Carolyn wrote down her financial status and studied it to see if she could manage on child support and her share of the family assets. She had made initial visits to two lawyers.

"She was getting herself very well prepared for this," Denise remembered. "She was ready to leave."

Although Bob Durall had never harmed Carolyn physically, her situation frightened her friends. Denise and Gary Jannusch owned a rental house, and their renters were moving out in mid-August 1998. It seemed providential. They were happy to rent it to Carolyn and her children. In late July and early August, the children stayed with her parents at their summer retreat on the island, going to camp during the day. If there should be an argument when Carolyn and Bob parted, the kids wouldn't have to witness it.

The only thing that troubled Denise was that she and her family were going to be in Lake Chelan for the week of August 3 to August 8. It was about a three-and-a-half-hour drive from Renton, and they would be far away on Thursday, August 6, when, as Denise knew, Carolyn planned to ask Bob for a divorce.

Although he had to know his marriage was moribund, Bob Durall's friends and coworkers saw no sign of stress in him. He had always had unexplained absences from work, but since he was a supervisor he didn't have to explain where he was. Of course, his job demanded that he be extremely proficient with computers, and he had access to the most complex and up-to-date ones available at the King County Housing Authority. He had an office with a door he could shut, and those who worked for him were used to finding him hunched over in front of a screen, tracking information vital to the department's records. He was the one who checked on other employees at the Housing Authority to be sure their computer skills were up to par and that they were performing well. He made sure that no one spent too much time on their personal interests on the department's computers.

But there was nobody who checked Bob Durall's computer.

On Thursday, August 6, 1998, Carolyn's friends at work could tell that she was distracted and a little depressed. She finally confided in several friends and told them what Denise already knew. She had made a decision: she was definitely going to ask Bob for a divorce that evening. She wasn't sure how he would respond, but she would never expose their children to an emotional scene. At the very least, there was bound to be an argument. This was the best time to do it.

"I'm going to tell him tonight," she told several coworkers who were her closest friends.

"Oh, Carolyn," one of the women cried, alarmed. "No! You mustn't be alone when you tell him. We'll all go out to dinner with you. You can tell him, but at least we'll be close by."

She shook her head. "Don't be silly," she said. "I can handle it." She said that her neighbors weren't that far away and, besides, Bob wasn't physically violent. He was suspicious and jealous—even obsessive about some things—and he always had to have his own way, but she didn't fear him. "He'd never hurt me," she said firmly. "He may cry, but I know he wouldn't hurt me."

Besides, it wouldn't be fair to him to have an audience when she broke the news to him. Divorce wasn't a spectator sport.

As Carolyn left her office that night, she was wearing a periwinkle-blue silk pants suit.

"She walked past my desk," one woman recalled, "smiling her beautiful smile. She said to me, 'Wish me luck. Tonight's the night.' I told her I would keep her in my prayers, and then I said good-bye to her. It was the last time I ever saw her . . ."

When several of her friends asked her to reconsider facing Bob alone, Carolyn turned back to them, trying to reassure them. "I'll be okay," she said. "I'll see you tomorrow."

Before she reached the parking lot and her 1990 maroon Ford Aerostar van, she turned around a second time and went back to calm her coworkers' fears. They will never forget what she said.

"If I'm not here tomorrow morning," Carolyn said

quietly, "just remember that my whole life is in my desk."

Her van was barely out of the parking lot when the phone rang. It was Denise, calling from Lake Chelan. She had been worried about Carolyn all week. "When I talked to her on Monday," Denise said, "I said, 'Keep your chin up and you can do it. You'll be fine, and it's going to work out okay.' It was a good conversation. She told me twice, 'Have a good vacation.'

"It was seven minutes after three when I called the office on Thursday afternoon, and Kim Arriza answered. She said Carolyn had just left, that she was very nervous and worried."

Kim told Denise that Carolyn intended to go ahead with her plan that night and was going to talk to Bob Durall as soon as she got home. Again, Denise felt that she should be there, close enough for Carolyn to come to the Jannusches' after she told Bob.

"We had given her our security code, though," Denise said, "so she could go to our house if she needed to.

"But Thursday night I had a bad dream about Carolyn, and I woke up needing to talk to her. It was a nightmare full of blood and she was in danger."

Carolyn was never late to work, *never.* She was due at Morgan Stanley Dean Witter at 8:30 Friday morning, August 7. After a mostly sleepless night, Denise called at 8:37 to talk to Carolyn, but she wasn't in the office yet. "I thought, 'No big deal,'" Denise remembered. "Maybe it was a tough night, and I thought I would call back later—but I did leave a voice mail asking Carolyn to call me just as soon as she got to work."

Denise's cell phone rang at nine. With a sigh of relief, she answered, but it wasn't Carolyn; it was the office calling to ask if she had heard from Carolyn. For the first time in anyone's memory, Carolyn was half an hour late. With anyone else, it might have been different. But not Carolyn.

Denise asked one of the male brokers to check across the street from their office where Carolyn's parents kept a small condo to stay in when they were in the Seattle area. "See if her van is there, would you?"

He came back on the line. "No van."

Kim Arriza, who had said good-bye to Carolyn the previous afternoon, lived just up the street from the Duralls. She worked a later shift, so the increasingly worried staff at Morgan Stanley called her and asked her if she'd drive down to Hoquiam Court to see if she could spot the van.

When Kim turned into the Duralls' driveway, she saw that Bob's 1997 green Nissan Pathfinder was there, backed up to the garage. There was no sign of Carolyn's van. Bob came around the house, and Kim noted that he was sweating profusely. He seemed surprised to see her. When she asked him where Carolyn was, he answered, "She left for work."

But Carolyn hadn't come to work at all that morning. Her friends and her supervisors were now worried in earnest. When they called her home, the phone rang and rang until voice mail with a standard message picked up.

They called Carolyn's next-door neighbor, Linda Gunderson, and asked her to check to see if Carolyn's car was in the driveway.

"Her car's gone," Linda said, "and so is Bob's. It looks as if there's nobody home."

Now Linda Gunderson felt a sense of urgency. She hadn't seen any activity around the house next door that morning, and as far as she knew, they weren't planning to leave a day early to go to Carolyn's parents' island cabin. After she knocked on the door and received no response, she glanced up at the master bedroom's window. It was shut. She felt a pang of fear. Bob and Carolyn always left that window open, even when they were away. It kept the house from getting stuffy, and it was too high for a burglar to reach unless he scaled the roof.

The whole house was locked up tight. It seemed to be zipped up completely and lifeless.

Carolyn's coworkers and Linda Gunderson gave up any pretense that everything was all right. They called the Renton Police Department and asked if a patrolman could go to Hoquiam Court and check on the Durall house.

An officer was dispatched to the pale green house shortly after ten to do a "check on the welfare of Carolyn Durall." No one answered his pounding on the door, either, but that didn't seem unusual to him on a Friday in summer. He noted there were no cars in the driveway and figured that the family who lived there had probably just decided to leave early for the weekend.

Their worries hardly eased, Carolyn's coworkers attempted to report her as a missing person, but the Renton officer explained that such a report had to come from someone in her family. Undeterred, they then called Carolyn's parents on the island. They hadn't heard from Carolyn, either. The island was accessible only by ferry, and on a summer weekend, there were long lines at either end. They all hoped that Carolyn was waiting in one of those lines.

Carolyn's parents were very concerned, too. It wasn't like her to be out of touch with them when her children were staying with them.

Some people go missing for a week or so and nobody thinks much about it. But Carolyn's friends at Morgan Stanley knew what her plans for the night before had been and that she had fully intended to be at work this morning. As Friday crawled by, they grew increasingly worried.

Bob Durall didn't go to work at the Seattle Housing Authority on Friday morning, but he wasn't expected; he was scheduled to attend a class in Fife, a small town near Tacoma. His coworkers, alerted by Carolyn's office, tried to call him there. They learned that he had called in to say he would be an hour late.

Denise Jannusch, still at Lake Chelan, learned that as she called everyone she could think of. Bob wasn't at home, and he wasn't at his office or the computer class. He finally answered the phone at his house in the early afternoon.

"Bob," she asked, "where's Carolyn? What is going on?"

He answered a little vaguely, saying she had gone to work.

"She never showed up at work."

Then Denise asked Bob if he and Carolyn had had a fight the night before.

"Yeah," he said curtly. "What do you know about that? I hear she told people she was going to have a serious conversation with me. What do you know about that?"

Denise backed off. "I don't really know. Have you checked her horse's stall? Maybe she just totally lost it,

ANN RULE

and she went—like maybe she's sitting in the corner of Drizzle's stall."

Bob Durall didn't appear to be worried about Carolyn, even when he heard she hadn't gone to work. Denise could hear no emotion in his voice, but that was like him. She asked him to run upstairs and check to see if Carolyn's makeup, her shampoo, the solution for her contact lenses, and the special gel she always used on her hair were there. He put down the phone for a few minutes then came back on the line. "Yeah, it's all there."

"Okay," she said firmly, "I want you to go and check the stall and see if she's there. Call me back at three."

He did call her back then, but he hadn't found Carolyn, and he had heard no news at all about her. No one had seen her. Still, he sounded calm, as if there was nothing to worry about.

By now, Bob's work associates had heard that his wife was missing, and they had also learned that he had called the class he was supposed to attend and said he wouldn't be able to be there at all. No one knew where he had been all day Friday.

Denise called Bob back at six. He said he still hadn't heard from Carolyn.

"Bob," she said, "you should call the police and find out what you should do. Just call the Renton Police Department and tell them your wife is missing and give them the information they ask for. Just report it, and ask them how long it takes before you can officially file a missing report."

"Okay," he said in a calm voice. "I'll do that."

• • •

Even if a husband or other close relative calls the police, the fact is that most departments don't take missing reports on adults—other than those with handicaps or mental disorders—until the person has been missing twenty-four to forty-eight hours. The vast majority of adults return to their homes safely within that time period, having left for reasons of their own. When there is evidence of foul play, of course, the rules change.

But there were no overt signs that something bad had happened to Carolyn Durall. Her husband certainly didn't seem concerned when he called the Renton Police Department to report her missing.

He had seen her early Friday morning, he said, as they were both preparing to leave for work, but she hadn't come home Friday evening.

"When did you see her last?" Detective Gary Kittleson asked.

Bob Durall spoke slowly, as if he was trying to remember helpful details. He said that he had awakened at about 5:45 Friday morning and that he had driven Carolyn's van down to the shores of Lake Washington, where he went jogging in Gene Coulon Park. After he returned home, he was taking a shower when he heard her call out that she was going downstairs.

". . . So she was headed down the stairs from our bedroom, and I assumed she was leaving for work," he said. "I didn't know until late afternoon that she didn't show up at Morgan Stanley."

The detective noted that Durall seemed very calm, very different from the panicky feelings of his wife's friends.

Bob Durall said there might be a number of reasonable

explanations for his wife's sudden disappearance, although he wasn't specific on this Friday night. "I have no idea why she would leave or where she might have gone."

The Renton police did send out a statewide computer request asking for "an attempt to locate" both Carolyn and her wine-colored van.

When her family compared notes, they realized that the last one to speak directly to Carolyn was probably her brother's wife, who called her about 8:30 Thursday night. Bob had answered on the fourth ring, sounding "very subdued."

"He didn't sound like himself," she recalled. "He sounded disturbed, and I asked him, 'What's wrong? You sound sad.' He said he was fine but 'really tired.'"

When she asked to speak to Carolyn, Bob said he thought she was probably asleep. She asked him to check. After a long wait, Carolyn came on the line, but she sounded odd, almost as if she "was talking in extreme slow motion."

"I said, 'What's up?'"

Maybe she was only sleepy, but her words were very deliberate, and she said that Bob had just mixed her a margarita. Although Carolyn rarely drank, a margarita was her preferred cocktail. However, as far as her sister-in-law knew, Bob had *never* mixed a drink for Carolyn. He disapproved of her drinking *any* alcohol and usually forbade her to drink except to grudgingly allow her to have an occasional drink at a family gathering. He himself drank only beer and that just a few times a year. It was hard to believe that Bob had actually mixed a drink for Carolyn.

Worried because Carolyn was speaking so slowly, her

sister-in-law asked her if she was okay. "She just said again that Bob had made her a margarita. She sounded happy enough but very unlike her usual self."

Asked if she had told Bob about her decision to separate from him, Carolyn said that she couldn't talk but promised to call her back the next morning.

Gary and Denise Jannusch packed up their children and their possessions and left Lake Chelan early Saturday morning, even though they weren't due back until Monday. As soon as they got to Renton, they drove to the Durall house, hoping that Carolyn would answer the door. But she didn't. They walked around the house and peered into the garage but saw nothing out of the ordinary. Both of the family cars were gone. They learned that Bob had left to catch a ferry to his in-laws' island home to spend the weekend with his children.

That seemed odd: how could he leave when his wife was missing? It seemed that the people who should be the most concerned about Carolyn weren't even looking for her. Bob certainly wasn't, and the police had said they could do nothing until Monday. From the very beginning it was Carolyn's coworkers and neighbors who looked for her.

The Jannusches drove to the property Bob and Carolyn had bought off I-90, planning to eventually build a house. They walked the property, not really sure what they might find. "We didn't really see anything," Denise recalled, "except for a wide trail where we could see a car had gone up in it and kind of turned around. We saw a tree where bark had been torn off, and it was fresh, white underneath the bark. And we saw what looked like fresh tire tracks on the property. We tried not to disturb anything, but we took note of it."

As far as they recalled, the tread on Denise's van tires were in a straight line and the tires that left marks in the mud were "windey." But how many people really look at their own tire patterns, much less someone else's?

For the whole weekend, Carolyn's friends and coworkers searched for some sign of her or her van. They found nothing.

Spending the weekend with his in-laws, Bob Durall received a call late Sunday night from the Washington State Patrol. The King County Police had located Carolyn's Ford van parked alongside the road between Renton and Issaquah (a small town further east, toward the mountain foothills). The van was only about two miles from the Duralls' house. To his host's consternation, Bob said he would wait until Monday to return to Seattle to check on it. By that time, he couldn't find it, he told her friends, suggesting that Carolyn had driven it someplace else.

As soon as they got word on Monday morning that her vehicle had been sighted, four of Carolyn's coworkers went out to look for it, driving slowly along the route where Bob said it was parked. If the van was ever there, it was gone. They called the State Patrol offices, giving them a description of Carolyn's van and the license number.

The patrol's radio operator confirmed that it had been seen again. "A citizen reported seeing it this morning at 4:55 AM on the freeway, headed toward Burien. The car was being driven erratically, weaving in and out of traffic lanes."

Burien is more than twenty miles southeast of where Carolyn's van had been parked on Sunday night in the Licorice Fern area. Burien is close to Sea-Tac airport. Her friends were relieved at the thought that she had been seen only about five hours earlier. But that hope was dashed when the driver was described as "dark-haired, slight build." Carolyn was a blonde. It might have been her van, but it didn't sound as though she had been driving it early that Monday morning.

It was Monday, August 10, and Carolyn hadn't been seen since the previous Thursday at three PM. She hadn't talked to anyone since six hours after that. Back in the Morgan Stanley Dean Witter offices, her coworkers did what she had asked of them. They weren't intruding on her privacy; they were carrying out her wishes. She had told them what they should do if she disappeared, "If I don't come back . . . my whole life is in my desk."

Still, they felt uneasy about looking through the drawers of her desk. Taking a deep breath, they went ahead, hoping there might be an address or a phone number—something—that would help them find her. They discovered that Carolyn's whole life was indeed in her desk, including her private financial records and her poignant writings about her failed marriage. They found a copy of a letter she had either sent to Bob or planned to send or give to him, perhaps on Thursday night.

"Our marriage was a mistake from the beginning," Carolyn had written. "I love you too little, and you love me too much."

Carolyn said that for years she had been "unhappy, guilt-ridden and humiliated. I am dying inside. There is so little left of who I used to be. My spirit is crushed. I feel that you are too controlling and obsessive and jealous."

There were numerous notes and a journal that told the same story, written by a woman who was being emotionally suffocated.

Carolyn had left the PIN for her private bank account in her desk, too. The balance was something over nine hundred dollars. A call to her bank showed that nothing had been withdrawn recently. If Carolyn had left of her own accord, surely she would have needed money to live on. She had noted that she had no independent access to the couple's credit cards or to Bob's bank account.

Carolyn's friends called the Renton police again to beg for an all-out search for her. Now she was officially a missing person but not classified as a possible homicide victim, something her friends feared she might be.

Only if her disappearance were reclassified as an urgent matter could the police call out Explorer Search and Rescue Scouts and their reserve officers.

On Monday night Bob Durall called Gary Jannusch and asked to meet with him at a local pizza parlor. Gary agreed, and the two men drove to Gene Coulon Park, where they sat and talked. Gary noticed that Bob's conversation wasn't about how worried he was about Carolyn; instead, his remarks were more derogatory toward her. At one point, Bob said, "Do you know that she *smokes?*" in a tone that suggested she was a scarlet woman. He stressed that Carolyn "yelled at the kids, too." It was as if he was building a case for himself as the injured party in their marriage.

Bob asked if he could move in with the Jannusches

"temporarily," but Gary said they really weren't set up to have a guest. If Bob Durall had done anything Monday, it was all about himself. He went to work for a while. He mentioned that he had seen a doctor earlier because he had injured himself lifting one of his sons into a swing. "I've got a torn biceps," he said, "and I'll need surgery."

A torn biceps muscle is a severe injury, one that would require delicate surgery to reattach the ends of the muscle so the arm wouldn't atrophy. It seemed unlikely that lifting one small boy into a swing would do so much damage, especially to a man who took pride in keeping in shape.

Bob also dropped into Morgan Stanley and spoke with a few of Carolyn's coworkers, women who weren't as close to her as Denise, Maria Benson and Tari Scheffer. Again, he spoke negatively about his missing wife. The women were both surprised and distressed.

It was Tuesday, August 11, when Detective Gary Kittleson met Bob Durall for the first time. Kittleson now knew about the information Carolyn had left in her desk and that she had planned to ask for a divorce the night she disappeared.

As he faced Durall, he found a man who was remarkably calm considering that his wife and the mother of his three children had been missing for five days. In fact, he wanted to tell Kittleson how disappointed he had become in his wife's behavior. He said he had "confronted" her about his suspicions that she was unfaithful in 1997. In his version, she confessed that she met men in a chat room on America Online and rendezvoused with many of them. Bob Durall was convinced she had had at least one affair with some man she met online.

In early 1998, Durall said, he found that Carolyn continued to communicate with men in chat rooms, and he became even more suspicious about her fidelity. He found women's underwear that he didn't recognize in their clothes hamper. He thought he detected semen on the garment.

"I thought she was having another affair," he said, "but I didn't confront her about it."

That didn't appear to upset him very much, either. Apparently he had dealt with it, and the marriage was intact.

When he was asked about the previous Thursday night, Durall said that he had taken Carolyn out to dinner and that nothing untoward had happened. "It was just a normal night."

He certainly had no hint that she planned to leave him or was about to run off with someone else.

"Which vehicle did you take to the restaurant?" Kittleson asked.

"Her van, the Aerostar."

"And you got home at what time?"

"About 8:40."

Carolyn's van had been spotted being driven erratically between Renton and Burien at about six on Monday morning. As Kittleson interviewed Bob Durall the next day, it was still missing. Noting that Durall was quite slender and had dark hair, he wondered if he was the one driving his missing wife's van.

Linda Gunderson, watching the Durall house, had

seen Bob drive up in his Nissan Pathfinder about 7:30 on Monday morning.

Witnesses living in the Licorice Fern neighborhood said that they first noticed Carolyn's van there sometime Thursday evening and that it remained there through Sunday. Who left it there and who moved it was anyone's guess. Perhaps Bob had left it there. He was an experienced jogger and could easily have run the two miles to his house. Or he could have run from his house to the van on Monday morning and driven it toward Burien, then gotten back to his Nissan Pathfinder, possibly by taxi.

Or if Carolyn herself had left her van two miles from home, maybe someone had picked her up and driven her away.

It was very confusing, particularly when a clerk at a minimart and gas station in Bellevue was sure that she had seen Carolyn alive and well there on Saturday, August 8. After she saw Carolyn's photograph on one of the hundreds of fliers her friends distributed, the clerk said she remembered her as the pretty blonde who had smiled at her.

Had she seen Carolyn Durall or another blonde woman? If she had indeed seen Carolyn, was it on August 8—or on August 1, the Saturday before?

Memory is not infallible, and it can be influenced by many factors.

When Gary Kittleson talked with Bob Durall on August 11, Bob never mentioned that he had been notified that Carolyn's van was found two miles from their home—or anywhere. Kittleson didn't say anything about that, but he did ask Bob where he thought it might be. He speculated that it could be parked somewhere near Sea-Tac airport.

Two days later, on August 13, Kittleson called Bob Durall and asked him if the two of them could check his residence to determine if Carolyn had taken any extra clothing with her when she left. Durall said he would call back later in the day.

Then Bob Durall, aware that he might be placed in the category of suspect because he was the closest person to his missing wife, decided to hire an attorney to represent him. When detectives asked to do a "walk-through" of his house, his antennae went up. He didn't like the idea of strangers swarming all over his home. He hired one of the most successful criminal defense attorneys in Seattle, John Henry Browne. The flamboyant, six-foot four-inch Browne had long flowing brown hair and a luxuriant mustache, and he rode motorcycles. Looking more like a renegade biker than an officer of the Court, he was in great demand. He often seemed to be the patron saint of lost causes, taking on the most difficult defense cases. More than twenty years earlier, it was Browne, then a public defender, who counseled Ted Bundy after his first arrest in Utah and during Bundy's trial in Miami.

Now Browne told the media that subjecting a worried husband to a search of his house would only add to his stress. There was no indication that Carolyn had met with foul play. In fact, Browne said, his client had reliable witnesses who reported seeing her alive and well on Saturday, August 8, and again on August 10, after she had supposedly vanished. He was speaking of the convenience-store clerk and the woman who saw the swerving van in the wee hours of Monday morning.

• • •

While Bob Durall continued to suggest that Carolyn had simply chosen to leave him and their children, no one who knew her well could accept that. She was much too loving a mother to do that. She just wasn't the kind of woman who would walk away from her responsibilities no matter how unhappy she was at being trapped in a cage-like marriage.

Carolyn's friends could not wait around for some word of her. They made hundreds of phone calls and continued to pass out fliers with her picture on them asking for information.

They organized search parties. Drawing a grid map with the Duralls' house in the center of a circle, they began a methodical search for Carolyn and her van. Sea-Tac Airport is a fifteen-minute drive southwest, and Bellevue approximately the same distance to the north. Within twenty miles they would come to the foothills of Snoqualmie Pass, where thousands of acres of national forest land, thick with fir trees, crept up to the I-90 freeway.

The volunteer search party began by driving slowly through the scores of parking lots outside hotels and motels, restaurants, and the airport. Carolyn's van was big and blocky, and its wine color would make it stand out even if it was hidden in the woods.

They looked in back of buildings and in private driveways. They found some similar Ford vans, but none was Carolyn Durall's.

On Wednesday, August 19, almost two weeks after Carolyn Durall was last seen, a party of volunteers searching for her turned into the parking lot of the Radisson Hotel at the corner of Pacific Highway, and South

170th. The hotel had parking on all four sides of the sprawling grounds. As they drove slowly around the hotel, they checked the scores of vehicles parked there, not really expecting their search to be any more successful than the previous sweeps of parking area. But this time, they spotted Carolyn's van.

It was parked next to the laundry area in the back of the hotel, just east of the north runways of the airport and the frontage road. The wine-colored van had plates whose number they had long since memorized: 166 CWI. It had obviously been there a long time: its windshield and roof were covered with leaves and twigs.

Their hearts in their throats, they peered into the van through its dusty windows. It looked normal enough, and there were no signs that anything violent had taken place there. They hoped fervently that Carolyn had taken the hotel van to the airport a quarter mile down the road and flown off to some tropical paradise but they knew that she probably hadn't. The only thing unusual they could see in her van were some bags of clothes marked for the Salvation Army.

They showed Carolyn's photo to the desk clerks, but no one recognized her. They notified the Renton police investigators, who had the van placed on a flatbed and taken to their headquarters to be processed. Later, detectives asked to check the registration log from August 6 to the present. Unless she registered under an alias, Carolyn had not stayed there.

Denise Jannusch wasn't surprised when she heard where Carolyn's van had been found. "The Radisson lot is where she and Bob used to park when they flew somewhere. It was cheaper than parking in the airport garage."

Carolyn hadn't used a credit card, made or received calls on her cell phone, accessed her bank account, bought a plane ticket on an airline flying out of Seattle, or contacted anyone who knew her.

She was simply gone.

That her husband didn't want them to look through the family home for any clues to her disappearance made the police look upon Bob Durall with unusual suspicion.

The consensus, as hard as it was to accept, was that Carolyn Durall was dead. On August 21, 1998, Gary Kittleson prepared an affidavit citing probable cause to obtain a search warrant for the green house on Hoquiam Court. Renton detectives, accompanied by criminalists from the Washington State Patrol crime lab, served the warrant and entered the last place Carolyn was seen alive.

John and Linda Gunderson stared at the CSI van from the Washington State Patrol as it turned into the Duralls' driveway. Linda had been distraught ever since Carolyn's disappearance, but as John admitted later, "Until I saw that CSI van, I didn't really believe that anything bad had happened to Carolyn; at that point, I had to wonder if Bob might really have done something to her."

With neighbors peering nervously through their blinds, the detectives and crime-scene specialists walked into the two-story home. It looked neat enough, although it had a stale smell of trapped air, a house left empty of its occupants for a long time. Bob Durall and his children had been living at his mother's house in Seattle while he waited for word of Carolyn.

They were armed with a search warrant signed by King County District Court Judge Robert McBeth that allowed them to search the Durall home, the Aerostar van, and the Nissan Pathfinder for cell phone records, weapons, trace evidence (which included blood, hair, fibers, latent prints, financial records, correspondence, diaries, journals, notes, calendars, computers and their electronic files, floppy discs, hard drives, etc., answering machines, and chemicals or appliances that might have been used to clean the vehicles or the residence). There were no signs of disarray in the downstairs portion of the house; the rooms looked as if someone had simply stepped away for a moment or gone to work, expecting to be home for supper.

They moved upstairs and into the master bedroom. It looked normal, too. But the carpeting under the bedside tables looked peculiar. The wall-to-wall carpet and the pad beneath had been cut out then patched with rectangles of the same color and weave. When they looked into the children's playroom, they saw that a piece of furniture was placed at an awkward angle. They lifted it and found bare subfloor; clearly, this was where the patches came from.

They returned to the master bedroom. Without speaking, they pulled up the patched section. Now they could see the reason for the repair job; the plywood subflooring was stained a dark mahogany, the color of dried blood. The crime lab technicians did a test on the spot and found the stain positive for human blood. Obviously, there had been so much blood that it soaked through the carpet and the pad and into the plywood beneath.

Next, they scanned the walls and saw almost invisible

spots and streaks. By spraying the walls and baseboards with a substance called Luminol, crime-scene investigators can bring out bloodstains. Reacting to the chemical, every drop, streak, or swipe of blood glows blue-green. Even when someone thinks he has scrubbed all vestiges of blood away, it isn't really gone. Luminol will detect a tiny scintilla of blood.

The investigators counted more than a hundred blood spatters. The stains were not in a spray pattern, which would have indicated the victim had been shot; it was medium-velocity blood that had probably flown out from someone's body or, more likely, head, after they had been struck by a heavy object. Tediously, they drew a circle in pencil around each drop that sprinkled the bedroom wall and attached a numbered sticker.

They found more stains and streaks of blood leading from the bedroom to the bathroom, mostly along the baseboards. Someone had been dragged from the bedroom to the bathroom. More blood streaks appeared when Luminol and special bright lights were used as the investigators worked from a doorway of the house into the garage.

Several sections of the Duralls' home were actually sawed away so that they could be used as physical evidence if a trial ever took place.

There was no bedding on the bed in the master bedroom. When Denise Jannusch and Linda Gunderson heard this, they had an eerie premonition. About a week before she disappeared, Carolyn had told them that she had purchased a lovely new matched set of linens: bedspread, pillow shams, and sheets. None of them were found in her house.

The blood in her home was Carolyn Durall's type and, if necessary, DNA testing could be done to absolutely ascertain that it had come from her. If she were still alive, which was increasingly unlikely, she had lost so much blood that she would have been critically injured when she was taken away. She would have needed to be in a hospital ER, so paramedics would have been called by anyone who cared about her. But there were no Jane Does in any area hospital or at the morgue in the Medical Examiner's Office.

After the lonely green house on Hoquiam Court had been searched, tested for physical evidence, and cleared for the family to take possession, several of Carolyn's friends moved slowly through it. What they had not wanted to accept, had fought to deny as impossible, was all too clear to them when they viewed the disfigured walls, the cut-up carpeting, the faint blood spots marked by stickers. They had seen crime scenes on television shows, but this was real. Carolyn had been here, but her spirit was gone from the house that she had tended so carefully. Seeing her makeup and hair-care products left behind in the master bathroom almost made the women cry. They knew she didn't need them any longer.

On August 22, 1998, Gary Kittleson went to Robert Durall's mother's home. There, he told Durall that he was under arrest. The suspect didn't seem to be upset or even surprised; he didn't even ask Kittleson what he was being arrested for. He was arraigned, pleaded not guilty, and was held without bail. He was charged with second-degree murder.

Durall, appearing for his arraignment in the orange coveralls of a high-risk prisoner and without his toupee, looked much diminished as he stood at the rail in the Regional Justice Center of King County. His mother did her best to rally their friends, his coworkers, and members of the church, where he had recently become an elder, to stand behind him and write letters attesting to his good reputation.

It was impossible not to feel sorry for this elderly woman whose life was nearly destroyed by her son's situation and who also grieved for the daughter-in-law she loved and for her three grandchildren who were being cared for by Carolyn's family. She could not even imagine that her boy could have done anything to hurt anyone.

The ripples that spread out from violent crime always wash over innocent people.

Durall wanted to get out of jail as soon as possible. Two King County deputy prosecutors, Patricia Eakes and Jeff Baird, asked that if bail were set for Bob Durall, it should be high.

"The State requests bail in the amount of $1 million. The defendant went to great lengths to conceal this crime. He has disposed of his wife's body and attempted to destroy the evidence that existed in the family home. For more than two weeks after his wife's disappearance, he continued to mislead people, including police, about her death. Given the nature of the crime, the potential for extended incarceration, and the defendant's actions, and the fact that his wife's body has not been recovered, he should be considered not only a danger to the community but a flight risk."

Durall's original attorneys, John Henry Browne and Tim Dole, asked that he be released on his own recognizance or on "reasonable bail" of $25,000, citing his three years in a supervisory position at the King County Housing Authority. They listed his more prestigious former jobs—Boeing (1987 to 1990), IPC Pension Services (1991 to 1995), and two short-term jobs at IBM, in 1983 and 1985—his loyalty to his mother and sister, and his three small children who were "dependent upon him for emotional and financial support." They quoted letters from his fellow church members who described him as "gentle, loving spiritual, full of honesty and integrity" and pointed out that if he were planning to flee Seattle, he would surely have done so before he was arrested.

None of their arguments did any good; bail was set at $1 million.

Bob Durall refused to discuss where his wife might be, claiming that he did not know. Her family and the more than a hundred people who had looked for her or her car kept up their search, determined that they would find Carolyn. If she was dead, she deserved to have a funeral or a memorial service and a decent burial. If she was miraculously alive somewhere, she needed to be found.

Bob Durall, the complete expert on computers, should have known that nothing is ever truly deleted from a hard drive. The bytes laid down might not surface in the same pattern that they had been typed in, but they are there, someplace. Perhaps he was confident that no one would have reason to check his computer.

He may not have been aware of it, but his supervisors had noticed that he spent an inordinate amount of time on his computer. Indeed, he had come close to being fired after people walked in on him and noticed that he wasn't doing agency business on it.

Durall's coworkers were not close to him, and most of their contact outside the office had been to play on company sports teams or to attend events he had at his house. He was involved in a multilevel marketing firm whose participants moved up the ladder by recruiting new members and also a long-distance phone plan that worked much the same way. For those who worked under him at the King County Housing Authority, it was a kind of command performance to show up for his demonstrations. Sometimes at the beginning of the football season, he would host a party for the guys to select players for their fantasy football teams. Hardly big-time gambling, it was more for fun; they bet small amounts on the players and teams they chose and settled up at the end of the season.

Female employees of the King County Housing Authority had often complained that they felt uncomfortable around Bob Durall. They found him too flirtatious. It wasn't that he touched them inappropriately, but his manner didn't mesh with what a husband and father, a church deacon and elder, and a Sunday school teacher should be. All in all, both female and male employees found him a bit of an odd duck.

None of the men were beer-drinking buddies or confidants of Durall's, but they did feel sorry for him when they learned of the sudden disappearance of his wife. In the weeks after Carolyn vanished, it was understandable that Bob hadn't been at work much. He called occasionally to question other employees about whether the police had shown up at his office. When she had been gone a week, he called employees into his office and asked them what they had heard from Carolyn's firm about the situation.

He seemed to be concerned that the police were tracking him, but he had little to say about Carolyn when his coworkers asked if she had been found yet. He usually frowned and said no, curtly. He explained that he had hurt his arm lifting his daughter into a swing and was having surgery on the torn biceps the next day, Friday. But he called again on that day, and it was obvious he hadn't had the surgery yet. He told police he injured himself lifting his son.

Bob Durall asked one man with whom he'd worked for several years what "bear tracks looked like." That came out of the blue. He hurried on to explain that he was an avid hunter and fisherman and had been to Tiger Mountain. It wasn't clear whether he was afraid that he might run into a man-eating bear or was just making conversation.

Durall didn't have the surgery to reattach his torn biceps on Friday, August 28. Instead, he was arrested and charged with second-degree murder. Now his coworkers were shocked.

Upper management at the Housing Authority asked a few of their sharpest computer experts to see if Bob Durall had left anything on his computer that might reveal his nonoffice activities over the past several months. The experts agreed to do that but didn't expect to find anything.

"He knew computers," one man said. "He knew that stuff remained on the hard drive even after it had been deleted. But he also would have known that all he had to do would be to put a new hard drive into his computer. It was a matter of loosening two or three screws. Switching hard drives would give him a clean slate, and anything he didn't want people to see would be gone when he junked the old hard drive."

Computer forensic investigations are a sign of the times; even a dozen years ago, it's unlikely that computer files were considered a fertile source to see what is truly going on in someone's life. Today, most of the civilized world understands how to send and receive email and how to use search engines to learn more about any number of things. After a visit to Google or Ask Jeeves, scores of sources flash across screens. It seems miraculous to anyone who remembers when keyboards were found only on standard typewriters.

In September 1998, one of the prime search engines was www.altavista.com. Bob Durall's coworkers used it to see if there was anything in his computer that might either help him or help the police investigators. Perhaps they might even find something that would lead them to Carolyn Durall.

The process is too complicated for me to explain or for most readers to follow. The information bubbled up in odd files and stray strings of text, and what surfaced was disconcerting to say the least.

Beginning on May 4, 1998, and continuing until June 23—more than seven weeks before Carolyn vanished— her husband appeared to have been looking for ways to kill her.

The Housing Authority pros found a search string that read "query?pg=q&stq=8o&what=web&kl=XXX&q=murder!"

As they clicked more links, they saw that most of Bob Durall's searches specified websites that had information on "kill + spouse." Then he narrowed the scope. He had gone to the internet for information on "smother," "homicide," "poisons," "accidental deaths," and just plain "murder."

It was a stunning discovery and hard for them to fathom. But Durall had clearly been studying various methods of homicide for months, and he had put the word "spouse" in the search slots. That left little doubt who the intended victim of a cleverly planned homicide was.

And now Bob Durall's wife was missing, his bedroom and hallways were full of blood, and he had been arrested for murder.

They looked for more clusters that were not work-related, wondering if their longtime boss had a secret life that involved more than they had located so far.

He had visited sites about Monica Lewinsky, prostitution, Venusians, photo sites with titles like "skin," and, surprisingly, a popular website that was the most up-to-date version of a lonely hearts column or dating service: Match.com.

Match.com is a perfectly legitimate way for singles to hook up with other singles who have similar interests. More active than ever today, Match.com claims that 200,000 people met "that special someone" through their service in 2004. Hundreds of couples go on to marriage. Of course, that doesn't mean that owners of the website or similar sites can guarantee that everyone who signs up and pays to post there is telling the truth. The website warns that online dating is no more or less safe than any other kind of dating and urges members to read their safety tips and to initially meet strangers in public places. Even so, it is easier when you are on the web to pretend to be something you are not. Even in a bar, women and men can see whom they are talking to. They can check for wedding rings or for the band of pale skin that shows that to appear single the person has recently removed a ring. Unless someone is really good at makeup and wardrobe, singles in a bar know whether they're communicating with a male or a female.

On Match.com, most of those looking for love or companionship have a handle or screen name, preferring not to have anyone who visits the site know who they really are.

Bob Durall's computer expert coworkers found emails from women to his computer address. They were written to someone called Freeedom. It wasn't a typographical error; Durall had deliberately added a third *e* to the word. They were all from correspondents who sounded intelligent and interesting, their grammar and spelling perfect.

One woman in Oregon wrote to Freeedom: "It's found within me first and foremost, but then if you and I 'connect' as we should, it will be found within our shared hearts as well. . . . I'm looking for (more) true opportunities for learning and personal growth, emotionally, spiritually and professionally. . . . I love to share strong, deep and true 'connections' with others. Good conversation, honest communication and being open to new ideas are all very important in my book. Playing games is not my deal, just want to be true to myself and to you."

This woman, a professional, wrote that she was beginning to correspond with a few other men. "But I also know full well that I am looking for someone extra special. Could you be him?"

Whatever Freeedom had written to this woman, she was apparently quick to trust him. She said she was "taking a chance" by giving him her real email address, since her subscription to Match.com was going to run out soon.

But did she *totally* trust him? Probably not. Her last email had a cheerful but veiled question in it.

"I look forward to hearing from you, Freeedom. (Does this handle mean you were married before and are feeling quite 'released' or what? <grin>)"

Clearly, she wanted to know if he was married.

The computer detectives kept going, finding more messages from single women directed to Freeedom, who seemed to have made quite an impression with his profile on Match.com.

Now, they looked for Freeedom himself, typing in anon. Freeedom. And there he was. They were even informed of how close he was to their location in the King County Housing Authority's offices: "Distance: 7 miles (11 km) from you based on registered location. This member's last activity on Match.com: August 5, 1998."

Only one day before Carolyn Durall had disappeared.

Freeedom's profile would indeed have been tempting to a middle-aged woman:

Romantic Spiritual Seeker, Lover of Life, and Dad
39-year-old male, located in Seattle, U.S.,
seeking 28 to 45 year-old female for email
pen-pal, activity partner, short-term relationship,
or long-term relationship.

Enjoying all the magical moments that life has to offer. I am confident, healthy, intelligent, attractive, a dreamer, love to laugh, kind, a romantic lover, and a moonlight walker. My focus is on nurturing my spirit by making great decisions. A common sense oriented man that someone can count on and a passion for life that enables me to enjoy the simplest of pleasures. A positive outlook on life has me smiling almost all the time and uplifting those around me. Always stretching my comfort zone to include new ideas and activities. Hiking, tennis, running, golf, basketball, and jet skiing are great fun. Professional with plenty of education (it's o.k. if you don't care). My preference is for a friend and partner who respects who she is and takes good care of herself spiritually, emotionally, and physically. Someone who can see the beauty even when it is not pretty every day. I have children and young ones at that. You must have an appreciation for children. If you have your own, then that is wonderful too.

 Ethnicity: Caucasian (White)
 Religion: Christian (Other than Catholic)
 Body Type: Athletic (Athletic/Slim)
 Smoking: Don't smoke
 Drinking: Drink socially/occasionally
 Children: Have children, living with me
  sometimes

His ad ended with only one proviso for women who might respond to him. They had to be nonsmokers.

There was no question that Freeedom was Bob Durall. He had not mentioned that he had a wife, only that he sometimes had his young children living with him. Perhaps he didn't expect to *have* a wife by the time he hooked up with just the right woman on the internet.

The Renton detectives hadn't asked that Bob Durall's computer be mined for evidence. The two men who held their breath as they scrolled through the internet sites and found *murder, murder, murder, murder, kill spouse* and all of the possible means of accomplishing that knew they had to tell the investigators what they had found. They printed out copies of all the web searches and Durall's handle on Match.com and gave them to the men and women who were investigating Carolyn Durall's disappearance.

When prosecutors Patty Eakes and Jeff Baird heard about Bob Durall's activities on the internet, particularly his searches for "kill + spouse," they knew that if Bob had killed Carolyn, it was not through a spontaneous act of rage, unplanned and perpetrated by a man gone suddenly out of control. No, from May 4 to June 23, he had been working on a plan to murder his wife.

On August 28, they amended the charges against him: he was now charged with first-degree murder, and his bail was raised to $5 million.

It was the first week in September, and Carolyn was still missing. Scores of people showed up for grid searches in an ever-widening circle around Renton. Jodie Kelly and Tari Sheffer planned the quadrants to be searched meticulously so that all sectors were covered and none gone over twice. They used a flag system to mark areas that had already been searched and a grid chart. They were headed away from Renton now, moving toward the foothills of Snoqualmie Pass.

Linda Gunderson and Denise Jannusch and their husbands still remember that terrible period from the night Carolyn disappeared to after Labor Day, 1998. Family life for all of the searchers virtually stopped. All that mattered was finding Carolyn or, as they now dreaded, her body. Most of their children were too young to understand the grim reality that overshadowed everyone's summer.

"We all lost months, years even," one friend said. "Our lives were totally caught up in the tragedy for such a long time."

The Renton detectives respected those who searched so diligently and realized that they might well be the ones to find Carolyn. After all, they had found her van, and they were even more determined now. "If you do," the investigators warned, "don't touch anything. Just call us."

The detectives learned more that added to their belief that Carolyn Durall was dead. They found that Bob had asked a dry cleaner how to remove bloodstains, saying, "My son had a nosebleed." Their sweep of the house had netted a gallon of solution designed to eliminate all traces of human fluids.

Bob was seen in a Fred Meyer store the day before Carolyn vanished. He was buying, of all things, several belts, men's belts. Why? That question was answered on September 9, after Carolyn had been missing for four weeks and five days. John Henry Browne talked with his client and impressed on Bob Durall that he should reveal where his wife's body was. It would be a kindness to her family and her friends, who needed to know where she was and to give her a decent burial. If Durall should agree to lead detectives to where he had left Carolyn, Browne, his associate, Tim Dole, and the prosecutors, Patty Eakes and Jeff Baird, had agreed to certain stipulations, if not an outright plea bargain: (1) he would receive some sentencing "consideration" after he pleaded guilty to first-degree murder; (2) the State would not reveal at trial that Durall had led investigators to Carolyn's body; (3) the State would not, however, reduce the charges to second-degree murder; and (4) if Bob Durall should take the stand in his own defense and deny that he had killed his wife, he would be impeached by the prosecution and the agreement not to mention that he had led the investigators to her body would be null and void.

He accepted that plea agreement. On that Monday in September, a caravan of cars followed the police unit in which Bob Durall rode with detectives and his lawyers. They took the I-90 freeway on its climb east through the foothills until they came to Forest Service Road 9031, ten miles west of the Snoqualmie Pass summit. There they turned down the heavily forested road, drove slowly for two miles, passing several turnouts (where people had illegally left bags of refuse). Finally, Durall told them to stop.

Carolyn was there, buried in a shallow grave beneath a pile of rocks. Using a litter connected to ropes, the search party carefully lifted her remains from the sylvan burial place.

Her body had been doubled over, cinched tight with several belts, and encased in a number of plastic garbage sacks.

The postmortem examination of Carolyn Durall's

body by the King County Medical Examiner's office verified that she had died of homicidal violence, blunt-force damage. Her skull had been shattered in several places by a heavy, dense object dropped on, or swung at, her head. It had to have been made of metal or hard wood. A fist or arm could not have done so much damage. More likely, the weapon was something like a baseball bat.

She was almost certainly unconscious immediately after the first blow. She might have continued to breathe for a short time. She had not suffered, very small comfort to those who loved Carolyn.

For all of Bob Durall's precise planning and internet searches on how to commit a perfect murder, it appeared that he had in fact flown into a violent rage, probably when Carolyn asked him for a divorce, and used the closest weapon at hand.

It was too late to determine whether Carolyn Durall had been drugged before she was attacked; there was little blood left in her body and she had lain in the woods for so many weeks. No poisons were identified in toxicology screens. The medical examiner was not surprised at those results because blood breaks down during decomposition.

There was no more searching. On September 16, a week later, a memorial service for Carolyn was held at Saint Thomas Episcopal Church in Medina, Washington, a church not far from Morgan Stanley Dean Witter where she had worked and where she had told friends of her dream to be free to live her life in peace. The theme of her services was a butterfly; she had always loved butterflies, and a picture of a beautiful Monarch was on the cover of the program. The minister reminded the mourners that Carolyn was no longer caged, but "as free now as a butterfly."

After the services, Morgan Stanley hosted a reception in honor of Carolyn. Her neighbors and friends held a final get-together in the Renton Highlands where she had once loved her home and doted on her children. They planted a flowering pink cherry tree in the park where the neighborhood kids played, they had a potluck dinner with dishes made from Carolyn's recipes, and, as the sun set, held a candlelit ceremony. They released white balloons, tying chocolates to the ribbons, Carolyn's favorite.

Her children's cat went to live with them at their grandparents house. Daisy, her parakeet, was adopted by the Jannusches. (Daisy lived until 2004.) Her friends cleaned her house and packed up her things. In a way it was over, but it was a long way from being truly over.

Robert Durall went through a succession of attorneys, most of them the very top criminal defense lawyers in Seattle. One of them declared him "the most difficult client I've ever had."

Durall wanted to run his own defense and to ignore any agreements previously made between his lawyers and the prosecutors. He intended to take the stand at his trial. He would not plead guilty to having anything whatsoever to do with Carolyn's murder. The public did not know yet that he was the person who led police to her body.

In jail he grew a beard, perhaps to make up for his jail-forbidden hairpiece. He had quite a few visitors, and his mother was often there to comfort and support him. She refused to believe that the son she cherished could have committed a crime like murder. At her urging, some of the men who had been neighbors or coworkers visited him out of friendship and the possibility that he had not been himself when he killed Carolyn. Some, however, frankly admitted that they went to the jail hoping he would say something that would help convict him.

He mentioned to one former associate that he had checked on his pension fund shortly after Carolyn vanished; he didn't want it to be claimed by anyone else if he was incarcerated. He expected to be acquitted or to receive a short sentence for something he "did not do," and he wanted to keep his investments and his pension fund protected.

When the news media publicized Bob Durall's arrest, a few women came forward to talk to detectives about their correspondence with him on Match.com. One said that she had begun writing to him in December 1997, some eight months before Carolyn's murder. They had met for lunch at a small restaurant a few blocks from the University of Washington. Theirs was not a romantic liaison, but Bob had been somewhat open with her about his feelings. He wasn't completely honest with her but did discuss the possibility of his "upcoming" divorce. He sounded very bitter about his wife and clearly had no love for her, but she noted tears in his eyes when he said he couldn't bear the thought of not seeing his children every day. As for his wife? "She would be better off dead," he had said bluntly.

On August 18, Bob's lunch date said, he wrote to her

about his situation. "I don't know how to say this," he wrote, "but Carolyn has vanished. I assume she's run off somewhere but no trace [so far]. I am worried and confused. Our family could use some prayers."

There were probably a number of women who did not come forward, women who held their collective breaths that they wouldn't be linked with Bob Durall in any way and that their correspondence and meetings with him would remain secret.

Durall and whichever attorney was representing him at any given time delayed his trial with a number of pretrial motions. Washington statutes grant defendants the right to a speedy trial, assuring them that their cases will be heard in court within sixty days. The accused, however, have the right to ask for more time. Durall exercised that right at least five times. And he would have five different attorneys who had to start from scratch in reviewing his case.

The defense team attempted to have the evidence seized at the Durall home excluded from his trial, claiming that the investigators had done a sloppy job of drawing up their search warrant.

Denied.

Bob Durall had other objections. He didn't want a corrections officer from the Regional Justice Center jail to testify about something he overheard Durall saying to himself: "Forgive me for what I have done."

He held that he had a right to pray without being overheard.

With his bail set high, Bob Durall remained incarcerated awaiting trial because of his own demands. It seemed further and further in the future. He made a close friend behind bars, a man in his cell block who seemed to have little in common with him, indeed nothing beyond their being close in age and in proximity. Clarence Burns* was a 39-year-old transient serving jail time for a third-degree assault and for taking a car without permission. He had no family that cared about him and he'd never had the kind of home that Bob Durall once owned or children he could dote on.

Burns and Durall passed the time by playing pinochle. The two men often appeared to be in intense conversation, with Durall doing most of the talking and Burns nodding in response.

The tragic summer was over, and the rains came to Seattle along with the holiday season. Thanksgiving and Christmas in jail are very pale imitations of happy family gatherings. Carolyn had always loved the baking and decorating of Christmas, and one wonders if her husband ever thought about what he had taken away from his children and, even, from himself.

Instead of reminiscing, he planned what he would do next. He had, according to Clarence Burns, come up with a diabolical scenario that would not only bring about the ultimate revenge for Carolyn's alleged affair but also lead to his own freedom. Bob Durall knew the name of the man Carolyn was attracted to and seethed to think that *he* was locked up while Dirk Lansing* walked around free. As far as Durall was concerned, Lansing was the one responsible for breaking up his family; his own infidelity and lies were entirely different matters.

Clarence Burns was due to be released in the spring of 1999. Durall had plans for him. Before he broached the subject, he groomed Burns to believe that they were good friends. Burns had no money to buy food, personal-care products, or anything else from the jail commissary, so Durall generously shared his purchases with him. He also arranged for money to be put into Burns's jail account. Durall said they would go on being friends on the outside once they were both free. If Burns did what he asked, Durall would not only pay him thousands of dollars, he guaranteed that the onetime street person would become much more than a friend; he would be a member of the family. "My kids will call you Uncle Clarence," Durall said. "You'll be visiting in our house often."

Burns had some dangerous assignments to fulfill before he would qualify as a beloved uncle. Once he was let out of jail, he was to track down Dirk Lansing and somehow overcome him, tie him up, and do whatever was necessary to hold him prisoner. Durall wanted Lansing dead and Burns was to eventually kill him, but first he had to force Carolyn's alleged ex-lover to write a letter admitting that *he* was the one who murdered her.

After the letter was written in Dirk Lansing's handwriting, Clarence Burns was supposed to kill him. His body and car had to be hidden where no one would ever find them. When that was accomplished, Burns was to make copies of the letter in which the now dead man admitted killing Carolyn and mail them to television stations, newspapers, the King County prosecutors, and to Bob Durall himself.

Since Lansing would never be found, Durall was sure the police would conclude that he had fled, perhaps to another country, to hide. They would believe that Dirk Lansing had felt guilty enough to admit to killing Carolyn, and to send his confession letters all over Seattle. That would lead to Bob's being let out of jail.

Instead of being a reviled murder suspect, Bob would be seen as a wronged man, a widower left with his motherless children. He would get his children back, his job back, his house back, his whole life back—except, of course, for Carolyn.

The two men had many discussions on how not to leave fingerprints on the letters or the car—should it ever be found—and how Burns could track Lansing down. The method he used to murder his prisoner didn't much matter to Bob Durall, just so long as it worked.

Clarence Burns had a checkered past, but he had never killed anyone, and he became afraid of his jail buddy as he listened to the cold-blooded plan. It had seemed to be only a fantasy at first; soon he realized that Durall was completely serious. Burns agreed that he would do what Durall wanted, partly because he didn't want to anger him and partly because he didn't want to give up the treats from the commissary.

In February 1999, Burns was written up for breaking one of the jail rules and moved to another cell block. There, he was no longer afraid of reprisals from Durall. He asked his jailers to tell the Renton police he wanted to talk with them.

Clarence Burns said that his jailmate had told him that he had killed his wife because she was going to leave him.

Now Durall faced not only charges of premeditated first-degree murder, but on July 9, 1999, the deputy prosecutor, Patricia Eakes, filed to amend the complaint against him to add a charge of solicitation to commit first-degree murder. Already facing up to twenty-six years in prison if found guilty of killing Carolyn, he now faced many more years.

His fourth attorney, Michelle Shaw, had done her best to convince Durall to plead guilty, as his earlier attorneys had, telling him that the State's case against him was extremely strong. But he was adamant that he wanted to go to trial. Shaw withdrew, and another attorney, Don Minor, agreed to represent him.

Two years had passed since Carolyn Durall's murder when her husband finally went on trial in Judge Deborah Fleck's courtroom in Superior Court in Kent in June 2000. The weather in King County was much the same as it was when Carolyn left her office for the last time, saying, "Wish me luck . . ."

Because the case had often been covered in the media during those two years, it wasn't easy to pick a jury. Ten of Carolyn's coworkers were in the courtroom for the opening statements, and at least one was present for the entire trial. It was usually her best friend, Denise Jannusch, who took careful notes so that she could share them with the staff at Morgan Stanley Dean Witter. The company granted her a sad kind of leave; they wanted only to see Carolyn finally receive justice.

Judge Fleck ruled that both charges would be considered in this trial; she would not separate the murder charges from the conspiracy charges. However, the prosecutor's office dropped the conspiracy charges halfway through the jury selection phase without comment. And they kept their promise not to tell the jurors that it was Bob Durall who led police and medical examiner's deputies to Carolyn's body deep in the lonely woods.

Now, finally, the trial, which took almost seven weeks to slowly unwind a complicated story of suspense and deception, had begun.

Deputy Prosecutor Jeff Baird made the opening statements for the State. They were succinct and horrifying.

"She wanted a divorce; he wanted her dead," Baird told the jurors. "She searched for the best way to leave; he searched for the best way to murder her. . . . He crushed her skull, stuffed her in a garbage bag, and dumped her in the hills."

While Carolyn was reading *Too Good to Leave: Too Bad to Stay* and trying to figure out if she had enough financial resources to raise her children on her own, Bob was writing down those things important to him. The Renton police had found an ominous list in one of his filing cabinets, one that harkened back to the sites his fellow workers found on his computer. It read "bat, gloves, pillows." Did he jot down those things after he read about "kill + spouse" and "suffocate . . . murder . . . poison (Sleep 2 pills (herbs), 3 Death?" He also wrote down chores he faced and forensic details: "disposal, tire tracks, footprints."

Bob Durall was dressed for court in a well-cut gray suit and a crisp white shirt and tie. As he sat beside Don Minor, his attorney, he looked like one himself. He showed no emotion as Baird spoke.

The State had so many witnesses, each one verifying and validating what had been said by the others. There was a mountain of both circumstantial and physical evidence. How could any "prudent juror" not decide that the man at the defense table had indeed plotted, planned, researched, lied, and manipulated almost everyone around him before and after Carolyn Durall died at his hands in a brutal attack?

But jurors are never predictable.

Don Minor had said he wanted to delay his opening statement until the defense case began. Apparently, Bob Durall was now undecided about taking the stand in his own defense. Across the board, defense attorneys in major felony cases advise their clients not to testify. The moment they do, they open themselves up to cross-examination by the prosecutors. But Bob Durall himself was really all the defense had going for it.

So far, Durall's witnesses hadn't had much punch. There was the woman from the minimart who was sure she sold gas to Carolyn a few days after the night she disappeared, testifying that she recognized her when she saw the Missing fliers her friends distributed.

A physical therapist said that Bob Durall already had an arm injury before the night of his wife's vanishing. Whether it was as serious as it proved to be when he consulted a physician a week later wasn't clear. A torn biceps muscle can't be fixed with physical therapy; it requires surgery to keep it from atrophying.

Would Durall testify? On Tuesday, July 25, he was still indecisive, and even Minor wasn't sure what he intended to do. The end of the trial was approaching, but Minor had no choice but to request a delay. Judge Fleck agreed to stop the trial in midflight so that Minor could read the computer disk that contained email messages police had seized from Durall's computers.

Even after Baird argued that the defense had had access to those disks for the past year, Judge Fleck went by edicts of discovery that said she had to grant the delay. She announced that court would reconvene the next Monday.

Jeff Baird was as frustrated as those in the gallery, a group that included relatives and supporters of each side. "This is a question about a defendant who has cold feet about testifying and, frankly, I think it's time for him to fish or cut bait," Baird said. "I don't think he's fooling anybody."

Judge Fleck urged the defendant and his attorney to make up their minds whether Durall *would* testify on Monday. Don Minor answered only that he couldn't promise. "On his way to the witness stand, he might change his mind," he said, a hint of resignation in his voice.

It was Monday, July 31, and the courtroom was hushed, everyone waiting to see whether Bob Durall actually would take the stand.

He did. What followed was one of the most stunning demonstrations ever seen in a courtroom. It's unlikely that even Don Minor knew what his client was about to reveal.

Bob Durall's testimony veered completely away from the evidence that had thus far been presented. He said that even he couldn't be positive about what had happened to Carolyn and then explained why. He discussed the night of August 6, 1998. "Nothing happened I consider way out of the ordinary," he told the jury in a calm voice. There was no fight, no talk of divorce. They awakened early on Friday and he saw her only briefly before she left to go to work.

Yes, he admitted that he told her worried coworkers

that he didn't know where she was or why she hadn't come to work. But he actually suspected that she was with another man. He had desperately searched for her van in motel and hotel parking lots but couldn't find it anywhere. "In my mind, I knew she was somewhere with somebody."

He had called the police later that day and attempted to file a missing persons' report, but he was still thinking that she was cheating on him with another man.

He didn't want to disappoint his children, and he wanted to be with them, so he had gone alone to the San Juan Islands to spend the weekend with his three youngsters and his mother- and father-in-law. When his 9-year-old son asked where his wife was, he said he had gently told him, "We can't find Mommy right now."

So far, Durall hadn't deviated much from the story he originally told the Renton detectives. Then Bob Durall suddenly began an incredible tale with a whole new cast of characters.

He testified that had returned from the San Juan Islands on Monday, August 10, in the early morning hours. (This would have been several hours after police had called to tell him that they had located Carolyn's van two miles from his house.) That was when he had become involved in a terrifying situation. While he was standing in his bedroom, a man with a gun had appeared. The man had held a gun on him, Durall said, and tied him up in a bathroom, all the while threatening to shoot him.

Everyone in the gallery, not to mention those at the defense and prosecution tables, stared back at the man on the witness stand, bemused and bewildered.

Durall continued to tell the story of what "really happened." Next, he said he was forced to drive several miles—he wasn't sure how many—to a place where they met a second man, who was waiting in a parking lot somewhere in Issaquah. The second man was shorter and quite tan and had bushy hair. He was sitting in a large SUV. Both men forced the still-bound Durall into the SUV and drove for what he estimated was about two hours until they came to a forested area off I-90. (It would not take anywhere near two hours to drive from Issaquah to the region Durall was describing; it was only about twenty-four miles east.)

It was of course the place where Carolyn's body was found. The mysterious strangers dumped a large bag there, which, he said, contained Carolyn's body, but he didn't ask.

Durall testified that he could not describe either man in detail, but knew they were both Caucasian. The one with the gun was taller and partially bald, while the other had a thick head of hair. "Bushy hair."

One of his captors told Bob Durall, "There wouldn't have been a problem. She should have kept her promise. She got caught on the phone."

He didn't ask about that either, apparently fearful that they might kill him too and leave him in the woods.

The men who had abducted Durall eventually returned him to his Nissan Pathfinder and warned him that he must not tell anyone about what he had seen. They ordered him to clean the bedroom of his home and remove all signs of blood in his house. If he told anyone, they threatened to harm his children, telling him that they would make him watch while they killed his children "one by one."

And so he had obeyed them, he said in a flat voice devoid of any trace of feeling. He had cleaned up the blood, and never told anyone what had really happened—not until now.

Unwittingly perhaps, he had invoked the most familiar of all phantom suspects—"The Bushy-Haired Stranger"— so familiar that cops and prosecutors usually just say "The BHS," for the little man who wasn't there, and never shows up at all.

After Bob Durall testified for most of two days, Jeff Baird approached him for cross-examination.

Just as his computer betrayed him by spitting out the websites he'd checked and his search for romance at Match.com, his emails came back to haunt Durall.

In one, he had written about hiring "an attorney and a private investigator" to find his missing wife. This was within days after he claimed that he had been warned not to talk to police or tell anyone.

Baird asked him if the "bushy-haired man who had a good tan" or the "taller man with the gun" had said, "No police, but go ahead and hire a private investigator?"

"No, those were not their words," Durall answered stiffly.

Hadn't he been suspicious that his wife had been killed in their bedroom? "When you removed the carpet," Baird asked, "did you associate the big bloodstain with the murder of your wife? There was a lot of blood there. You cleaned up the blood, knowing or assuming it was evidence of a murder?"

"I thought there was a good chance my wife was killed there but did not know for sure." He added that he didn't know the "definition of murder."

It was like shooting fish in a barrel. Durall's story of the deadly strangers would have been unbelievable even in a soap-opera script.

When he was asked about his list of "bat, bag, pole, hill, gloves, pillow, place, tire, tracks, footprints and disposal," he said none of these words referred to what had happened to Carolyn; instead, he had written them down to remind himself of baseball, his property in the foothills, and a trip out of town.

His affect was so flat that it was easy to see why an acquaintance had said, "He's a cocky guy, but I wondered 'Is anybody in there?'"

At a time when even a trace of emotion would have helped him get through to the jurors, he spoke of ultimate horror as if he were an automaton.

Would any of these jurors believe the tale of the killers who had just waltzed out of left field to confuse a flabbergasted gallery?

Jeff Baird called Durall's testimony absurd and termed it "the desperate act of a desperate man."

After the two hundred exhibits that were entered into the record, the DNA evidence, the scouring of the internet by the experts, and the sophisticated forensic science that connected the defendant to the crime, after dozens of witnesses, things looked bleak for Bob Durall.

Don Minor did his best, insisting there was no direct evidence. "What you have been presented with is circumstantial evidence," he told the jury. "You should understand that circumstances can be misleading."

Minor wisely did not put Durall's assertion that he had been abducted by the real killers and then released into the main thrust of his final argument. It's quite possible that even he didn't know about that tale until he heard Durall's testimony along with the rest of the bewildered courtroom. He tried to make the State's case look as if it were made of smoke and mirrors and assumptions not based in fact.

"Things that were innocent in nature have been given a sinister meaning," Minor argued. "Mr. Durall has a need for attention but not a need to kill his wife."

Perhaps not. But Bob Durall had told some of his other women that Carolyn would be "better off dead" and that his life would "be easier if she were dead." He had sighed that he couldn't bear the thought of her raising their children even part of the time.

The jury stayed out only two hours. When they returned, they announced that they had found Bob Durall guilty of First Degree Murder. It was August 6, 2000, exactly two years after Carolyn Durall died.

Jeff Baird spoke to several jurors after they were dismissed. They were curious about one aspect of the case. How had the police known where Carolyn's body was? Now that it was over, he was able to reveal that Bob Durall led them to it and that the State had stuck to its agreement not to introduce that detail during his trial.

Carolyn's family, friends, and coworkers hugged each other. They knew they could never have a truly happy ending, but her boss, Roseann Watson, could say, "We wish we could bring her back, but at least he didn't win this one."

On October 6, 2000, Robert Durall appeared in Judge Deborah Fleck's courtroom for sentencing. He had shown no feelings during his trial. But now in the sentencing phase, video images of Carolyn brought her back to life one more time. She was there on the screen as music played. There was Carolyn on horseback, showing her skill as she gracefully controlled her beloved horses. There she was ice-skating, pregnant with their babies, cooking in her kitchen, hugging her children, laughing with her family. There was Carolyn with Bob and Denise and Gary. There was Bob's hand resting protectively on his wife's shoulder.

For the first time, the prisoner's eyes filled with tears. Was he weeping for her or for himself?

Judge Fleck looked at him with disdain. She remarked that he was a man with an education, a church leader, one who was flourishing in his job and well thought of by his community, but also one who was typical of abusers—apparently successful men who dominate their partners with psychological abuse and intimidation. The murder he committed was an example of "aggravated domestic violence, preceded by a pattern of psychological abuse."

The judge was not impressed with him, and characterized him as a "sniveler" by his behavior during the trial. He might have gone into her courtroom expecting a twenty-six- to thirty-year sentence, but Judge Fleck delivered an exceptional sentence. He would spend forty-six years and eight months in prison for the premeditated murder of the wife who had sought only freedom.

"Freeedom," the web prowler, had lost his. At 43, he was headed for a cell.

Carolyn and Bob's children live with her parents in another state, and their last name is no longer Durall. Nor is that name on her gravestone. The children are doing well, as well as they can, given their great loss at a tender age. They see their old friends and are exceptionally gifted. Carolyn's children can look at the memory books her friends made for them so that they will always know who their mother was.

The family that raised Bob so lovingly suffered, too, and no one blames them for what he became. But nothing, of course, will ever be the same.

Whenever those who loved Carolyn see a butterfly, they think of her. They can be proud that they did their very best to find her and to be sure that her killer is paying for the loss of her life.